Francis A. Drexel
LIBRARY

Books For College Libraries
Third Edition

Core Collection

SAINT JOSEPH'S UNIVERSITY

George N. Peek *and the Fight for* Farm Parity

George N. Peek
and the Fight for
Farm Parity

by Gilbert C. Fite

Norman : University of Oklahoma Press

By Gilbert C. Fite

George N. Peek and the Fight for Farm Parity (Norman, 1954)
Mount Rushmore (Norman, 1952)
Peter Norbeck: Prairie Statesman (Columbia, Mo., 1948)

Library of Congress Catalog Card Number: 54-5934

*With sincere appreciation
to Elmer Ellis and Lewis E. Atherton*

Foreword

THIS book is the story of a man and a movement. The man is George Nelson Peek; the movement is the campaign for farm parity, which he led and directed. The two are so closely related that it is impossible to write about one and not the other. Farm parity has become a well-known national policy in the mid-twentieth century, having been accepted by both major political parties. The man who was most instrumental in developing and promoting this concept, however, is less familiar. The impact which George Peek made on his times deserves better understanding and wider recognition. It is hoped that this book will fill that need. "When the last chapter in the great farm relief struggle has been written," said William Hirth, himself an important farm leader, "the farmers of the United States will owe this 'smiling soldier of fortune' from Illinois a debt of gratitude which they will never be able to repay." Indeed, farmers who enjoy parity or near-parity prices owe George Peek their undying gratitude.

My interest in farm problems originated as a boy on a South Dakota farm. In the late 1920's I was struck by the fact that my parents had to teach rural school intermittently to supplement their meager farm income. They worked many acres and toiled from dawn to dark, as did most farmers in Jerauld County. It was not that. Their farm management could have been better, but it was probably average. Hard work and fair management, however, were not enough. Prices of farm commodities were too low in relation to the prices of nonfarm goods. There was a marked disparity. About all I understood at the time was that after taxes and interest were paid little remained for the pleasures and comforts of life. What was wrong? This was the question in the minds of men and women on millions of American farms.

While farmers were struggling to make ends meet in the face of this basic problem, George Peek and a little band of followers were insisting that the federal government had the responsibility to help farmers get parity prices, and that they be placed on an equality with labor and industry in the over-all economy. After a long, hard struggle of over ten years the parity concept was written into the Agricultural Adjustment Act of 1933. It is an interesting and important chapter in recent American history, and, as Hirth wrote, it "should be preserved for future generations."

Many people and organizations have helped to make this book possible. I am indebted to the American Philosophical Society for a travel and research grant awarded from its Reserve Fund in the summer of 1952. The Faculty Research Committee of the University of Oklahoma also gave me financial help.

I am grateful to Dean Herbert S. Schell of the University of South Dakota, who first interested me in the academic phases of farm problems. I want especially to express my appreciation to the following persons who read all or part of the manuscript and made helpful suggestions: Deans William L. Bradshaw and W. Francis English of the University of Missouri; Stuart R. Tompkins, research professor of history, and Professor Jim Reese, Department of Economics, University of Oklahoma; Professors John D. Black of Harvard University; and M. L. Wilson, recently extension director, United States Department of Agriculture. Mrs. Mavis Martin helped check and proofread the manuscript. Many librarians and members of their staffs rendered great assistance, but those to whom I must give special credit are Miss Opal Carr, reference librarian, University of Oklahoma, and Miss Vivian Wiser in the Natural Resources and Records Division of the National Archives. They were of inestimable service.

I owe an unusual debt of gratitude to Burton F. Peek and Chester C. Davis. Mr. Davis has more complete firsthand knowledge of the farm relief campaign and of Peek's activities than any living person. He read the entire manuscript and gave unstintingly of his time and understanding. He also made a distinct contribution when he placed his private papers and files in the Western Historical Manuscripts Collection at the University of Missouri.

Foreword

Mr. Burton F. Peek laid the foundation for this book when he deposited George Peek's files in the Western Historical Manuscripts Collection and made all of the material available to me without restrictions of any kind. He also permitted me to use pertinent records of Deere and Company which relate to Peek's business career. He gave generously of his time and energy, and co-operated wholeheartedly and unselfishly in every way.

Despite the help which I have received from so many persons, it is needless to say that any errors of fact or interpretation are entirely my own.

My greatest and most lasting debt of gratitude is to my parents, Clyde and Mary Fite. For over thirty-five years prior to their untimely death on August 2, 1953, they cheerfully made untold sacrifices which made possible the opportunities for me to study and write. Their interest, encouragement, and wise counsel during the period when this book was being written will never be forgotten.

GILBERT C. FITE

Norman, Oklahoma
September 10, 1953

Contents

Illustrations

George N. Peek *and the Fight for* Farm Parity

Chapter I

Troublous Times

A DESPONDENT Georgia sharecropper wrote to Secretary of Agriculture Henry C. Wallace on December 13, 1921: "I have 8 head of children and my wife. We work hard but I am not able to take care of them. I have children who are of school age .... I am not able to school them. My family are in bad shape, they are naked and barefooted." Six months before this pathetic communication reached Washington a slightly more affluent Southern farmer wrote to President Harding: "This fall not only will I lose my home and everything in it, but hundreds, perhaps thousands, will be in my condition, homeless. Unless the farmer gets 35c to 40c for his cotton, we will all be ruined, . . ."

Early in 1921 a Colorado farmer commented: "I have farmed or hired farming done west of the Missouri for fifty-five years, gone through drouth seasons and grasshopper seasons, but never seen as discouraging times for the farmer as at present." And a North Dakotan, who "as a barefooted boy" had helped his parents "pick buffalo bones" off the prairies, told the same story. "I have witnessed the ups and downs of North Dakota nearly forty years and . . . the situation is the worst we have ever seen," he said.

A wheat rancher in Washington State explained to Secretary Wallace that he had not bought a new suit of clothes for eight years and that the future seemed to offer no hope for better things. An Oklahoma citizen pleaded with the Secretary to work for a farm-debt moratorium. "Why should we all have our homes taken from us," he complained.[1]

[1] Letters in the files of the Secretary of Agriculture for 1920 and 1921. National Archives, Washington, D. C.

Thus, beginning in late 1920, letters from the great agricultural sections of the United States cluttered the desks of President Wilson, and later President Harding, the secretaries of agriculture, congressmen, and senators, describing in pitiful detail the effect of the deepening farm depression. One story was told of a Great Falls, Montana, banker who received a letter which read: "I got your letter about what I owe you. Now be patient. I ain't forgot you. Please wait. . . . If this was judgment and you were no more prepared to meet your Maker than I am to meet your account, you sure would have to go to Hell. Trusting you will do this, I remain, sincerely yours. . . ."

The depression hit millions of American farmers suddenly and without much warning in the summer of 1920. The prices of most basic farm commodities began a precipitous decline in June and July, or shortly thereafter, and continued downward for nearly two years. For example, No. 1 dark northern wheat brought $2.94 a bushel in Minneapolis during early July, 1920. But in succeeding months, statements like "Grain Market Hits Toboggan" were typical captions for agricultural news releases. By December, wheat had dropped to around $1.72. The farm price was much lower and the downward trend continued until farmers were receiving a paltry 92 cents or less by December, 1921.

Good beef steers sold for $14.95 a hundred pounds in September, 1920, but fourteen months later they brought a mere $7.31. The farm price of cotton averaged 37 cents a pound in July, 1920, but by December, when much of the crop was being marketed, it had declined to 13 or 14 cents. During a five-month period, corn on the Chicago market dropped from $1.83 to less than 70 cents a bushel.

Staple producers were not the only ones who suffered. An official of the Ohio Farm Bureau Federation wrote: "One Ohio onion grower stored 40 carloads. He was able to sell seven carloads . . . the balance was hauled back to the field and plowed under. There were thousands of tons of cabbage the country over plowed under . . . and much of that which was sold was sold at a loss."[2] Based on prices received at the farm, the total value of agricultural products dropped from $18,328,000,000 in 1920 to

[2] Joint Committee of Agricultural Inquiry, *Hearings,* 67 Cong., 1 sess., Vol. I, 268.

$12,402,000,000 in 1921.[3] This was, indeed, a catastrophe for many farmers.

The price drop hit most farmers especially hard because the cost of producing the 1920 crop had been one of the highest on record. Labor, machinery, fertilizer, and other supplies all commanded high prices and kept the cost of production at a record level. In October, 1920, a North Dakota citizen wrote to President Wilson emphasizing how expensive it had been to raise his crop, and he pleaded with him: "For God's sake . . . keep these poor farmers facing a winter on these bare prairies from going bankrupt."

To be sure, this was not the first panic which had left farmers in financial ruin. Agriculture, along with other segments of the economy, had experienced periodic ups and downs for over a century. The panics of 1819, 1837, 1857, 1873, and 1893 had all taken their toll. But for farmers, the panic of 1920–21, and the depression years which followed, was not just another low swing in the economic pendulum. The condition was more grave and fundamental. Agriculture was a sick industry, with a sickness resulting from its position in a society that was becoming predominantly industrial.

Comparatively, the economic and social rewards of agriculture had been declining for over a half century, and the rural way of life had lost prestige. Certainly, some farmers had made money, and agriculture had experienced tremendous expansion following the Civil War. But the most ambitious young men looked to the city rather than to the soil. Sturdy, independent yeomen, once considered the backbone of America, were often ridiculed by members of an increasingly urban society, and sometimes contemptuously referred to as "hicks" and "hayseeds." Thomas Jefferson had thought of farmers as "the chosen people of God, if ever he had a chosen people," but the Jeffersonian concept was rapidly losing validity in the public mind. The old familiar phrases concerning the importance of agriculture were constantly repeated, but fewer and fewer industrial-minded citizens really believed them.

Following the Civil War, business and industry became the arbiter of American life. An industrialized America became a reality. By 1890, for the first time, the value of industrial production exceeded that of the output of the nation's farms. Although

3 *Yearbook of Agriculture*, 1922, p. 985.

more farms and greater acreages were rapidly added to the agricultural domain in the generation after Appomattox, the number of people engaged in nonfarm occupations exceeded those working in agriculture during the 1870's. And by 1920 more Americans were actually engaged in manufacturing than in agriculture. In the same year the census showed that the rural population had dropped to less than half of the total, and that portion actually living on farms was probably not over 30 per cent.

Growing industrial predominance was also reflected in the American export trade. In 1860 agricultural exports made up 81 per cent of the total, but by 1910 only 52 per cent of United States foreign shipments were farm commodities. Agriculture was still a vitally important part of the American economy in 1920, but it had gradually become subordinate to industry. The question was being seriously asked, Have farmers simply become gardeners for the rich and powerful industrial community?

Part of the farmer's trouble was that he continued to operate under a philosophy largely repudiated in both theory and practice by other major groups in the economy. Historically, farmers had been among the strongest advocates of freedom, independence, and equality. They believed that competition was the staff of economic life. And farming was highly competitive. Millions of American farmers not only competed with one another but with Canadian, Argentine, and Australian producers as well. But while farmers were still shifting for themselves, business and industry were combining and stabilizing their operations. The formation of trusts, holding companies, and other types of combinations were characteristic of the late nineteenth and early twentieth centuries. An excellent example of price stabilization in business is seen in the figures for the depression period from 1929 to 1933. During those years the price of agricultural implements and motor vehicles dropped only 6 and 16 per cent respectively, while production was cut 80 per cent in both industries. In the case of agricultural commodities over which there was no similar control of price and production, prices declined 63 per cent and production only 6 per cent. Labor also organized and gained some of the advantages which came from combination and co-operation. The farmer, still clinging to the idea of competition, finally awakened to the fact that he was operating at a distinct disadvantage. He was an old time operator in a new, streamlined economic age.

Of course this was not the first time that farmers had recognized their unfortunate position. Goaded by hard times, they had organized periodically for mutual protection between 1865 and 1896. The Grange and Populist movements had been organized to fight against monopoly and special privilege. These were followed in the twentieth century by the Society of Equity, the Farmers' Union, and the Nonpartisan League. Through their organizations the farmers struck at the problems of the "money trust," business monopolies, railroads, marketing abuses, and others. Feeling their individual helplessness, they called on the government for aid—not for themselves, but aid in governing and restricting those they feared would plunder agriculture. Farmers were obviously at odds in their own thinking. On the one hand, they preached a doctrine of independence and individualism; yet on the other, they asked for government regulation of banking, industry, and transportation. Farmers in the late nineteenth century seemed to feel confident that they could achieve prosperity if the currency were inflated and if monopolies were strictly regulated or government-owned. However, they largely overlooked their main difficulty, namely, their growing position of inferiority in the over-all economy of the nation.[4]

Important changes also took place within the agricultural industry itself during the four decades before World War I. The basic development was the spread of commercialized farming as more and more farmers produced for a cash market. The tendency was to specialize in wheat, cotton, dairy products, or some other crop. The general farmer, who supplied many of his own needs, was rapidly passing from the scene. But as farmers produced some specialized crop for the commercial market, their problems increased. Capitalization and expense of operation grew, making it more essential than ever to raise a good crop and dispose of it at fair prices. In fact, the commercialization of agriculture made the matter of price more important to farmers.

There were many problems for a commercial farmer in an increasingly industrial and urban society. He was affected by the

4 Consult Theodore Saloutos, "The Agricultural Problem and Nineteenth-Century Industrialism," *Agricultural History*, Vol. XXII (July, 1948), 156–74.

condition of distant markets, by transportation costs, by the price which he had to pay for machinery and other equipment, by government monetary policies, and by other factors over which he had little or no control. Furthermore, between 1870 and 1897 there were long periods of low farm prices which caused widespread distress and discontent.

Beginning in 1897, however, American farmers set out on one of the longest periods of prosperity recorded in the annals of American agriculture. For over 20 years, or until 1920, farmers enjoyed unprecedented prosperity. Commodity and land prices rose, and the purchasing power of farm crops increased. From 1900 to 1910 the prices of nonfarm commodities climbed only 18 per cent, while farm prices shot up 47 per cent. Land values also rose more rapidly than the general price level. Thus Secretary of Agriculture James Wilson could write in his annual report of 1909, "Most prosperous of all years is the place to which 1909 is entitled in agriculture." Concerning the greatly increased income in the first decade of the twentieth century, the Secretary stated that it "has paid off mortgages, it has established banks, it has made better homes, it has helped to make the farmer a citizen of the world, [and] it has provided him with means for improving his soil and making it more productive." Indeed, the period between 1900 and 1914 has sometimes been called the golden era of American agriculture. This did not mean that everything was satisfactory in rural America. There were many problems, both economic and social. But relatively speaking, times were good. Since the purchasing power of agricultural products was favorable to the farmer, he approached what depression-ridden farmers after 1920 called "parity."

At the same time, however, basic adjustments were becoming necessary in American farming. For one thing, exports of cereals and meats began to decline about 1900. The gradual loss of some important export markets was due to competition from new agricultural regions like western Canada and Argentina, to the better use of fertilizer and improved livestock breeding in Europe, and to foreign tariffs and embargoes. Fortunately, however, domestic markets held up because of increased industrialization, the large migration of people from farms to factories, and heavy foreign immigration. For instance, the average number of industrial workers totaled 4,700,000 in 1899, but had grown to 6,600,000 ten years later. Thus, if there was less call for American wheat and beef in Europe, there was more demand at home. Furthermore, the market for sugar, dairy products, fruits, and vegetables increased and farmers placed more emphasis on production of these crops to meet home requirements.

In those fields where exports were declining, farmers were tending to adjust production so as to be less dependent upon foreign sales. Although production of exportable surpluses had been fundamental in American agricultural history, the lessening dependence upon foreign markets after 1900 seemed like a desirable trend, unless American farmers were prepared to compete with producers abroad who were exploiting highly productive virgin soils. This competition, however, already had created hardships for farmers in the United States, who no longer had that advantage. Therefore, the trend in the direction of an effective equilibrium between supply and demand in the home market looked toward reducing the probability of farmers being confronted with a "surplus problem."

And then came World War I. The war was a great disruptive force in the normal development of American agriculture, and in some respects it was an extreme calamity. Under the stimulus of high prices, patriotism, and inflation, American farmers greatly overexpanded production to meet both home and Allied demands. For example, wheat acreage jumped from about 48,000,000 acres to over 75,000,000 between 1914 and 1919. Hog production also increased sharply, and in 1919 the South had a previously unequaled $2,000,000,000 cotton crop. As commodity prices soared and gross farm income reached about $17,000,000,000 in 1919, land values climbed to unprecedented heights. Good Iowa plow land had sold for $82 an acre in 1910, but in 1920 the same land commanded a price of $200. Some Iowa farm land sold for as high as $400 an acre in 1919.

American farmers, feeling secure and prosperous under wartime conditions, turned to enjoy the fruits of their labors. Farm buildings were painted and improved, and obsolete and worn-out machinery was replaced. Moreover, farmers bought automobiles and trucks and installed telephones and electricity. The census of 1920 revealed that in the West North Central States, 57.6

per cent of the farmers owned automobiles and 69.5 per cent had telephones. Over 15 per cent lighted their homes with gas or electricity. In Iowa, where the fires of agricultural revolt were shortly to burn fiercely, the percentage of farmers who owned automobiles, enjoyed telephones, and had other conveniences was considerably higher than the average in the Midwest. In other sections, particularly the South, living standards were much lower, but, on the whole, farmers enjoyed a fairly comfortable position.[5]

Little, however, did farmers realize the economics of war and peace. They did not seem to recognize that the war had renewed and increased their dependence upon foreign markets. The depression about which farmers were bitterly complaining in 1920 came, to a large extent, because of shifting national and international events over which as individuals they had no control.

The immediate causes of the depression are not hard to find. A major factor was the loss of European markets for basic products like wheat and pork, which resulted from a curtailment of United States loans abroad. Although unexciting, figures best tell the story. In 1919 agricultural exports totaled $4,107,158,753, but by 1922 they had fallen more than 50 per cent to $1,883,315,000.[6] Foreign countries were not only without funds with which to buy farm products in the United States, but they encouraged production at home. This was especially true as the United States raised tariff barriers and restricted European industrial imports from entering the American market. Not only were foreign demands shrinking, but in many areas of the world, American grains and meats were crowded from the market by similar items from Canada or Australia.

The withdrawal of government price supports was another factor in the farm depression of the early 1920's. After early March, 1919, there was no price guarantee for hogs, and the government support price for wheat continued only through the 1919 crop. Thus when prices began to fall in 1920, there was no government policy to cushion the shock. With contracting foreign markets, the absence of government price supports, foreign competition, and the general deflationary movement, United States farmers

[5] Bureau of the Census, *Fourteenth Census of the United States,* V, Agriculture, 1920 (Washington, 1922), 514.

[6] *Yearbook of Agriculture,* 1922, p. 960.

slumped into the trough of depression. Not all producers, of course, suffered alike. The condition among dairy farmers and fruit growers was not as serious as that of wheat producers. There was, in fact, no single farm problem, but multiple problems requiring different solutions.

It must be emphasized that hard times were not confined to American farmers. The agricultural depression was world-wide. Furthermore, the depression hit other industries as well as agriculture. But the farm situation was different because, as one observer has said: "Agricultural prices fell first, fell fastest, and fell farthest."[7] As a result, farmers dropped into a position of serious disparity with industrial groups. The prices they received were much lower in terms of purchasing power than the prices they had to pay for nonagricultural commodities. The relative position of a great many producers was extremely unfavorable.

Considering the purchasing power of several basic farm products in 1913 as 100, it had dropped to only 67 in 1921. Some crops remained distressingly low. Professor George F. Warren, of Cornell, figured the purchasing power of wheat at 72 and hogs at 58 as late as 1924.[8] Authorities do not agree on the exact extent of the disparity, but all concede that it was a serious handicap to the farmer.

Figures, however, are cold and impersonal. They do not tell the human story or assess the social and economic effects of depression. As shown earlier, the flood of letters to Secretary Wallace and President Harding early in 1921 presented a graphic picture from the grass roots. Farmers may not have fully understood the intricacies of economics, but they felt the drop in purchasing power of their products. In his annual report of 1923, Secretary Wallace pointed out that a suit of clothes which had cost a North Dakota farmer twenty-one bushels of wheat in 1913 cost him thirty-one bushels in 1923.

No farmer could miss the significance of these developments, particularly if he were in debt. Farm mortgages in the United

[7] Clarence A. Wiley, *Agriculture and the Business Cycle Since 1920* (Madison, Wisconsin, 1930), 14.

[8] George F. Warren and F. A. Pearson, *The Agricultural Situation* (New York, 1924), 67. See also Warren's estimate in the *Cong. Rec.*, 67 Cong., 1 sess., June 21, 1921, p. 2792.

States increased from $3,320,470,000 in 1910 to just short of $8,-000,000,000 in 1920. In view of falling farm prices, many farmers found the heavy fixed charges on this debt an intolerable burden. Other fixed expenses were equally burdensome. Taxes on farm lands in Kansas increased 171 per cent between 1913 and 1921, and as much as 237 per cent in twenty counties of Eastern Washington.[9] Between July 1, 1920, and October 14, 1921, there were forty-five bankruptcy cases filed in the United States District Court at Creston, Iowa, to mention a single locality in the Midwest.[10] A director of a Malvern, Iowa, bank wrote to Secretary Wallace that "next year landowners will be going the same route tenants are now going."

Farm life could not help but be deeply affected by these developments. There was a decline in rural morale, more rapid movement away from the farms; living standards had to be cut, farmers had to work harder and longer, and many of them lost their farms and homes. And the psychological effect of the depression could hardly be overlooked. Some farmers were stunned and disheartened; others were in an ugly, fighting mood.

The general attitude of farmers caused Secretary Wallace grave concern. The agricultural situation might have political repercussions for the recently victorious Republican Party. On August 29, 1921, he sent a large sampling of farm letters to President Harding with the comment: "Knowing your deep heart interest in the farmer and your earnest desire to do what is possible to build our agriculture on an enduring foundation, it occurs to me that you might like to look over a few typical letters." A short while later Wallace mailed a group of similar letters to John T. Adams, chairman of the Republican National Committee. He urged Adams to read them carefully in order to "get a fairly good understanding of the farmers' psychology at the present time." William Allen White, writing in December, 1920, said there might be a dangerous political reaction to the current economic maladjustment in the Midwest. He explained that seventy-five "well-fed, God-fearing, staunch Republican farmers" of Lyon County, Kansas, had recently met and had taken a dim view of conditions. Farmers were out of patience, the Emporia editor declared, and

9 *Yearbook of Agriculture,* 1921, p. 141.
10 Notice in the files of the Secretary of Agriculture dated October 22, 1921.

he added that unless they got relief, a revolution "not unlike the agrarian uprising of the nineties" might take place in 1922.[11]

The diagnosis and suggested cures for farm troubles were almost as plentiful as the diagnosticians. There was considerable unanimity that something was seriously wrong, but little agreement on what should be done. Many felt that the farmer must work out his own salvation, either individually or by co-operating with other farmers. On the other hand, a large group of farm doctors prescribed a medicine to be mixed by the federal government. A long background of federal aid to farmers served as a precedent for those who demanded government action. The Morrill and Hatch Acts, rural free delivery, parcel post, federal aid for road building, regulation of cotton futures, the Federal Farm Loan Act, and the Smith-Lever and Smith-Hughes Acts were all a part of the government program to assist farmers. There was also the wartime experience of setting minimum prices for wheat and pork.

But despite the indecision and disagreement regarding a course of action, one thing was certain. Farmers were no longer content with such cures as cheap money and monopoly control. The antidotes offered by Daniel Shays and William Jennings Bryan fell far short of what farmers demanded during and after 1920. Caught between rapidly falling farm values and fairly rigid industrial prices, farm leaders began to think in terms of either direct or indirect government price supports. Letters in the files of the secretaries of agriculture at this time indicate clearly that farmers understood the matter of disparity, and many of them outlined the general farm problems with clarity and accuracy. In fact, farm thinking at the grass roots was often more intelligent and realistic than that which was done in the hallowed halls of agricultural colleges or in government offices. The depression sharply pinched the pocket nerves of farmers, and, as Oliver H. Kelley, founder of the Grange, had once said, "You must get into the farmers' pockets to reach their hearts, and a lively palpitation there invigorates their minds."

A flood of proposals on how to solve agriculture's difficulties began hitting Washington in late 1920. "The agitation for relief became hysterical," said Secretary of Agriculture David F. Hous-

11 *Emporia Gazette,* December 3, 1920.

ton.[12] Most of the plans called for some kind of federal aid. *The Farmer,* published at St. Paul, declared in November, 1920, that "to completely solve the problem of getting for agriculture her proper return for labor and investment, we must link up with co-operative growth the strong arm of the Government."[13] Shortly afterward, a representative of the New Orleans Cotton Exchange wrote to Senator Kenneth McKellar: "The problem which confronts us is beyond the ability of individual enterprise, calling for joint action which can only be secured through government intervention."[14]

It was widely suggested that the War Finance Corporation, whose activities had been suspended in May, 1920, be re-established to finance the export of surplus farm commodities. In December, Congress passed a resolution approving this proposal, but it was vetoed by President Wilson upon Secretary Houston's advice. Although Congress passed the resolution over the President's veto, it was not until August of 1921, after the Republicans had returned to power, that Congress specifically amended the War Finance Corporation Act to provide special agricultural credit.

Since wheat growers were among the chief sufferers, the idea of a government-guaranteed price gained much support. On March 1, Harry N. Owen, the editor of *Farm, Stock, and Home* at St. Paul, urged Congress to set a minimum wheat price of $2.00 a bushel for the 1920 season, $1.75 for 1921, and $1.50 for 1922. Another price-fixing scheme was offered in 1920 by W. H. Lyon, a lawyer of Sioux Falls, South Dakota. He advocated that the federal government buy up the surpluses of four major crops—wheat, oats, flax, and corn—at a minimum price of $3.00 a bushel for flax, $2.25 for wheat, $1.00 for corn, and 75 cents a bushel for oats. Lyon presented his stabilization plan before a Congressional committee on December 14, 1920, and a bill incorporating these principles was later introduced by Congressman C. A. Christopherson of South Dakota.[15]

---

12 David F. Houston, *Eight Years With Wilson's Cabinet* (New York, 1926), II, 109.

13 *The Farmer,* Vol. XXXVIII (November 20, 1920), 2556.

14 Quoted in the *Cong. Rec.,* 66 Cong., 3 sess., December 13, 1920, p. 272.

15 *Reviving the Activities of the War Finance Corporation,* Joint Hearings Before the Committees of Agriculture and Forestry, 66 Cong., 3 sess., pt. II, 1920, p. 247ff.

Congress and the executive branch of the government were steadily bombarded with similar proposals. G. W. Gieger, a Huron, South Dakota, landowner, said that legislation fixing the price of wheat, corn, and cotton "seems to me . . . the best antidote of the ills now overtaking agriculture."[16] A Des Moines lawyer urged Secretary Wallace to get behind a government program to set minimum prices at cost of production plus a fair profit. Another Iowan explained to Wallace that Congress ought to guarantee farmers "a reasonable profit and a fair return on everything they produce."[17]

Several price-fixing bills were presented to Congress in late 1920 and during 1921. Congressmen Christopherson and James H. Sinclair, of South and North Dakota respectively, both introduced bills to fix and stabilize the price of certain farm products. Neither of these measures, however, received serious consideration. Congressman Christopherson also presented a memorial passed by the South Dakota legislature favoring "the enactment of a law by congress . . . requiring the President, through a commission of experts . . . to fix and guarantee the prices of certain farm products."[18]

The most seriously considered proposal along this line was that advanced by Senator George W. Norris. He suggested that an export corporation be created to buy American farm products and sell them abroad on credit. The Norris plan had the approval of the Senate Committee on Agriculture and Forestry, and called for a $100,000,000 appropriation. It was aimed at the problem of removing the price-depressing surpluses from the domestic market in what amounted to financing our own exports. Norris's bill was defeated in August, 1921, when, over the opposition of some farm bloc members, expansion of the activities of the War Finance Corporation was approved as a substitute.[19] Republican opposition was intense to anything bordering on price-fixing, or any program which would put the government in business. And Democratic opposition was nearly as militant. Commenting on the measure, Senator H. C. Lodge expressed a common attitude held by the ruling Republican hierarchy: "It puts the United States into

16 Gieger to Wallace, July 6, 1921. Files of the Secretary of Agriculture.
17 Letters to Wallace, May 10 and August 24, 1921. *Ibid.*
18 *Cong., Rec.*, 66 Cong., 3 sess., December 6, 1920, p. 11.
19 *Ibid.*, 67 Cong., 1 sess., August 4, 1921, p. 4641.

active business. I think at this time the more we take the United States out of business and the less we put it in the better." He added that it was "a dangerous bill." Senator Walter Edge of New Jersey charged that the Norris bill would result in "absolutely changing the traditional policy of the government. . . ."[20]

The metropolitan press echoed these sentiments. On December 1, 1920, the Chicago *Daily News* warned farmers to beware of "quack proposals," while the Indianapolis *News* remarked that no class was entitled to government relief. The editor concluded, "Nor is it the business of government to maintain prices, or to intervene to prevent their fall." After discussing some of the farm relief schemes, the *New York Times* said on January 6, 1921, "The proposal that a market shall be made artificially for their benefit can fairly be countered by the proposal that they shall learn their business better, . . ."

Despite the number of price-stabilization plans which would have put the government in the business of buying and selling farm products, there was no lack of more traditional relief proposals. Bernard Baruch saw the solution to agriculture's problems in the restoration of foreign trade. This could be accomplished, he said, only by making peace with Germany and determining what reparations must be paid. Baruch added that better storage facilities and additional credit would be helpful, but that the farmer's real hope rested on revived foreign markets.[21]

Herbert Hoover, writing in 1920, recommended that American bankers loan money abroad so that foreigners could finance agricultural purchases in this country. Some "immediate co-operative action should be taken between the American farmer and the American banker," he said. But beyond this, he had little to offer, and Hoover was careful to insist that the federal government should not extend such credits. He did deplore the wastefulness of farm marketing and advocated the creation of commodity co-operatives. Showing more wisdom than he did in later years, however, Hoover discounted the power of farm co-operatives to control prices—the thing in which farmers were most interested.[22]

20 *Ibid.*, July 19 and 21, 1921, pp. 4039 and 4156.
21 Bernard Baruch to the secretary of the Kansas State Board of Agriculture, November 3, 1920, in *Twenty-Second Biennial Report of the Kansas State Board of Agriculture* (Topeka, 1920), 19–31.

Other solutions included raising the general tariff rates on agricultural commodities and placing a complete embargo on such items as wool, butter, meats, and vegetable oils. Senator Porter McCumber, of North Dakota, wrote to President Wilson on October 12, 1920, saying that he had received many urgent requests that an embargo be placed on Canadian wheat. Diversification of farm production was another standard remedy which received its quota of supporters in 1920 and 1921. Farmers should quit specializing, it was said, and join in the program typified by the slogan "a cow, a sow, and a hen." More liberal credit facilities, prohibition of trading in grain futures, and establishment of commodity co-operatives were also among the proposals receiving considerable support. Indeed, if farmers could have cashed the advice they were given on how to solve their problems, they would have been rich.

One of the major attacks on farm problems was launched by the farm bloc. It had become evident by the spring of 1921 that the new Republican administration had no positive agricultural program. Addressing Congress on April 12, President Harding conceded that farming was in a bad state of affairs, but he offered only a higher tariff and lower transportation rates as a solution. Thus, on May 9, a bipartisan group of senators from the South and West, under the leadership of W. S. Kenyon, of Iowa, met in the offices of the American Farm Bureau Federation to discuss a legislative program. Twelve senators were present at this first meeting, and others soon became affiliated with the movement. A similar group was formed in the House shortly afterwards.

Although the eastern press pretended to see the ghosts of Marat, Danton, and Robespierre rampaging about the nation's capital, formation of the farm bloc was not a radical move, or even a threat to the two-party system. In fact, members of the bloc fought for no drastic reforms and did very little to relieve the basic difficulties confronting agriculture. Because of farm bloc pressure, however, Congress passed several bills of interest to farmers. Among them were the Future Trading Act, the Packers and Stockyards Act, the Capper-Volstead Co-operative Marketing Act, and expansion of the activities of the War Finance Corporation. Two minor amendments to the Federal Reserve Act were passed as well as the Intermediate Credits Act. But the farm bloc was unable, and to some

22 Herbert Hoover, "Farmers' Problems," in *ibid.*, 3–18.

extent unwilling, to go beyond these or similar measures. Although the power of the bloc was formidable up to late 1923, it never achieved its original goal of passing legislation which would bring substantial aid to farmers.

While the farm bloc was pushing its legislative program, the Joint Committee of Agricultural Inquiry met in Washington during July and August, 1921, to seek answers to the farm dilemma. Congress had directed the committee to learn the causes of the depression, to study the state of credit resources, and to investigate marketing and transportation problems. About half of the three volumes of printed hearings were taken up with the question of agricultural credit. Other matters touched upon included the tariff, railroad rates, farm co-operatives, and marketing. Officials of the Federal Reserve System, economists, farm leaders, and a sprinkling of dirt farmers were among those questioned by eager congressmen seeking a method to solve farm ills. Although this inquiry produced some worthwhile information on agricultural conditions, it failed to get at the heart of the difficulties. Of those who testified, the actual farmers got closest to the crux of the matter when they mentioned the effect of surpluses on the market, and emphasized the problem of ratio-prices.

A few plans for farm relief approached the ridiculous. One correspondent suggested to Secretary Wallace that farm products could be profitably marketed directly by parcel post. And buy-more-flour and eat-more-bread campaigns were common in the wheat raising areas. The businessmen of Walla Walla, Washington, staged a contest to see who could make the most attractive window displays with loaves of bread. There were those, too, who said that farmers were trying to maintain a standard of living beyond their means. In effect, it was argued, farmers should forsake their automobiles and go back to the horse and buggy. This was an old charge against discontented agrarians. In the 1780's, before Shays' Rebellion, it was said that trouble among farmers was due to the fact that they could not maintain living standards gained during better times!

Proposals to help the farmer so flooded the United States Department of Agriculture in 1920, 1921, and 1922 that Secretary Wallace declared: "Visionary schemes of all kinds are presented. Some would have the government take charge of the large business enterprises; others would have the government undertake to fix prices either arbitrarily or indirectly by buying up surplus crops. The experience of 3,000 years shows the impracticality of such efforts."[23] In reply to a plea from W. P. Manley, a banker of Sioux City, Iowa, Wallace said that "there seem to be no short cut methods which will insure prompt relief, but no suggestion which seems to hold out a promise of being helpful is overlooked here."[24]

Actually, Wallace was about as perplexed as farmers at the grass roots. Neither he nor his economists in the department really had anything to offer except the usual and well-worn remedies of more credit, better marketing facilities, lower transportation rates, better statistical information, and the like. Improvements in these fields certainly should not be discounted. They offered real and substantial help to agriculture in the long run. But as relief which they could see and feel such proposals were as sounding brass and tinkling cymbals to depressed farmers.

Throughout 1920 and 1921 farmers were unorganized and could not unite on any common objective. Some of them struck out blindly as prices began to toboggan. There were threats of holding wheat until the price advanced to $3.00 a bushel. The Farmers' Union, including leaders like John A. Simpson, and editors of various farm journals and newspapers urged this course. Holding farm products for a better price was not new in American agricultural thinking. As far back as 1873 a convention of farm leaders in Chicago had urged a fruitless "hold your hogs" campaign, and the idea had bobbed up at later times. But all previous attempts by farmers to control marketing voluntarily or to restrict production had failed.

In the cotton belt, night riders, reminiscent of 1908, attempted to keep cotton off the market. Farmers were warned not to pick their cotton while it was selling under 40 cents a pound. Gin owners were told not to buy cotton and several gins were burned when the warnings went unheeded. Notices were posted on some cotton gin establishments signed by "The Black 75" and "The Citizens of Everywhere." At Earle, Arkansas, in October, 1920, the Earle Compress Company building was burned, destroying

23 *Yearbook of Agriculture*, 1921, p. 15.
24 Wallace to W. P. Manley, November 9, 1921. Files of the Secretary of Agriculture.

about 5,600 bales of cotton at an estimated loss of $600,000.[25] On the night of January 22, 1921, a band of twenty-five masked riders visited farmers in Bath and Fleming counties, Kentucky, and advised them not to haul any more tobacco to market. Unless they complied, the raiders threatened to burn their barns.

The threat of wheat farmers to withhold their crops and the actions of night riders to keep cotton and tobacco from going to market were not cures for the problem of low prices or reduced farm income. They were only symptoms of a very sick industry. The all-consuming question was, What should be done? Obviously, there was no generally accepted plan for relief, and the disorganized agrarians had no leader. The plan and the leadership, however, were soon to come from the same man—George N. Peek. But who was George Peek?

[25] Oklahoma City *Times,* October 8, 11, 16, and 23, 1920.

Chapter I I

The Man from Moline

G EORGE NELSON PEEK was born on November 19, 1873, at Polo, a small village in northern Illinois. He was among the eighth generation of Peeks (originally spelled "Peake") in America, the first of whom, Christopher, had emigrated from Essex, England, to Roxbury, Massachusetts, in 1634. George's grandfather, John Peek, was the first member of the family to leave New England. In 1838 he had followed his brother-in-law, John Deere, to Grand Detour, Illinois, on the Rock River. Deere had left Vermont a few months earlier and was about to start a career which would bring him world-wide fame as a manufacturer of steel plows.

John Peek traveled from Vermont to Illinois in a covered wagon, taking his own and Deere's family to Grand Detour. Two baby boys about six months of age were cradled in the feedbox of the wagon. They were cousins, Charles H. Deere and Henry Clay Peek. Probably John Deere then had no idea that some day his son would head the largest manufactory of steel plows in the United States; and certainly Peek did not conceive of the prominent part his grandsons, George and Burton, would have in building up Deere and Company.

Peek did not join Deere in the business of making plows, but settled on a prairie farm about sixteen miles from the town of Oregon, not far from Polo. There his son Henry Clay Peek grew to manhood. At the outbreak of the Civil War, young Peek enlisted in the Fifteenth Illinois Cavalry. He served four years and came out of the war a captain. In 1864, Henry married Adeline Chase, whose parents were Quakers of New York background.

Back from the war, Henry Peek engaged in the livestock business in Polo. But in 1874, as economic distress spread over the nation, he sought the job of sheriff of Ogle County, and was elected. The salary was not much, but it was steady, and a regular income was welcomed by a man with a growing family. Later his son George humorously remarked that he spent the first ten years of his life in jail!

Henry Peek was a popular county official and he served six two-year terms, or until a state law prohibited a sheriff from succeeding himself. In 1885 he moved to a farm near Oregon. There George and his older brother, Burton, got their first steady taste of farm life. And they did not like it. In the 1880's little modern machinery was available to lighten the backbreaking toil of farm work. The elder Peek was a hard worker, and the boys remember him knocking on their bedroom door and saying, "Get up, it's 'most four."

Not many boys in the Oregon community received more than a grade school education, but George graduated from the Oregon public highschool in the spring of 1891. During the summer he was employed by C. D. Etnyre, a realtor in Oregon. Meanwhile, Burton, who attended highschool for two years, had gone to Moline, where he found employment in the shops of Deere and Company.

George had no intention of returning to the farm; so he went to Evanston and enrolled at Northwestern University. He entered the School of Liberal Arts on September 15, 1891. For some unknown reason he enrolled for only one course, mathematics. He received satisfactory grades, but academic life had no special appeal to him. George Peek was not the philosopher type; he was a young man of action. His eye was on the business world, the world of Rockefeller, Carnegie, and Mark Hanna.

After school closed in June, 1892, young Peek got a job with Alexander H. Revell and Company in Chicago. As an office assistant, he made eight dollars a week. But after nearly six months in the furniture business, Peek decided to seek his fortune in the Northwest. In December, 1892, he pocketed a flattering recommendation written by his former employer and headed for Minneapolis. "He came to us totally unacquainted with practical office work," read the recommendation, "but being bright and alert

. . . , he invariably did the right thing at the right moment and we believe his promise of future usefulness . . . will make him a valuable acquisition." By January, 1893, Peek had found a job in the credit manager's office of Deere and Webber, a branch house of Deere and Company. His salary was forty dollars a month.

Deere and Webber officials soon recognized that they had employed a young man of singular energy and ability. Peek rapidly acquired the techniques of a business office and he seemed to be a natural-born salesman. Impressive in appearance, his six foot, 180-pound frame suggested firmness and solidity. There was decision in his square jaw, and his piercing blue eyes were fired with enthusiasm and determination. He just looked like a man who prevailed. And he usually did. His whole character was positive; yet, he was likeable and made friends easily wherever he went. Peek talked fluently and convincingly, generally converting others to his point of view. Customers found him persistent and doggedly determined.

Peek was forceful. In fact, he had more force than tact. He usually won his positions by frontal assaults rather than through diversionary tactics. Once, after he had become vice-president of Deere and Company, he was attending a conference of dealers and manufacturers. The dealers were sharply critical of the high prices for machinery repairs. One speaker for the manufacturers tried to humor the dealers, but not Peek. When he rose to speak, he said sharply: "I've been in the implement business 24 years, but never until now have I ever been accused of robbery, highway or low-way. Furthermore, I can't say that I like it a dambit." He snapped off the "dambit" in such a way that it had a meaning all of its own. Later he and the dealers got along fine, but Peek would not be bullied or pushed around. If there was any pushing, he would do it. He was sure of himself, inclined to be stubborn, and found compromise difficult.

Peek was baptized into the business world during a critical period. The panic years of the 1890's thoroughly tested his mettle as a salesman and collection agent. It was not easy to settle accounts with dealers who did business with farmers selling wheat for twenty-five to fifty cents a bushel.

On one occasion, after he had been in Minneapolis only a short time, he was sent to collect an account from a dealer in a small North Dakota town. When he arrived, representatives of other firms were ahead of him. Swearing loudly, the delinquent but rough and boisterous dealer cajoled the other collectors into leaving without getting a cent. Then turning to Peek with a scowl, he said in his booming voice: "Well, kid, you're next."[1] But bluff and bluster did not scare Peek. Before he left he had made the collection.

Peek's first big opportunity came out of adversity within the Deere organization. The John Deere Plow Company of Omaha, although located in the heart of the rich Missouri Valley, had consistently failed to make money. The depression of the 1890's was partly responsible, but even after good times returned in 1898, conditions in the Omaha branch continued bad. President Charles H. Deere wanted a new manager, as did the directors of the Omaha house. In looking over the field, Deere's eye fell on George Peek.

Peek's aggressive and efficient work in Minneapolis had already brought his promotion to head of the collection department. And more important, his leadership had attracted the attention of Deere and Company officials outside of the Twin Cities. Earlier Deere had remarked to Burton Peek: "I like that brother of yours. He thinks of things." Somebody needed to think of things if the Omaha branch was to show a profit.

So in 1901, just a few months before his twenty-eighth birthday, George Peek went to Omaha as general manager of the John Deere Plow Company. One of Deere's competitors in Omaha was heard to remark, "Well, Deere is about through out here and they have sent a boy to wind up the company."

Indeed, Peek did wind it up. He wound it so tight that the firm ran as never before. Soon things were humming around the Deere offices in Omaha. Sales began to climb and the books showed a substantial profit. In 1902, sales of the Omaha branch totaled only $793,756, but by 1910 they had risen to $4,577,715.[2] Such progress was unprecedented within the organization. By 1910, Peek had made the John Deere Plow Company of Omaha one of the most profitable branches of the firm. The early years of the twentieth century were fairly good ones for farmers, and this fact

[1] George F. Massey, "Considering George N. Peek," *Implement and Tractor Trade Journal*, Vol. XXXIV (May 3, 1919), 23.
[2] Records of the John Deere Plow Company of Omaha.

undoubtedly helped account for business increases at Omaha. But Willard D. Hosford, who later served as general manager, wrote, "I . . . think that George Peek was entitled to the bulk of the credit."[3]

Peek knew how to sell and, equally significant, how to collect. He also recognized the importance of credit and made friends with Omaha bankers, helping the dealers in his territory to make proper financial arrangements.

He worked hard to get his dealers to handle only Deere and Company implements. The John Deere name was good among farmers, and thus his task was made easier. He did not demand exclusive contracts or agreements which would force the dealer not to handle competitor's goods, but replies to his letters indicate that he sold many of the dealers in his territory on the principle of handling only Deere machinery. A dealer in Sioux City wrote, "Our trade on John Deere goods for 1910 will be between 15 and 20 times as large as it was 8 years ago."[4] Thus, he rapidly built up business for Deere and Company in his trade territory, which included Nebraska, Wyoming, western Iowa, and southern South Dakota.

A man of vision, Peek possessed a shrewd insight and general business wisdom which many of his associates lacked. His recognition of the decline of the use of horses on American farms illustrates this point. While absent from Deere and Company and serving on the War Industries Board in World War I, he advised a member of his firm that the "horse is going out of commission so rapidly that I fear an overproduction of horse drawn implements and an underproduction on tractor drawn tools." He added a short time later, "The trade on horse drawn tools is going to gradually grow less and the trade on tractor tools rapidly grow greater." Peek probably did not recognize how accurate his prediction was, and it contrasted sharply with the opinion of some other Deere and Company officials. He usually made the right business decisions and made them at the right time.

When Peek arrived in Omaha, he was single, a little cocky, and supremely self-confident. He was a hard-working, serious young man who tended strictly to business. Yet, he lived a full, well-

---

3 Willard D. Hosford to author, September 26, 1950.
4 Quoted in Deere and Company's *Salesman's Manual*, 1912.

rounded life. Although he had inherited the Puritan virtues of hard work, thrift, and diligence, George was uninhibited by Puritan social standards. He liked expensive cigars, an occasional drink of whiskey, golf, and Saturday-night poker games with the boys. He lived well and enjoyed the pulsing life found in a rapidly growing town like Omaha. At first he had bachelor quarters at the Paxton Hotel, but in 1902 he moved to the Omaha Club.

On December 22, 1903, Peek married Georgia Lindsey, daughter of Zachary T. Lindsey, president of the Interstate Rubber Company. The Peeks had no children of their own, but adopted a daughter, who died in 1911 at the age of three. Mrs. Peek was a spirited and talented woman, who was a match for her energetic husband. She was a devout Episcopalian. George was largely indifferent to organized Christianity, and took little or no active part in church activities. Rather than attending church, he was more apt to be on the golf course or in his office on Sunday morning.

While Peek was building up the John Deere Plow Company in Omaha, he closely observed the prevailing economic winds. The dominating characteristic in the business world during the McKinley–Theodore Roosevelt Era, especially from 1898 to 1903, was consolidation and concentration of both management and production. The trust, popularized in the 1880's by Rockefeller's Standard Oil Company, had given way to other types of organization among the larger firms. Holding companies were being organized to bring new business efficiency, and as a means of cutting down or eliminating competition. Illustrative of the holding-company development was the formation of the Northern Securities Company, a railroad combine, in 1901, United States Steel the same year, and the International Harvester Company in 1902. In most instances, but not always, holding companies brought competing firms together under one unified and noncompetitive management and operation.

To Peek and a number of other young executives, the Deere and Company organization was sadly outdated, a replica of the mid-nineteenth century. The original company had been incorporated in 1868 for fifty years. It owned a controlling interest in the branch distributing houses located in Minneapolis, San Francisco, Kansas City, Portland, Dallas, and other cities. The Deere branch companies jobbed machinery manufactured by allied, but noncompeting firms like Deere and Mansur of Moline (corn planters and disc harrows); Moline Wagon Company (farm wagons); Union Malleable Iron Company of Moline (malleable iron and castings); Dain Manufacturing Company of Ottumwa, Iowa (hay tools); Syracuse Chilled Plow Company (plows); Kemp and Burpee of Syracuse (manure spreaders); and Van Brunt Manufacturing Company of Horicon, Wisconsin (grain drills).

But Charles H. Deere, head of the company, was in ill health. He did not have the strength and energy to carry through plans for consolidation. In 1907, however, Deere died, and William Butterworth, his son-in-law, became president. After that plans moved ahead rapidly for a reorganization of the company. A committee was appointed in 1909 to direct the reorganization, and Peek was a member of this seven-man group.

Although there were others of equal importance, Peek was among those who worked hard to bring about a company reorganization. He believed that the allied factories and distributing houses should be unified under Deere and Company's control and direction. This was in keeping with the general business trend. Moreover, he believed that Deere would be more able to compete successfully in all lines with the International Harvester Company. Thus, it was George Peek who offered the formal resolution "to purchase and hold the capital stock of companies manufacturing goods handled by Deere and Company and its branches." By 1911 plans were completed for reorganization along this line. Now Deere and Company, a new holding and operating company, was able to produce and distribute a more complete line of farm machinery.

The first official act of the new company was to invite Peek to become vice-president in charge of sales. President Butterworth said that the firm should "have the benefit of the experience of a man who was familiar with branch house organization and the various lines."[5] Other officials heartily supported the move to bring Peek to Moline. Although Peek said he was reluctant to leave Omaha, he was willing to do whatever seemed best to the board of directors. Actually, he was less modest than would appear from his statement. He was not the kind of a man who would

[5] Deere and Company Corporate Records, Vol. I, Moline, Illinois.

pass up an opportunity to get to the top in his business or profession.

The Peeks moved to Moline in the summer of 1911. Shortly afterwards, George began to build a spacious country home, Fairacres, on the south edge of the city, overlooking the Rock River. His brother, Burton, also lived in Moline, having become general counsel and treasurer of Deere and Company in 1907.

Peek's first major job was to write a salesman's manual which was designed for the information, guidance, and instruction of traveling salesmen. This seems to have been the first attempt to formalize the company's sales policy. Although he advised salesmen to seek full-line representation for John Deere goods among dealers, Peek did not demand exclusive contracts. In this regard, he anticipated the Clayton Anti-Trust Act of 1914 by at least two years. Among other things, this law prohibited the sale of goods upon the condition that the dealer should not handle competitive articles.

Peek told his salesmen: "There will always be competition in the implement business . . . . Your position as a salesman is strengthened rather than weakened by wholesome competition. . . . The stronger your position in the trade, the more you advertise a competitor by mentioning his name or seriously discussing his proposition. All the money, energy, and talent that any or all of us have to expend along the line of advertising should be devoted wholly to the merits of our own goods . . . ."[6]

After the Clayton Act was passed, Peek emphasized that Deere and Company must follow both the letter and spirit of the law. "It means," he wrote, "that our prices and terms cannot vary between dealers who give us a like business; that cash discounts cannot vary; that we must treat all customers alike in interest charges and in allowances for pre-payment. The rules that we adopt for quantity discount cannot vary. All must be treated by the same rule." He added that Deere and Company was not seeking a monopoly and said that "we will get exclusive trade only when we earn it."[7]

Peek forged ahead in the implement trade and was soon recognized as one of the outstanding young executives in the business.

6 Deere and Company, *Salesman's Manual*, 1912.
7 *Ibid.*, 1919.

In 1914 he gave the main address before the Retail Implement Dealers Association, and by 1917 he was serving on the executive committee of the National Implement and Vehicle Association. While he was popular within his own organization, there was little likelihood that he would ever become head of the firm, since the presidents were generally chosen from the Deere family.

Peek did not confine himself exclusively to the implement business. He liked the business of living. He was a member of the Rock Island Arsenal Golf Club and played golf one or two afternoons a week. He was also a member of the Chicago Club and of the Fort Smith, Arkansas, Country Club. He traveled widely for both business and pleasure.

His growing financial affluence made possible a way of life which he thoroughly enjoyed. Peek's salary was $12,000 a year, but the basis of his later financial independence was laid when he, along with other executives in the firm, took a large block of common stock in the reorganized company. This stock was sold to a selected group at $100 a share, half of which was to be paid in cash and half in services. At first the stock was worth little and paid no dividends, but as Deere and Company prospered it increased in value and sold for over $600 a share in the late 1920's. Peek disposed of most of his holdings prior to the crash of 1929. As Bernard Baruch said, "He knew when to buy and when to sell."

Despite growing prominence in the farm implement business, it was not until the United States entered World War I that Peek won national attention. Early in December, 1917, he was appointed as industrial representative on the War Industries Board. Board member Alex Legge, general manager of International Harvester Company and Peek's chief business rival, first suggested that he be brought to Washington.

The job of the industrial representative was to convert the country's manufacturing to war work. He was to advise agencies on locating new production facilities, help industry find the necessary supplies, and divert commodities to military or civilian uses, depending on where they were needed. "He was to be a sort of generalissimo of industry under the War Industries Board," wrote Grosvenor B. Clarkson.[8]

[8] Grosvenor B. Clarkson, *Industrial America in the World War* (Boston, 1923), 240.

Neither Peek nor other members of the board were able to accomplish much in late 1917 and during the early weeks of 1918. The board drifted along with inadequate authority and leadership until President Wilson appointed Bernard Baruch as the new chairman in March, 1918.

Baruch was a man of many unusual talents. Starting with next to nothing, he had by shrewd trading and speculation built a fortune estimated at $10,000,000. He was unobligated to any group or faction and had the courage of his convictions. Most of all he was devoted to the public interest. Not the least of his attributes was his knowledge of men. When he became chairman of the W.I.B., he surrounded himself with up and coming young executives who could get the job done. As Clarkson has said, he passed over the "old warhorses," despite their reputations, and picked the coming business leaders for his most important positions.

Under the reorganized board, Peek was appointed commissioner of finished products. He had the real responsibility of co-ordinating American industry with civilian and military needs, and seeing that industrial conversion to war needs was accomplished.

Peek had great faith in the American economy. He believed with proper organization and co-operation between government and industry that necessary supplies could be produced for the war without interfering too seriously with civilian production. Under Baruch's administration, Peek had an opportunity to bring about more effective co-operation between government and industry. Commodity sections were established, and specialized government representatives worked directly with corresponding industrial groups. Businessmen now found it relatively easy to do business with the government, and the government in turn was able to get the supplies it needed. Peek administered five divisions of commodity sections, plus the facilities division. He proved to be an excellent administrator in government as he had been in private business. The success of the War Industries Board is a permanent testimony to the ability of Peek and others on whom Baruch relied.

Peek did not concern himself with the affairs of Deere and Company while he served in Washington. His company did not profit from his government connections, and he carefully observed the niceties of a businessman serving temporarily in Washington. At one time Deere and Company planned to build a steel shed, but the scheme was dropped when Peek advised that the use of critical material might be subject to criticism.[9] When he later became head of the Industrial Board, he resigned his executive positions in Deere and Company. Peek said that he regretted having to disassociate himself from the company with which he had been connected for twenty-six years, but he believed that he could not properly undertake such an important government job and still maintain his private interests.

Government service fascinated Peek. He enjoyed the administrative opportunities and he liked to be in the center of things. Shortly after arriving in Washington, he wrote his friend C. D. Velie: "Really, Charley, this is the most interesting thing in the world down here. The problems which I run into . . . and have more or less a part in straightening out are absorbing to the last degree."

The experiences which Peek gained on the W.I.B. made a deep impression upon him. To him, the war demonstrated the desirability of business co-operation. He hoped that "conditions of highly competitive situations" would not be restored with the return to peace. In his letter of resignation of December 17, 1918, he told Baruch:

> It has been demonstrated, I think, that co-operation among the members of industry is beneficial, not only to the members of the industry, but to the general public, and the benefits of proper co-operation should not be lost in return to peacetime conditions of highly competitive situations brought about by the normal operations of the law of supply and demand. Proper legislation should be enacted to permit co-operation in industry, in order that the lessons we have learned during the war may be capitalized in the interest of business and the public in peacetimes. Such questions as conservation to avoid wasteful use of materials, labor and capital; standardization of products and processes, price fixing under certain conditions, . . . should continue with government co-operation.

9 F. R. Todd to Peek, September 30, 1918. Peek Papers.

Here Peek seemed to have been advocating several of the principles incorporated in the National Recovery Act, passed some fifteen years later.

Peek was not only impressed with the desirability of co-operation among industries but also with the fact that policies of the federal government could greatly help or hinder business. Within a short time he was arguing that the government should be used as an instrument to help American agriculture.

The beginning of Peek's lifelong friendship and affection for "My dear chief," Bernard Baruch was the highlight of his career in Washington. It made no difference that Peek was a Republican and Baruch a Democrat. Peek became commonly known as one of "Baruch's boys." Later when Peek headed the campaign for agricultural equality, Baruch aided him with both his influence and his financial backing.

By late December, 1918, most of the work of the War Industries Board had been completed. On December 11, Peek's associates gave a dinner in his honor and presented him with "a beautiful cigarette case" inscribed with the words "a true finished product." He was proud of this loyalty, and it was clear that he prepared to leave government work with some reluctance. Yet business was his real career, and opportunities awaited him. He wrote President Butterworth on December 20 that he would return to Moline shortly, but that he wished to stay on a few days longer to see that the War Department canceled government contracts "in the proper spirit." He thought it was his duty to "see that the business interests of the country are properly protected after their loyal co-operation with the Government."

Peek was being urged to return home quickly. His brother Burton said that he would be much better off to forget government work and return to business. However, he did not act hastily. He went to New York on December 31 to see Baruch off to Paris, where he was to join President Wilson. Although the War Industries Board was officially disbanded on January 1, 1919, Baruch had asked Peek to remain until February 1 to see that the board's work was completed in "an orderly way." And then he could not dismiss the postwar problems from his mind. Even before the armistice Peek had pondered the necessary readjustments to a peacetime economy. Shortly after his appointment by Baruch, he stated that it was not enough simply to organize industry for war purposes. "The second problem," he said, "is to insure continuance of our industrial strength after the war." About the same time, he wrote to C. C. Webber, his former employer in Minneapolis, that he would use his influence to see that industry emerged "after the war strong and intact for the economical conditions which will face us."[10]

The uncertainties in business following the armistice brought deep concern to many officials in Washington. The highly inflationary wartime prices, it was thought, could not be maintained if business was to expand and prosper. Secretary of Commerce W. C. Redfield, wrote on February 6, 1919, that unemployment was partially due to "reluctance of buyers to purchase more than their emergency requirements at the present level of prices."

Peek was among those who hoped that the general price levels might be lowered through voluntary agreements between industry and government. He thought that if the producers of basic raw materials would lower their prices, public and government agencies would then go into the markets and buy freely. The scheme seemed simple—reduce prices, stimulate buying, increase employment, and eliminate the social unrest so prevalent in the country early in 1919.

Following conferences between members of the Cabinet and former War Industries Board officials, Secretary Redfield cabled President Wilson for permission to set up a special board or commission to work with industry in establishing lower price levels on basic commodities. "Business has become stagnant," Redfield said, and "industrial activity has slackened because of lack of orders from consumers who are buying merest necessities waiting for prices to fall. As a result the number of unemployed already large is increasing rapidly. If this condition continues, social disturbances will result and financial failures sufficient to induce a condition of panic may be expected." The Secretary asked that Peek be made head of a new board within his department to deal with the situation.[11] On February 13, President Wilson authorized

10 Peek to Webber, February 4, 1918. *Ibid.*

11 Cablegram, Redfield to Woodrow Wilson, February 6, 1919. Cited in George N. Peek, *History of the Industrial Board* (n. p., n. d.), 7.

the establishment of the Industrial Board and five days later Secretary Redfield formally asked Peek to act as chairman.

Peek undertook the new job with his usual enthusiasm. If the problem of unrest throughout the country was not met, he said, "we are going to have state socialism." He constantly referred to the dangers to the "American system" unless a proper price adjustment was made. He told industrialists that they had made good profits during the war and now must "stand the first shock of readjustment." To do this, he expected industry to "go down in its pocket, if need be."[12]

On February 24, Peek wrote Baruch: "You played a hell of a trick on me in relieving me for this job. I do not know whether or not you appreciate the difficulties. . . . Everything depends upon the co-operation of industry." Baruch agreed that it was a "most difficult undertaking" but predicted that Peek's "courage and patience, knowledge and experience, and good judgment" would pull him through.[13]

Despite the difficulties of operating on a voluntary basis, Peek was optimistic about obtaining lower prices through conferences with different industries. Although the board had no power to force price declines, Peek wrote that "we are going to make a success of it." "I have great faith in the fairness of American businessmen and in the ability to accomplish things by co-operation."[14]

The importance of steel in the industrial structure pointed toward seeking price reductions there first of all. On March 19 and 20, following preliminary conferences, Peek met with representatives of the steel industry in New York. After considerable discussion a new and substantially lower schedule of steel prices was agreed upon. For example, the price of steel rails was reduced $10 a ton, or from $55 to $45. This, indeed, was an auspicious beginning and negotiations proceeded next in the glass, coal, lumber, cement, and other industries.

But the Board's program was short lived, and its death came from a most unexpected source—departments of the United States

[12] Quoted in the record of a meeting of the Industrial Board with James Bell, March 17, 1919. Copy in Peek Papers.

[13] Peek to Baruch, February 24, and Baruch to Peek, February 27, 1919. *Ibid.*

[14] Peek to D. R. McLennan, February 24, 1919. *Ibid.*

George N. Peek, about 1918

government. Peek shortly discovered that Walker D. Hines, director general of the railroads, would not co-operate. Hines informed Peek that the Railroad Administration would not buy rails at the price agreed upon between the steel industry and the board. He argued that the board was attempting to fix prices, a policy which he abhorred and which the President had not intended. The Railroad Administration, he said, could buy at lower prices "unless the government . . . shall lend its aid to the steel and iron interests to support prices . . . on the level now fixed."[15]

Hines' refusal to co-operate with the board led to a bitter but fruitless quarrel between him and Peek. It was obvious that the whole program would have to be abandoned if government departments refused to purchase at the agreed prices. A number of conferences were held with Hines during April but he would not budge from his position.

Peek realized that it was a conflict which only the President could solve. He knew, too, that most of Wilson's advisers, except Secretary Redfield, were supporting Hines. Thus he wrote on April 10, "I may be out of a Government job very shortly."

As a last resort, Redfield appealed to President Wilson who cabled on April 18 that he did not think it wise to extend the work of the board. This was the death knell, and Peek submitted his resignation four days later. Although some further last minute attempts were made to iron out the differences, Redfield accepted the resignations of Peek and other members of the board on May 9. The next day in a parting blast Peek charged that not only Hines and the "old railroad guard," but Secretary Glass and partisan politics had destroyed the program. Glass replied that "there is scarcely one accurate assertion or sane deduction in all of Mr. Peek's intemperate screed."[16] And there the matter rested.

Generally speaking, the country's press did not mourn the board's passing. "That such a body could straighten out and guide the price situation was only an evanescent dream," said the Philadelphia *Press*. The New York *Mail* stated that price fixing was dead and "most of us are satisfied with that admitted fact." A widely published chain editorial was extremely critical of the

15 Hines to Carter Glass, April 4, 1919; in Peek's *History of the Industrial Board*, 29–33.
16 Washington *Post*, May 12, 1919.

board and said Peek was "mourning at its bier."[17]

Businessmen and industrialists were much more inclined to support Peek. The *Manufacturers Record* said that administration politics had defeated "the only constructive program the administration had attempted to assist in readjustment and reconstruction." The *Implement and Tractor Trade Journal* also supported Peek's position.

The program of the Industrial Board foreshadowed some aspects of the National Recovery Act. The idea of permitting uniform prices throughout an entire industry with government support was not unlike policies followed by the Franklin D. Roosevelt administration in 1933. Although labor was not to be protected by law, it was Peek's intention that price adjustments should be made without cutting wages. At least, he said, not until the cost of living had dropped. Furthermore, Peek argued that his board was not fixing prices but just suggesting a guide.

It is not surprising that Democrats like Carter Glass, imbued with Wilsonian philosophy of business competition, should oppose the Peek plan of stabilized prices. And a generation raised on the "law of supply and demand" as the determinant of economic action could only be expected to oppose a peacetime program bordering on price-fixing. Also Peek's unfortunate experience with economic planning reflected a dissatisfaction with wartime restrictions and a desire to return to "normalcy," where government control and influence over the economy would be held to a minimum.

Swallowing his bitter experience, Peek took a short vacation and then returned to Moline. By this time he did not regret shaking the Washington dust from his feet. However, he surprised many of his associates by not assuming his old job at Deere and Company. As early as December, 1918, he had confided to his brother Burton that "I may get a chance to go to the other side of the street . . . and if I do, I want to avail myself of it." "The other side of the street" meant the Moline Plow Company, which had offices directly across from Deere and Company.

Since Peek had resigned as a director and vice-president of Deere and Company when he was appointed head of the Indus-

17 Philadelphia *Press,* April 9, 1919; New York *Mail,* May 13, 1919; and Niagara Falls *Gazette,* May 20, 1919.

trial Board, he was free to accept the presidency of the Moline Plow Company owned by John N. Willys. He was to get $100,000 a year. Peek was an ambitious executive, and the idea of being top man in a large farm-implement business had a strong appeal. By August, Peek was in his new office, writing, "I have some real big things in mind and hope to be able to pull some of them off."

One of his first steps was the employment of Hugh Johnson. Peek had first met Johnson in 1917, when the General represented the War Department on the War Industries Board. After the war Johnson had established an office in Washington to represent contractors who were seeking settlements with the government. "General Johnson," Peek said, "is one of the best men I know."[18]

Willys could scarcely have found a more able team of executives than Peek and Johnson. Yet, within less than a year, the Moline Plow Company was on the verge of financial ruin. In fact, it was virtually bankrupt before Peek took over, something which, surprisingly, he did not know until it was too late. The internal condition of the company was such that it could scarcely have remained solvent in the most prosperous times. To make matters worse, the market for plows and other types of farm machinery began to decline sharply as the farm depression hit the country in the summer of 1920. For the next four years Peek struggled to put the firm on its feet, but he failed.

As a member of the industry which felt the first shock of the agricultural depression, Peek now turned his attention to the causes and remedies for the farmers' ills. For all practical purposes he dedicated the rest of his life to obtaining "equality for agriculture." The implement industry lost a vigorous, capable executive, but the farmers gained an influential and persistent friend.

18 Peek to W. M. Ritter, August 9, 1919. Peek Papers.

Chapter I I I

Equality for Agriculture:
The Campaign Begins

URING 1920 and 1921, while government officials, farm leaders, politicians, ordinary dirt farmers, and others were anxiously seeking a solution for farm ills, George Peek sat in his office eyeing bleak sales charts of the Moline Plow Company. They showed only one thing—mounting losses. Peek was a man who came quickly to the heart of a problem, and this time was no exception. "You can't sell a plow to a busted customer," he exclaimed.

For more than a year he and Hugh Johnson had discussed the plight of agriculture in connection with the sad predicament of their own company. By December, 1921, they had developed a plan of "equality for agriculture." This was the genesis of the McNary-Haugen bills, the most celebrated farm relief proposal of the 1920's. The phrase "equality for agriculture," which they coined and popularized, became the battle cry of the farm crusade which continued with only occasional abatement until the Agricultural Adjustment Act was passed in May, 1933. Here was the idea of parity, which finally became an accepted part of American farm policy.

Peek and Johnson saw the farmer's trouble in the operation of the protective tariff. In considering the problem, they concluded that agricultural tariffs did not protect farm crops of which the United States produced a surplus. For instance, the world price of wheat determined the domestic price, despite the tariff, because American surpluses forced the home market down to world levels. But while producers of surplus farm commodities had to take world prices, they were required to buy manufactured goods in a protected market, where industrial tariffs were effective and caused higher prices. In other words, farmers were buying in a protected market and selling in the competitive markets of the world. The result was a marked disparity or inequality between agriculture and industry.

To restore any degree of farm prosperity, Peek and Johnson declared, the protective principle had to be amended so that "it will do for agriculture what it does for industry." The tariff should be made effective for the farmers, they said, and this could be done by removing or segregating the surplus which depressed the domestic price to approximately the world level. They thought that agriculture must be placed in a position to do for itself what industry did, namely, to "regulate supply to demand on the domestic market."[1] Unlike industrialists, farmers could not easily control their production because of weather, pests, and diseases, their inability to co-operate, and other factors. Therefore, the effective arm of government must be called on to bring farmers together for their own benefit.

Surpluses were the burdensome factor. If they could be eliminated from the domestic market, then the price of farm commodities could rise behind a tariff wall. In order to remove surplus crops, Peek and Johnson proposed dumping them abroad at the world price. Peek was familiar with such sales tactics in industry, and it is significant that he, a businessman, should point to this two-price system. He did not cite specific examples, however, and dumping was not practiced by Deere and Company. Nonetheless, it was common for industries such as United States Steel and Standard Oil to sell surpluses in foreign countries at less than domestic prices. Dumping made it possible to produce in excess of domestic requirements, yet preserve higher prices at home. But because of its ability to regulate production, industry could carry on the two-price system much more successfully than agriculture.

If the farmer could achieve effective protection, Peek declared, his products would have a "fair exchange value" with those of industry. Thus, equality for agriculture would be achieved. Since farmers had been relatively prosperous before World War I, he defined a fair exchange value as "one which bears the same ratio

[1] George N. Peek and Hugh S. Johnson, *Equality for Agriculture* (1st. ed., Moline, 1922), 20.

to [the] current general price index as a ten-year pre-war average crop price bore to [the] average general price index for the same period." To get this result he suggested that a fair exchange value or ratio-price be established by law and a fluctuating tariff created to protect that price on the domestic market. The price of farm commodities would, therefore, rise and decline with the general price level and provide a farm dollar with a fair and stable purchasing power. Peek's idea of a fair price was cost of production, plus a profit. He mentioned this in the first edition of *Equality for Agriculture*, as well as in his personal correspondence.

Under the Peek plan surplus farm commodities must be removed from the domestic market. To do this, he said, a government corporation should purchase the surpluses and sell them abroad at world prices. Losses on foreign sales were to be paid by the farmers themselves through a tax or equalization fee on each bushel or pound of a commodity sold. This was the essence of the ideas presented by Peek and Johnson in an unsigned forty-eight-page pamphlet entitled *Equality for Agriculture*. Proof copies were ready for distribution in the last days of December, 1921. The ideas were primarily Peek's, and some three thousand copies of the first brief were printed.

Essentially an economic nationalist, Peek was devoted to the principles of high protection. He never seriously entertained the idea of trying to help agriculture by lowering industrial tariffs. He abhorred free trade as the worst kind of economic poison. "America could make no greater blunder at this crisis than to abandon protection," he wrote. And he added, "We erected a tariff to protect our industry and our living standards from cheap foreign competition, but we left a breach in the agricultural curtain of defense."[2]

For years farmers had realized the ineffectiveness of tariff protection except for such specialized crops as sugar, wool, and butter. In the 1890's, David Lubin of California, along with others, emphasized how "manufactures are sold in our country at enhanced or artificial prices, while agricultural staples are sold for export and home use at the world's free-trade prices." He added that agriculture was the "only great industry . . . that must sell its products at the world's free-trade prices, and must through the operation

2 *Ibid.,* 13 and 40.

Chicago Tribune Syndicate

McCutcheon's "Unequally Protected"
The situation for agriculture had been anomalous

of the tariff, pay protection prices for necessities."[3] Despite the fact that increasing duties on staple farm commodities had little or no effect in raising the domestic price, tariffs continued to have a strong appeal to American farmers.

It is also clear that by 1920, farmers and farm leaders had caught the over-all significance of the surplus problem. In November, 1920, more than a year before the publication of Peek's first brief, the idea was admirably stated by a Kansas farmer. He discussed the effect of agricultural surpluses and said that manufacturers did not permit the foreign market to determine their domestic prices. To meet the problem, he suggested that a national farmers' corporation might control wheat marketing by segregating the small surplus and selling it abroad.[4] Several of the plans offered in Congress during 1920 and 1921 were aimed at eliminating price-depressing surpluses.

As previously shown, the post-war depression had brought the matter of relative values into sharp focus. Although they did not use the exact term, farmers emphasized the ratio-price idea. An Idaho farmer wrote to Secretary Wallace in January, 1922, that "Relative values are what we are after."[5]

Thus, it is seen that Peek did not invent any novel or original ideas. Most concepts, in fact, are not actually new when they become accepted. As Fritz Redlich has written, "What actually makes the great business leader and statesman is the instinct for choosing the idea suited to the day or the ability to effect a new combination of ideas, a combination in which an older thought can suddenly become a propelling one."[6] It was in the over-all grasp of the situation and his forceful presentation that Peek had no peer. Agricultural economist Henry C. Taylor said that Peek and Johnson had thought "out this whole question of the relation of tariff to agriculture more completely than any one else I know of."[7]

[3] *McNary-Haugen Bill,* Hearings Before the House Agriculture Committee, 68 Cong., 1 sess., 349–50. Lubin suggested an export bounty as the best solution to this problem.

[4] A letter to *Wallace's Farmer,* Vol. VL (November 12, 1920), 2616.

[5] William Potter to Henry C. Wallace, January 16, 1922. Files of the Secretary of Agriculture.

[6] Fritz Redlich, *History of American Business Leaders,* II, pt. I (New York, 1947), 2.

[7] Taylor to Peek, December 14, 1922. Peek Papers.

Peek was an agrarian at heart. The fact that plow sales were slow only partially explains his intense interest in the farm problem. Although he had achieved prominence and wealth in the field of industry, he believed fervently in the importance of agriculture. Like Jefferson, his ideal America was one where independent and self-reliant farmers were a dominant group. "Red doctrine thrives in industrialism," he wrote in his first brief. But he concluded: "It fails in a community of land owners. There was never a red upheaval without an agrarian question. We are rapidly incubating such a question. The essence of our political genius flows from a land-owning agricultural community." Here, then, was the driving force behind Peek's campaign to achieve equality for agriculture. And these same Jeffersonian concepts won many recruits for the ensuing battle.

Peek had first begun serious study of the farm problem in the early summer of 1920, even before prices commenced to drop. He and Johnson prepared a thirty-page memorandum entitled "An Analysis of Present Day Agricultural Problems," which was edited by officers of the American Farm Bureau Federation. At the time, almost no one knew of the memorandum's origin. It was distributed to a select group of interested citizens in August. Copies were given both to Warren G. Harding and to James M. Cox during the presidential campaign, and Peek presented it to Senator Medill McCormick, who took up the matter personally with Harding. Although the statement dealt largely with problems of transportation, finance, and labor, Peek's basic ideas were evident. "The earth is the source of all wealth. . . . Agriculture is the basic foundation of every human endeavor," said the memorandum. To this physiocratic concept was added the statement, "Industrial peace and agricultural prosperity will only be assured when the men whose labor feeds the world shall receive in exchange, products of industrial labor representing an equivalent in human effort."[8] From this beginning, Peek and Johnson expanded their idea the following year.

As the depression worsened and farmers bitterly complained, it is not surprising that officers of the American Farm Bureau Federation lent a willing ear to Peek's plans when he approached them early in 1921. After preliminary discussions with President

8 Typescript dated August, 1920. *Ibid.*

James R. Howard in Chicago, Peek presented a more complete outline of his ideas in October to Howard and to J. W. Coverdale, secretary of the Farm Bureau.

During the next few weeks, Peek disclosed his views to a number of influential people, including his old chief, Bernard Baruch. Baruch received a copy of the brief in the first week of January, 1922. On January 9, he wrote that he had studied the tentative proposal and "I have not yet been able to punch a hole in the plan." At about the same time, Johnson communicated with Secretary Hoover, explaining, "We consulted the best minds among our confidential friends on the economic questions and were invariably assured that the plan was sound."

The first stroke of luck for publicizing the surplus-control plan came when Secretary Henry C. Wallace called a national agricultural conference in January, 1922. The day after Wallace announced the forthcoming meeting, W. M. Ritter, one of Peek's Washington friends, wired him, "It would seem to me . . . that you and General Johnson should by all means take an important interest in this conference and why would that not be the place to develop the plan that you have started?"[9] On January 10, Secretary Wallace asked Peek to be a delegate. This was the opportunity for which he had been waiting.

Peek and Johnson acted immediately to lay the groundwork for their campaign in Washington. Copies of the unsigned brief were distributed to key people, and they called on their main supporter, Baruch. Johnson wired Baruch of Peek's appointment to the conference, and added: "Howard favors plan and thinks it can be put over. No one has punched a hole. We are going to Washington latter part of next week and with your help put plan over."[10]

Arriving in Washington on Friday morning, January 20, Peek and Johnson settled comfortably at the old Shoreham Hotel. Johnson left at once to confer with Secretary Hoover, who had previously received a copy of the brief. Hoover strongly objected to the principles, but agreed to give the plan further study. His main criticism was that if farm prices were raised, the general price

9 Ritter to Peek, December 31, 1921. *Ibid.*
10 Johnson to Baruch, January 11, 1922. *Ibid.*

index would rise.[11] Johnson later declared that it had been a mistake to discuss the scheme with Hoover, "who was intent on building export trade and would consider nothing that would raise the cost of American industrial products."[12]

In the afternoon Peek and Johnson called on Secretary Wallace. He had not yet read the brief, but they discussed the general ideas. Although the Secretary favored broad discussion of agricultural conditions, he did not want the conference to get off on the political aspects of the tariff. Peek and Johnson agreed. Wallace believed that the ratio-price idea was so encompassing that if it were mentioned, nothing else might come out of the meeting. The Secretary told Peek and Johnson to see Sydney Anderson, permanent chairman of the conference.

They hurried to Anderson's office. The Minnesota congressman said that it would be inconsistent to raise this question because the official position of the Republican party on the tariff already had been stated. Higher agricultural rates, Anderson said, was the accepted remedy. He also remarked that he would not permit the conference to enter into a discussion which might lead to such broad considerations. Besides, the program was prepared.

Having been unable to make much progress with Wallace, and none at all with Hoover or Anderson, the "Men from Moline" met with Henry C. Taylor, chief of the Bureau of Markets. But Taylor was so busy with conference arrangements that he did not have time to discuss the proposal at length. Moreover, he had not read the brief.

The National Agricultural Conference opened on January 23 with a speech by President Harding, probably written by Judson Welliver, but sounding as though it might have come from the pen of Herbert Hoover. There was certainly nothing in it to encourage those who were seeking unconventional remedies for the agricultural situation. "It can not be too strongly urged," the President said, "that the farmer must be ready to help himself. This conference would do most lasting good if it would find ways to impress the great mass of farmers to avail themselves of the best methods. By this I mean that, in the last analysis, legislation can

11 Peek and Johnson, "Memorandum on What Happened in Washington," February 20, 1922. Typescript. *Ibid.*

12 Hugh S. Johnson, *Blue Eagle from Egg to Earth* (New York, 1935), 105.

do little more than give the farmer the chance to organize and help himself."

Self-help through co-operatives or better credit and transportation facilities fell far short of what actual farmers were asking. There was an obvious discord between the tunes coming from the grass roots and the White House. Secretary Wallace had received scores of letters from farmers just before the conference opened, demanding quick and positive government action to raise farm prices. Over a hundred Montana farmers signed a petition asking for a revival of the United States Grain Corporation. "We propose this," said the request, "as the only thing that will prevent another disastrous year for grain farmers. . . . We see no hope of relief within a reasonable time unless the government . . . undertakes to pool all the country's wheat, and sell it as it did in the war."[13]

Farmers tended to scorn more credit and co-operative marketing as solutions to their immediate problems. A fair price is what we need, they said. From the great wheat-raising sections of the country a strong plea was made for a government-guaranteed price. J. S. Wannamaker, president of the American Cotton Association, expressed similar sentiments for the cotton south. No immediate good could come from discussing the St. Lawrence waterway, he said, when farmers were daily going bankrupt. Wannamaker declared that it was the duty of the government to use its vast power and wealth to raise farm prices.[14] Wartime price guarantees had deeply impressed farmers, and they often mentioned that experience in their letters.

This is not to say that a majority of farmers were asking for some kind of price supports, but many of them were. A digest of farm opinion, gleaned from letters in the Department of Agriculture, was made for Secretary Wallace. Out of about one hundred communications from all sections of the country, twenty-three of them called for price-fixing, guaranteed cost of production, or similar measures. At about the same time Senator Norris declared that a strong feeling existed among farm leaders that Congress should set a minimum price for a selected list of farm crops.[15]

[13] John A. Fox to Wallace, January 12, 1922. Files of the Secretary of Agriculture.

The Peek plan was actually much more conservative than many of the ideas being urged upon the Department of Agriculture. Peek never considered the ratio-price idea as price-fixing, and he was as much opposed to this as the most loyal Hooverite. Early in 1922 he predicted that the price-fixing bills then before Congress would be defeated, and he added, "I think there is a very great difference between fixing a price and establishing a relationship, the effect of which is to allow a free play in price fluctuations but which makes it possible to secure a fair price, which is cost of production, plus a profit."[16]

The conference was divided into twelve groups and Peek was assigned to the committee on farm marketing. The first afternoon he briefly discussed the principles of equality for agriculture, but was informed that his ideas more properly belonged in the subcommittee which was studying price-fixing. Peek attempted to meet with this group, but was denied a hearing. The subject, he was told, had been definitely closed by the resolution of Julius Barnes. Barnes, one of the nation's leading grain exporters, was a close friend of Hoover and president of the United States Chamber of Commerce. He had opposed calling any conference and was unhappy with Secretary Wallace for doing so. Barnes' resolution declared: "With respect to the question of government price guarantees, we feel that there should be a comprehensive study of this subject; therefore, we urge that the Congress cause a careful investigation of this whole problem."

Thus during the first day of the conference, Peek had been able only to mention his plan. The next morning, however, he told Henry C. Taylor of his problem, and Taylor arranged for him to appear before the committee on agricultural price relations. The chairman said he would allow Peek ten minutes. Peek launched into a discussion of the inequality of agriculture, followed by an explanation of his ratio-price plan. Among those who listened carefully to his arguments were Henry A. Wallace, L. J. Taber, of the National Grange, and Samuel Gompers, president of the American Federation of Labor. Before finishing, Peek had spoken for an hour and a half. At least one conference committee

14 Wannamaker to Wallace, February 17, 1922. *Ibid.*
15 Norris to G. W. McConaughy, January 20, 1922. Norris Papers.
16 Peek to W. H. Lyon, March 20, 1922. Peek Papers.

had become thoroughly familiar with Peek's ideas, and he won some converts.

The same evening he returned to a general session of the committee on marketing, where resolutions were being considered. The Barnes resolution on price-fixing was looked upon as worthless by such members of the committee as W. H. Lyon, and John A. Simpson, militant president of the Oklahoma Farmers Union. Simpson presented a minority report which declared that in light of agriculture's importance and condition, "it is the sense of this committee that the Congress and President take such steps as will immediately guarantee a price below which no farmers in this country will have to sell his 1922 crop of corn, wheat, and cotton."

Peek saw immediately that Simpson's resolution would not be approved by the hostile committee, so he hastily amended it to read: ". . . it is the sense of this committee that the Congress and the President of the United States should take such steps as will immediately re-establish a fair exchange value for all farm products with that of all other commodities."[17]

The Peek amendment was unanimously passed and became a part of the marketing committee's formal report and recommendation. He had succeeded in getting his basic idea of farm parity incorporated in the proceedings of the conference.

This was a fair beginning, but Peek had only begun to fight. As Russell Lord has written, he was a man of "magnificent stubbornness," and he would not leave Washington until his ideas had received a better hearing. He was in dead earnest about doing something for agriculture. Peek had not gone to Washington just for a change of scenery. He meant to get results. The pious platitudes and thirty-seven general legislative recommendations of the conference might pay the administration's political debt to farmers, but they did not satisfy Peek. While other delegates were leaving for home, he was devising new strategy. On Saturday, the day after the conference closed, Peek and Johnson met with Secretary Wallace. They asked him to call together a small group of "competent critics" to pass upon the practicability of the plan.

First, however, Wallace said that he wanted the economists of his own department to study the brief. The first week of February

17 *Report of the National Agricultural Conference,* 1922, 67 Cong., 2 sess., *H. Doc. No. 195,* p. 171.

then was devoted to discussing the proposal with Taylor, B. H. Hibbard of the University of Wisconsin, George F. Warren of Cornell, and others. At first the agricultural economists scoffed at the plan, but Peek kept hammering away at them. When the question arose as to what kind of legislative mechanism might be devised to determine the ratio-price, to segregate the surplus, and to levy a tax or fee on farmers to pay for export losses, Peek said that he did not feel qualified to develop a full-fledged plan. If the principles were sound, he argued, members of Congress or some other group could develop a workable mechanism. Though the economists may have remained doubtful, at least Secretary Wallace was friendly to Peek's ideas. Taylor, if not yet in complete agreement, kept an open mind. In a memorandum for the Secretary dated February 5, he concluded, "Some plan of this kind must be added to the tariff idea in order to make the tariff effective in holding up the prices of products."[18]

Peek was a clear thinker and unusually convincing. But he was single-minded. He did not see all of the economic relationships, or show much interest in taking all of the intellectual excursions which a professional economist might want to consider. Part of his economic argument was weak, because he failed to take into consideration the over-all complexity of economic conditions, both national and international. He saw a practical problem and believed that he had the correct answer. Peek drove straight ahead in a manner characteristic of men of action.

Peek and Johnson also discussed their ideas with several senators, including W. S. Kenyon, Arthur Capper, Reed Smoot, James W. Wadsworth, J. W. Harreld, Robert L. Owen, Medill McCormick, and William B. McKinley. They were offered several opportunities to discuss their proposal before Congressional committees, but their first aim was to sell the administration. Above all, they wanted action, and action could be secured most readily by getting support of the Republicans in power.

Within a few days, Secretary Wallace consented to call a group of business and financial leaders together to discuss the ratio-price plan. Peek declared that he "desired to lay the whole situation before the representative heads of industry which would be most affected by governmental intervention."

[18] Henry C. Taylor, "Memorandum to the Secretary." Files of the Secretary of Agriculture.

This meeting is one of the most interesting and significant steps in the early drive for agricultural equality. The conference met on February 13. Those present were suggested by Peek and Johnson and included: Julius H. Barnes; Charles G. Dawes, director of the budget; Otto Kahn of Kuhn, Loeb and Company; Fred J. Lingham, of the Lockport Milling Company; George McFadden, a cotton exporter; Frederick B. Wells, of the Peavey Elevator Company; Thomas Wilson, president of the American Institute of Meat Packers; J. R. Howard and Gray Silver, of the Farm Bureau; Judson Welliver, of President Harding's staff; Henry C. Taylor; Secretary Wallace; and Peek and Johnson.

General Johnson spent most of the morning outlining the principles of the ratio-price idea. Only infrequently did Peek comment. But he was carefully analyzing the reactions of those present, trying to keep one step ahead of their objections in his thinking.

Barnes was the most vocal opponent of the plan. Such a scheme, he said, would interfere with American milling practices and break down the export machinery. Furthermore, he declared that the proposal was objectionable from a constitutional viewpoint and that, besides, conditions were improving. General Dawes also reacted unfavorably. Although he later helped Peek in the fight for agricultural equality, Dawes then strongly opposed the plan. He did not dispute the principles involved, but, as Peek said, he "applied the usual number of cuss words to what he called a 'half-baked plan.' "

Of the businessmen present, Otto Kahn was the most sympathetic. He considered the plan economically sound, but was not sure that it was practical from an administrative viewpoint. In any event, Kahn believed it would be wise to wait sixty days, or more, to see if the relationship between farm and nonfarm prices did not improve. If conditions did not get better, he was in favor of trying the Peek and Johnson scheme.

Wallace and Howard both spoke favorably of the plan, particularly the ratio-price feature of it. The Secretary warned, however, that "any price-fixing plan which does not control production is a thoroughly hopeless effort." Peek and Johnson agreed with this position, but they believed that an increase in the tax or equalization fee would deter greater output. After hearing the criticisms of Barnes and others, Wallace said, "I hope that none of you will close your mind to it until you consider it further." He then gave a somewhat gloomy report on farm conditions at the grass roots, and intimated that a serious political upheaval might result if conditions did not become better. But Dawes and others discounted any danger of radicalism. Farmers were not "turning red" Dawes said, and Kahn added that just a few hairbrain radicals were making a lot of noise. At this point, Peek broke his silence and reminded his business friends that much more radical price-fixing measures were then under consideration by Congress.

At the close of the morning session, Secretary Wallace asked Barnes, McFadden, Wells, Wilson, and Lingham to study further the plan as it might affect normal marketing procedures and to report back that evening. Speaking for members of the group at the night session, Barnes said they all favored restoring ratio-prices, but that the Peek-Johnson proposal was unsuitable. It would stimulate production, he declared, destroy the ordinary marketing channels, make food cheaper abroad than in the United States, and necessitate the creation of a vast bureaucracy.

Barnes also mentioned the complications of administering such a plan. In reply, Peek admitted that it would work best if applied to wheat, where the exportable surplus could more easily be segregated and sold abroad. The amount of wheat exported usually did not exceed 20 or 25 per cent of the total crop. As to cotton, however, the part of the crop which entered the export trade was around 50 per cent. A problem also arose in the case of corn, which was marketed largely in the form of pork products. Peek conceded that the administrative problems required much more study. But he took the position that "if the plan was applied to wheat alone it would inspire such confidence as to immediately stimulate general activity."

It was General Dawes who took the parting shot for the critics before the meeting adjourned at 11:00 P.M. If the plan works, he said, it would help "these fellows sell plows" but "where you undertake to institute a new theory that is revolutionary and paternalistic you want to go pretty slow."[19]

[19] The best sources on this important conference are Peek and Johnson, "Memorandum of What Took Place in Washington" (February 20, 1922), typescript, Peek Papers; and H. C. Taylor, "Conference Called By Secretary Wallace, February 13, 1922," Taylor Files.

After this special conference, Peek and Johnson conferred further with Howard and Silver, who asked them to prepare a bill incorporating their ideas. The next day the "Men from Moline" decided to go home "to get out of the atmosphere." They promised the Farm Bureau officials to work out a measure which might be introduced by friends in Congress.

Some things had become crystal clear to Peek as a result of his three-week stay in Washington. He saw that any new or nontraditional attack on the farm problem would have rough sledding. More particularly, he learned that most representatives of the business community would bitterly resist any attempt to raise farm prices artificially. Low prices for foodstuffs and raw materials were definitely favorable to American industry as it sought to compete in world markets. Especially, Secretary Hoover left no doubt that his chief concern was to press the export of industrial products over those of the farm. But regardless of how formidable the obstacles might be, Peek had no intention of quitting. Opposition only strengthened his determination to get his plan accepted.

Actually, the outlook was not as dim as it might have appeared. Peek and Johnson had accomplished more during and after the agricultural conference than could be seen at first glance. The friendship of Secretary Wallace for surplus-control legislation was of utmost importance. Here was an avenue through which other members of the administration might be reached. Other than Wallace, Baruch, who had been a member of the conference, became their most effective supporter. Shortly after the conference closed, Baruch wrote to Wallace: "I am sorry that the Peek matter came to nothing. . . . I believe that if those who were interested in the trade had really wanted to work it out, they could have easily shown the way."[20]

Although Baruch and Peek agreed on the need for helping farmers, they differed markedly on the tariff question. Peek favored high protection, while Baruch believed that general trade barriers should be lowered. He said that if the United States hoped to sell abroad, European prosperity must be restored through reduced tariffs. "There is no use talking, George," he wrote, "you can't get prosperity by a spirit of isolation; and you had better throw out some of these 'best' minds like Hughes and Hoover and

[20] Baruch to Wallace, March 1, 1922. Files of the Secretary of Agriculture.

put in some of the old dodo birds like we had in Washington."[21] Peek, however, never accepted this principle. His whole thesis was built on the validity of the protective tariff, and he thought in terms of economic nationalism.

Originally Peek had not intended to become active in the political fight to get his ideas accepted. "It was our thought at that time," he declared, "that if the American Farm Bureau Federation decided to adopt and promulgate the principle we would drop out of the picture." By the end of the agricultural conference, however, it was apparent that the Farm Bureau would not undertake an aggressive campaign to obtain surplus-control legislation. In its annual conventions of 1921 and 1922, the Farm Bureau went no further than to ask for the extension of credit to finance agricultural exports through the War Finance Corporation. President Howard favored the Peek plan but he apparently made no effort to commit his organization to it as early as 1922.

There were several reasons why the Farm Bureau did not begin an aggressive fight in 1922 for legislation similar to that recommended by Peek and Johnson. In the first place, the organization was in the midst of a campaign to build up co-operative marketing along the lines advocated by Aaron Sapiro, the country's greatest propagandist for commodity co-operatives. Another factor was that President Howard stepped out in December of 1922, and Oscar E. Bradfute of Ohio succeeded him. Bradfute was essentially conservative in his approach to farm ills, and he continued to emphasize co-operative marketing as a solution to agricultural problems. He refused to be led into new and untried paths. Some of the state Farm Bureaus urged the national body to get behind surplus-control legislation, but the official policy continued to be directed along other lines.

And neither the Grange nor the Farmers Union, the other leading farm organizations, were willing officially to endorse the Peek proposal. A large element in the Farmers Union was demanding government price-fixing on the basis of cost of production, and the Grange was more inclined toward co-operatives.

It became apparent to Peek that, if his idea ever received legislative approval, he would have to spearhead the drive himself. At least this would be true until sentiment for his plans developed

21 Baruch to Peek, August 9, 1922. Baruch Papers.

among the regular farm organizations or until special pressure groups could be formed. So upon their return home from the agricultural conference, Peek and Johnson revised the brief and published it under their signatures. It was ready for distribution about the middle of March. Peek told Baruch that the next step was to circulate the pamphlet among county Farm Bureau officials and county agents "followed with a series of articles for the agricultural press."

The second booklet was confined to general problems of the tariff and agriculture, and no specific administrative mechanism was mentioned for activating the Peek-Johnson principles. Subsequently, Peek explained to Secretary Wallace, "you will recall that the principles involved were never seriously questioned but the suggestion of a plan, in the first edition, drew fire from every direction." Peek wanted to avoid the heat of criticism until he could build up more support. Certainly, he thought, no one would oppose the *principle* of equality for agriculture.

Arguing in general terms, Peek and Johnson repeated that agricultural tariffs were not benefiting the farmer and that the doctrine of protection must be revised "to insure agricultural equality of tariff protection and a fair exchange value with other commodities . . . or the protective tariff principle must perish." This could be done, they asserted, only by equalizing "supply with demand on the domestic market, at not to exceed fair exchange value with other commodities, to protect that value by a tariff, and to divert surplus to export and sell it at world price."[22]

The heart of Peek's and Johnson's thinking was aimed at developing a method whereby agriculture could regulate price in the recognized industrial pattern. Yet, as will be shown later, farmers and most of their spokesmen who *wanted* the same control over price as that enjoyed by industry, were generally unwilling to accept production control, which was a vital factor in permitting businessmen to regulate prices.

Throughout the remainder of 1922, Peek sent out hundreds of copies of *Equality for Agriculture*. They went to senators, congressmen, farm leaders, editors of agricultural journals, friends and acquaintances in business, and others. In April, a four-page mimeographed letter summarizing the ratio-price idea was printed

[22] Peek and Johnson, *Equality for Agriculture* (2nd ed., Moline, 1922), 3.

on Moline Plow Company stationery and addressed "To All Who May Be Interested In Equality For Agriculture." This statement also received wide distribution.

The scheme to bring equality for agriculture swept like a cyclone across the western prairies in late 1922 and 1923. A. H. Stafford, a leader of the Montana Farm Bureau, wrote to Senator Thomas J. Walsh that he had never seen anything gain so rapidly in public favor. The plan, he declared, "is spreading like wildfire from mouth to ear among the farmers and smaller businessmen."[23]

Peek's proposal especially gained momentum when it became certain that the administration or Congress had no effective plan. In 1922 the Capper-Volstead Act, which legalized co-operative marketing associations, was passed. About the same time the Fordney-McCumber Tariff raised rates on many agricultural commodities, and early in 1923 the Intermediate Credits Act was approved. But these laws did not meet the basic problems as farmers saw them. They were interested in one thing above all others— higher prices.

By 1923 the demand for surplus-control legislation was reaching avalanche proportions between the Red River of the North and the Columbia. Senator Walsh, who opposed Peek's plan, was forced to admit that "the farmers of my state, who border on desperation, quite generally, if not unanimously, are giving their endorsement to the so-called Johnson-Peek plan for an agricultural export corporation."[24]

Perhaps more important was the support which Peek was gaining among national legislators. By late 1922, Senator Peter Norbeck of South Dakota indicated his conversion to the Peek scheme. "Slowly but surely," Norbeck wrote, "the idea is getting home that it is the surplus, and that the way to stimulate the market is to find some way to dispose of the surplus. Sell it at a good price, if we can; sell it at a poor price if we must, give it away if we cannot do better. . . . In other words, let agricultural products have the same benefit of a similar control that big business gives its products."[25]

And Baruch continued to use his influence among congress-

23 Stafford to Walsh, December 20, 1923. Walsh Papers.
24 Walsh to George W. Norris, December 27, 1923. *Ibid.*
25 Norbeck to C. M. Henry, December 7, 1922. Norbeck Papers.

men and senators. At every opportunity he supported the idea of agricultural equality. He carried on a sizable correspondence with many who were in a position to lend official support. "The condition of agriculture in this country," he wrote Senator Norris, chairman of the Committee on Agriculture and Forestry, "will require some drastic and direct action."[26] Baruch's work for farm relief is probably the least known among his many services to the nation, but actually he made one of his greatest contributions in this field and was of inestimable help to Peek.

The situation continued so bad in the northwestern wheat regions that in October, 1923, Secretary Wallace dispatched Henry C. Taylor to make a first hand investigation. Wallace wanted Taylor to talk with actual dirt farmers. Taylor had already indicated his support of the Peek principles. In September he had written a memorandum for the Secretary on "The Agricultural Situation and the Means of Setting It Right." After discussing various problems, he said that the idea of dumping surpluses abroad in order to maintain a higher domestic price "is the only method thus far proposed which would quickly re-establish the pre-war ratio between the prices of farm products and other products." This memorandum may have been the deciding factor in causing Wallace to announce publicly his support of the Peek plan.

Stopping first at Madison, Wisconsin, where he owned a farm, Taylor found only a little complaint. Dairy farmers, he wrote, were doing quite well. But the situation began to change when he got farther west. In North Dakota there were hundreds of insolvent farmers. After a meeting in Fargo, he noted, "Hard-headed men, but want a more advantageous price ratio established." He talked with scores of farmers in North Dakota and Montana. One Montana farmer told him: "We farmers have done all we can ourselves. We are looking to Washington." Another wheat producer declared disgustedly, "I don't believe a man can live on a farm and be a Christian!"

At Helena on October 13, Taylor met with Chester C. Davis, Montana's commissioner of agriculture, and M. L. Wilson, professor of agricultural economics at Montana State College. Davis

26 Baruch to Norris, March 9, 1923. Norris Papers.

and Wilson were then spearheading the fight for agricultural equality in that area. After talking over the situation with both farmers and farm leaders, Taylor telegraphed Wallace on October 17: "The farmers from the Red River Valley to the Columbia River are solid for the restoration of purchasing power of farm products through an adequate tariff and export commission." Here was further evidence that Peek's plan had captured the imagination of people at the grass roots in the Northwest.

On November 14, shortly after Taylor's return to Washington, Secretary Wallace gave his first public, although somewhat timid, endorsement of the Peek export proposal in an address before the Chicago Association of Commerce. Then in his report to the President on the wheat situation dated November 30, Wallace officially recommended that the "most careful consideration" be given to establishing an export corporation to handle surplus farm crops. The duty of the corporation, he said, "would be to restore, so far as possible, the pre-war ratio between wheat, and other farm products of which we export a surplus."[27]

The fact that conditions remained so acute in some agricultural regions was favorable to the rapid acceptance of Peek's plan. But, apart from the immediate depression, his scheme of equality for agriculture had inherent merits which appealed to many farmers and their perplexed leaders. Public support had come quickly because Peek presented a direct and positive approach to the question of prices. Higher prices were what primarily interested farmers. Furthermore, Peek had been careful to emphasize that his proposal would not disturb existing marketing conditions to any extent. His plan also did less violence to the popular ideas of the proper relationship between government and business. This fact becomes clear when it is compared with the outright price-fixing bills favored by Simpson and Lyon. Thus Peek presented a formula which seemed to promise quick relief; the ratio-price was not price-fixing in the ordinary sense; and it seemed reasonably fair to ask for equality of treatment. The factors of simplicity, directness, fairness, and promised effectiveness were all in the plan's favor. L. R. Clausen, president of the J. I. Case Company, who strongly opposed the scheme, had to admit that "at first glance

27 *Yearbook of Agriculture*, 1923, p. 150.

the argument appeals to one and seems very proper, plausible and correct."[28]

The great significance of Peek's thinking was that he put aside the familiar agrarian panaceas of trust busting and currency regulation. He concentrated attention on more immediate farm problems. Although his plan would not have given farmers full parity prices, he believed it would lessen their disparity. Producers of surplus crops would receive substantially more than the world price.

By late 1923 the Peek plan of equality for agriculture had been widely studied and publicized. The time had come to make the principles effective by legislation. Peek, Wallace, and other supporters believed that their chances of success rested with the Republican Party.

[28] Clausen to Peek, April 12, 1922. Files of the Secretary of Agriculture.

Chapter IV

"Eyes on Washington"

B Y NOVEMBER, 1923, the Department of Agriculture was preparing a bill incorporating the Peek principles. Secretary
Wallace had asked Charles J. Brand, a consulting specialist
in the department, to reduce the principles of equality for agriculture to a workable legislative formula. Brand went to Moline
and conferred with Peek. He also had a memorandum written by
Peek and Johnson in October, which outlined the main points
to be stressed and avoided. Peek emphasized that the plan should
be put into effect with "the very slightest possible dislocation of
existing mechanism," a point of view which exemplified his basic
conservatism.[1]

The Brand draft was not satisfactory; and in December,
George C. Jewett, manager of the American Wheat Growers Associated, asked Senator Charles L. McNary of Oregon to revise it.
Senator George Norris, chairman of the Senate Committee on
Agriculture and Forestry, was not requested to sponsor the legislation because his own Norris-Sinclair bill was then pending.
Coming from a state where wheat farmers were up in arms and
demanding relief, McNary immediately went to work. He referred
the Brand version to the Senate Drafting Bureau, where it was
revised prior to introduction on January 16, 1924. At the same
time Representative Gilbert N. Haugen of Iowa, chairman of the
House Agriculture Committee, dropped it in the legislative hop-
per of the House.

[1]Peek and Johnson, "Some of the Matters to be Considered in the Draft of
Legislation for the Department of Agriculture" (October, 1923). Typescript.
Files of the Secretary of Agriculture.

The first McNary-Haugen bill was designed to restore and maintain ratio-prices for basic farm commodities by establishing a government corporation with power to buy and dispose of surpluses. Eight basic commodities were included in the bill—wheat, flour, corn, cotton, wool, cattle, sheep, and swine—and any food product manufactured from the three last-mentioned commodities. Farm relief advocates generally believed that if the prices of certain important crops were raised, the main problems of agriculture would be solved. Furthermore, the inclusion of commodities from several agricultural regions had a practical political value in winning support for the measure.

In order to determine the ratio-price, the secretary of labor was to compute the average all-commodity price for the period 1905 to 1914. Some 404 items were included by the Bureau of Labor Statistics in deciding the wholesale-price index, and the average index figure was 100. Together the secretaries of agriculture and labor were then to compute the basic-commodity price of each benefited crop for the same period. The prewar years were chosen because the purchasing power of farm products had been relatively good at that time. The bill was based on the idea that "the price of agricultural commodities should bear a proper relation to the prices of other commodities."

The secretary of labor was to compute monthly ratio-prices, which would bear the same relation to the current all-commodity price for the month as the pre-war basic-commodity price bore to the prewar all-commodity price. In this way the price of basic agricultural products would give them about the same purchasing power as they had had in the prewar period. Peek and his followers were seeking farm parity. For example, in the case of wheat the farm market price in August, 1924, was around $1.16 a bushel, but if the ratio-price had been operating it would have brought $1.40.

Surplus crops were to be handled by an agricultural export corporation consisting of the secretary of agriculture and four presidential appointees. The government was to supply the corporation with a capital of $200,000,000. After an emergency had been declared and the corporation found domestic prices of a basic farm commodity lower than the ratio-price, it was to buy the surplus at the ratio-figure. The corporation could sell its purchases abroad at the world level. The plan was not price-fixing in the strict sense of the term. Prices were free to go as much above the ratio-price as supply and demand would determine, but they were not to be allowed to fall below that figure in the domestic market. To that degree the bill fixed prices.

For instance, if the corporation bought wheat at the ratio-price, it was obvious that substantial losses would result on the amount sold abroad. To make up this deficit, farmers were to pay an equalization fee, or tax, on every unit or bushel of a commodity sold. Peek and other promoters of this plan insisted that farmers did not want a federal subsidy. Those who received the benefits, they argued, should share the losses. Thus the directors of the corporation were to estimate the probable loss on each commodity and charge it to the particular product. In the original bill, the purchaser of each basic commodity was required to pay the amount of the fee in script which could be bought at any post office. An equalization fund was to be built up out of which losses on each commodity could be paid. If the losses were less than anticipated the holders of script would be paid a dividend on a prorata basis. If the corporation suffered greater losses than expected, the fee, of course, would have to be raised the following year.[2]

By artificially lifting the price of basic farm commodities the likelihood of imports would be greater and might obviate the purpose of the law. Therefore, a flexible tariff provision which authorized the president to raise rates sufficiently to protect the corporation in its operations was included. Although Peek had first emphasized the principle of making the tariff effective for agriculture, the original McNary-Haugen bill stressed the ratio-price idea. By concentrating on the principles of equality and fair exchange value, it was hoped to avoid raising the general tariff problem, which was always full of political dynamite.

The McNary-Haugen bill was basically a marketing device. It was built on the philosophy that farmers could be helped if they were forced to participate in a great pool or co-operative enterprise. This was to be accomplished by making all the producers of a commodity share the responsibilities of keeping prices up by paying the equalization fee. The farmers, wrote Henry A. Wallace, "were to be given the centralizing power of the Federal Govern-

2 *McNary-Haugen Bill,* Hearings before the House Agriculture Committee, 68 Cong., 1 sess., 1924, p. 19ff.

ment so they could dump enough of their surplus abroad to raise prices in the domestic market."[3]

The bill scarcely mentioned other aspects of the agricultural problem. Nothing was said about production except that the corporation was to study the matter and advise producers on probable demands. Extraordinary high output would increase the surplus, which in turn would necessitate levying a higher equalization fee. This would reduce much of the benefit which might come from the plan. Therefore, the corporation was to have the difficult responsibility of trying to get farmers to restrict or regulate production on a voluntary basis while, at the same time, attempting to obtain for them a ratio-price. Most McNary-Haugenites believed that a surplus was desirable and necessary. It was needed, they argued, "to save the population against uncertainties of yield and to retain foreign markets."

There is no doubt but that the plan was complicated. Yet, Peek made it sound simple, especially when applied to wheat. Explaining a later version of the bill, he wrote:

America raises about 800,000,000 bushels of wheat. Of this production we use at home about 650,000,000 bushels. The remaining 150,000,000 must be marketed abroad. If the world price is $1.00 a bushel, then the farmer gets not merely $1.00 on 150,000,000 bushels, but on 800,000,000 bushels. His total crop revenue is $800,000,000, and the existence of a 42-cent tariff does not alter the case practically. But let us assume that the McNary-Haugen plan is operating, that the surplus is segregated in the market, and that the price rises to $1.40 a bushel. The total revenue now would be $1,120,000,000, an improvement of $320,000,000. However, there would still be 150,000,-000 bushels of wheat that would have to be sold abroad at $1.00 a bushel, the assumed world price. It is plain that a loss would be suffered on this surplus wheat of 40 cents a bushel, or $60,000,000 in all, plus costs of administration. Now the question arises where this money is to be found. . . . A charge would be placed against each bushel of wheat brought to market at the most convenient point of collection. . . . To arrive at this charge, costs and losses would be spread out over the

3 Henry A. Wallace, *New Frontiers* (New York, 1934), 148.

whole crop. A total loss of $60,000,000 on 800,000,000 bushels means that each bushel is liable for 7½ cents. A fee of 8 cents a bushel would be ample to cover all possible costs and losses on the operation. The elevator man, therefore, being subject to a charge of 8 cents a bushel, would be able to bid, not the full $1.40, but only $1.32. The farmer would thus get $1.32 for his wheat, instead of only $1.00 and his crop would be worth $1,056,000,000 instead of $800,000,000, a net gain of $256,-000,000.[4]

On January 21, five days after the McNary-Haugen bill was introduced, Congressional hearings began. For nearly two months, or until March 19, the House Agriculture Committee listened to forty witnesses express all shades of opinion. Inquisitive legislators heard Secretary Wallace, Peek, farm leaders, businessmen, exporters, bankers, and others. The testimony and statements filled 741 printed pages. Then the committee spent a month in executive session amending and improving the bill. Almost another month was devoted to further discussion and consideration before House debate commenced in earnest. During the three months from January to April, the House Agriculture Committee was in session every legislative day except two, and most of the time was devoted to the McNary-Haugen bill. Few measures have ever been presented which received such intensive study by a Congressional committee. Because of the tariff features of the bill, it was first considered in the House.

Before Congressional debate started a few significant amendments were made to the bill. On April 17 the House committee voted to eliminate the script provision. Rather than forcing buyers of farm commodities to purchase script with which to pay part of the selling price, farmers were to be paid cash for their products and receive an "equalization certificate" for the amount of the fee. If losses were less than the corporation had figured, they would be paid a prorata amount on their certificates. The principle was not much different than the use of script and the change was made for political reasons, since there was bitter opposition to the term "script."

[4] George N. Peek, "The McNary-Haugen Plan for Relief," *Current History,* Vol. XXIX (November, 1928), 274–76.

A more important change in the original bill was the elimination of cotton from the list of benefited crops. Representative James B. Aswell of Louisiana called a meeting of congressmen from the cotton-producing states, and they unanimously agreed to drop it. The South was then mostly interested in co-operative and orderly marketing. Co-operative leaders felt that federal loans to hold and market their cotton might help them, but they opposed levying an equalization fee to finance this development. Thus, southern representatives could see little value in the bill for their main crop. Moreover, cotton was then selling above the ratio-price.

By the time the measure was introduced, tremendous pressure had built up for it in the Northwest. During the latter part of 1923 and early 1924, export leagues were formed in all of the northwestern wheat states. One of McNary's constituents wrote him on January 18 that his section was practically 100 per cent organized. On February 8, 1924, following a call by the Minnesota organization, an Interstate Export League was formed at Crookston. C. H. Zealand became secretary with offices in St. Paul. Within a few days an executive committee was created for the express purpose of promoting the McNary-Haugen bill in Congress. C. G. Selvig was sent to Washington to lobby for the measure.[5]

This was the first pressure group of an interstate nature organized specifically to foster the Peek proposal. By the spring of 1924, some three hundred organizations or associations had actually endorsed the plan, about half of which were farm groups. In agricultural circles these varied from the guarded support of the National Grange to the militant backing of the Illinois Agricultural Association, from influential associations like the Montana Bankers to inconspicious groups like the Kiwanis Club of Creston, Iowa. Endorsements were plentiful, but an endorsement is far short of active and positive aid. Early in 1924 the scores of organizations which supported McNary-Haugenism did not send lobbyists to Washington, spend money, or exert the kind of pressure which makes Congress act. It took a battle of three years before Peek and his friends were able to funnel agricultural pressure to the legislative chambers in such a powerful manner that Congress was forced to pass the McNary-Haugen bill.

There was relatively little effective and organized agricultural

[5] C. H. Zealand to Thomas J. Walsh, dated March, 1924. Walsh Papers.

support behind the first McNary-Haugen measure. Most of the burden of getting Congress to consider the scheme was carried by Secretary Wallace and a few members of his department, some interested congressmen and senators, Peek and a number of his personal friends, and a scattering of state farm leaders. Most of the backing was spontaneous and miscellaneous and quite ineffective; above all, it was sectional.

The major farm organizations lent only moderate support. They were divided and confused on surplus-control legislation, or for that matter, on any legislation. Early in January, the Washington office of the American Farm Bureau sent a memorandum to members of Congress saying that "something helpful should be done for the distressed wheat growers."[6] But no mention was made of Peek's plan for agricultural equality. It was not until *after* the first McNary-Haugen bill had been defeated that the Farm Bureau officially endorsed it. At the annual convention held in December, 1924, the Farm Bureau recommended an export corporation with sufficient powers to "preserve the domestic market for the American agricultural producers at an American price." Much credit, however, is due state farm organization leaders, especially in the Farm Bureau, who went to Washington and worked hard for the bill notwithstanding the opposition or lukewarmness of their national officers. Individual leaders in the Farm Bureau such as Charles Hearst of Iowa, Sam H. Thompson and R. A. Cowles, president and secretary respectively of the Illinois Agricultural Association and Gray Silver of Missouri, the Washington Representative, performed yeoman service for the first bill. Thompson and Cowles went to Washington in March to lobby for the measure's passage. Throughout the spring a series of "revival meetings" was held by the Illinois Agricultural Association in all parts of the state and many supporters were gained. On one occasion, President Thompson presented petitions to a House Committee carrying sixty thousand signatures of Illinois farmers who said they favored the McNary-Haugen bill. But lack of unity throughout the organization weakened these efforts.

The Farmers Union had no united policy. At the national convention in November, 1924, President C. S. Barrett frankly ad-

[6] American Farm Bureau Federation, "Memorandum on Agricultural Legislation," January 12, 1924. Files of the Secretary of Agriculture.

mitted this. Speaking of farm legislation in the previous session, he declared, "even our own great organization was divided as to the proper course." One group favored co-operative marketing while the other wanted some federal program to stabilize prices. This split was apparent in the ranks of all major farm organizations.

Likewise, the Grange was lukewarm toward the bill. In February, the executive committee endorsed the McNary-Haugen bill as an emergency measure.[7] Master L. J. Taber wrote President Coolidge in May, expressing the hope that he would not oppose the bill. Yet, he added: "I have never looked upon this as a perfect piece of legislation; I have always thought of it somewhat of an experiment, but have felt and now feel that its adoption is justified in view of the conditions."[8] Such pussyfooting was not likely to sway opposition which was rapidly developing against the measure. Farmers eventually learned that they must *demand* what they wanted. Humble supplications had no effect.

Only a few farm journals came out boldly for McNary-Haugenism in 1924. *Wallace's Farmer,* The *Dakota Farmer* and a few other agricultural papers favored it, but that is all. The editor of the *Dakota Farmer* warned his readers to awaken and fight for their rights. "This plan," he wrote, "by all odds will bring a greater measure of prosperity than any other government plan now in operation or promised."[9] Many farm papers, while not especially opposed to the Peek plan, were too indifferent to be effective. The *Farm Journal* said that the proposal was "not very good, but the other schemes are far worse. Let's try it a year or two anyway."[10]

If the major farm organizations and the agricultural journals were lukewarm, divided, or indifferent to the McNary-Haugen bill, this could not be said of the American Wheat Growers Associated, headed by that giant of a man George C. Jewett. Early in 1924, Jewett set up offices in the old Franklin Square Hotel at Fourteenth and K streets and employed a small but active staff to promote surplus-control legislation. Jewett and his little organiza-

[7] L. J. Taber to Gilbert N. Haugen, February 19, 1924. Files of the Secretary of Agriculture.

[8] Taber to Coolidge, May 23, 1924. *Ibid.*

[9] *Dakota Farmer,* Vol. XLIV (February 1, 1924), 128–29.

[10] *Farm Journal,* Vol. XLII (April, 1924), 12.

Henry Cantwell Wallace
secretary of agriculture, 1921–24

tion made up the hard core of grass roots support during this first drive for farm parity.

Besides Jewett, numerous state agricultural officials, and independent leaders like Frank W. Murphy of Wheaton, Minnesota, lent influential support. Secretary Wallace acted as the main behind-the-scenes director of the initial campaign. Brand and Henry C. Taylor were his principal aides and advisers in the department. Testifying before the House committee on January 30, Wallace argued that it was the most hopeful plan suggested. He admitted that the proposal would probably be difficult to administer, but he regarded it as "the best bet."[11]

Others who came to the plan's support early in 1924 included Otto Kahn, who, two years before, had been somewhat skeptical. "It would seem to me," he wrote Wallace, "that the government would be justified in giving its endorsement to a measure along the lines of the principle on which the McNary-Haugen bill rests." Kahn was one of the few eastern financiers who finally concluded that the plan was sufficiently practical to deserve a trial. It should be tried, he thought, regardless of how "novel in conception and . . . at first flush out of line with accepted economic doctrine."[12] Essentially, this was Wallace's position. Wallace explained to his brother Dan that agriculture was in such bad condition that "in my opinion the time has come to make a very determined effort to improve it, even if this effort involves doing some things which a few years ago we might not have been disposed to do."[13]

Bernard Baruch continued to do everything possible to aid the farm cause and his old friend Peek. On March 6 he gave a dinner at his New York home for a number of leading journalists, at which time Peek and Johnson explained their ideas. He also paid the expenses of several farm leaders to a New York meeting, where he and Peek briefed them on the entire situation.

Probably Baruch's most significant contribution, however, was his contact with Democratic members of the House and Senate. The result of his extensive correspondence was not felt as early as 1924, but partly through Baruch's influence more Democrats gradually came to support the McNary-Haugen bill. He was less

11 *McNary-Haugen Bill,* Hearings before the House Agriculture Committee, 68 Cong., 1 sess., 1924, p. 119.
12 Kahn to Wallace, March 8, 1924. Files of the Secretary of Agriculture.
13 Henry C. Wallace to Dan A. Wallace, March 8, 1924. *Ibid.*

confident than Peek in the economic soundness of the plan and kept arguing that tariffs should be lowered and foreign markets opened. This was "more important than anything else," he said. At the same time he advised limiting the bill's operation to wheat. If it worked with wheat, other agricultural products could be added; but if it failed, "the mistake would not be so great," he wrote Senator Thomas J. Walsh.[14]

McNary, Norbeck, and others agreed that it would be best to experiment first with only one crop, wheat. In early 1924 McNary often referred to the measure as "my wheat bill" or "the McNary-Haugen wheat exportation bill," indicating the scope of his thinking. At first even Peek had been forced to admit that it might be more practical to apply the bill only to wheat. "I should make a beginning with wheat alone," he wrote in June, 1923. But within a short time he became convinced that the plan was also administratively feasible for corn and hogs. In any event, it was not politically expedient to confine the bill to one crop, even for experimental purposes. Therefore, other crops were added in hopes of gaining support from important agricultural elements in the West and South.

Banker and small business support of the measure was militant in the depressed agricultural regions from Iowa to Washington State. Letters in the files of the Secretary of Agriculture show that small country banks were counting on better farm prices to save them. Debts made to buy costly land and machinery in 1918 and 1919, when crops sold at high prices, could not be repaid with $1.00 wheat and 8-cent hogs. Many country bankers in Iowa, for instance, had a lot of uncollectable farm paper in their vaults, and higher commodity prices were nearly as vital to them as to their customers. "Bankers in Iowa are for this bill because they have got to the end of their string on renewing paper," one Iowa farm leader told the House Agriculture Committee. By 1923 and 1924 they found it was not safe to renew notes and mortgages, and the number of foreclosures increased.

Iowa bankers, both individually and collectively, rushed telegrams and letters to President Coolidge and Secretary Wallace, urging passage of the bill. The same was true of those from other western states, particularly Oregon and Washington. And speak-

14 Baruch to Walsh, April 14, and May 14, 1924. Walsh Papers.

ing of South Dakota, Senator Norbeck wrote, "Every letter from the banks, relating to the McNary-Haugen bill, is practically a wholehearted endorsement."[15]

Businessmen in rural towns of the Northwest also endorsed the scheme. Scores of resolutions passed by commercial clubs and chambers of commerce testify to this support. Fred Falconer, president of the Oregon Wool Growers Association, informed Coolidge, "I have found them [bankers and business men] almost unanimously in favor of the McNary-Haugen bill."[16] Senator Thomas Sterling of South Dakota, a conservative and friend of Coolidge, wrote in March, "The sentiment in favor of this bill is not by any means confined to farmers, but there is a strong sentiment among bankers and business men for the endorsement of this bill into law."[17]

It was the farmers themselves, however, who had the most at stake. Those who lived in distressed regions bombarded the President and Secretary of Agriculture with urgent communications. The cry was for government help. "Every farmer in this county have their eyes on Washington," wrote C. G. Ramer, of Minnesota, to Coolidge.[18] Farmers could not afford telegrams, but lead-pencil letters were sent to Washington in large numbers.

Opponents of the bill charged repeatedly that farmers did not understand and really did not want the McNary-Haugen type of farm relief. This was untrue. Probably most farmers did not comprehend the complicated mechanics of the measure, but they understood the problem of ratio-prices and believed this bill would best meet their needs. This was especially true in the corn-hog and wheat areas. The files of the Secretary of Agriculture, which contain letters to both Coolidge and Wallace, probably reflect farm sentiment as accurately as it can be gauged.

W. F. McCauley, president of the Columbia County Export Commission League in Washington, told Henry C. Wallace that farmers in that area had been studying the plan for two years and were nearly unanimous for it. Farmers were distressed, he said, that Coolidge seemed to be taking advice from Hoover, Barnes,

---

[15] Norbeck to S. X. Way, February 12, 1925. Norbeck Papers.

[16] Falconer to Coolidge, February 21, 1924. Files of the Secretary of Agriculture.

[17] Sterling to Coolidge, March 2, 1924. *Ibid.*

[18] Ramer to Coolidge, February 12, 1924. *Ibid.*

and Meyer "all of whom sing the song of the Chicago Board of Trade."[19] The *Dakota Farmer* reported, on May 15, that farmers in that section favored the McNary-Haugen bill "almost to a man." A Minnesota citizen explained to McNary that "the people of this state are practically unanimous in their support for your measure."

Although economic conditions were not as bad in Iowa and other corn-hog states as in the wheat belt, farmers there were equally active in behalf of the bill. Walter Burge, a livestock producer, wrote, "here in Iowa we are moving rapidly toward the same conditions which are reported to be prevailing in the Northwest."[20] The McNary-Haugen bill, he added, was the best measure offered. Farmers in Illinois also got behind the legislation. Some of them were extremely critical of Democratic Representative Henry T. Rainey who opposed Peek's plan. One of Rainey's constituents declared that if he had nothing better to offer "for God's sake go way back and sit down."

The Department of Agriculture attempted to summarize and evaluate the sentiment on the McNary-Haugen bill while it was under consideration between January and June. There were 669 letters and telegrams received by Coolidge and Wallace favoring the proposal. Some of these were petitions representing scores, and in a few instances hundreds, of farmers. In addition, congressmen and senators had listed 328 more in the *Congressional Record,* making a total of 997 supporting communications. On the other hand, there were only 91 letters and telegrams opposed to surplus-control legislation.[21]

Some of the farm organizations also attempted to gauge farm sentiment. The Minnesota Farm Bureau sent out 19,327 ballots in the spring of 1924, asking farmers' opinions on the McNary-Haugen bill. Only 116 reportedly opposed the measure. The Missouri Farm Bureau received 1,550 letters favoring the proposal and only 8 against it. The secretary of the South Dakota Farm Bureau reported, as had Senator Sterling, that farmers there were "unanimously for the McNary-Haugen bill."[22]

19 McCauley to H. C. Wallace, February 5, 1924. *Ibid.*
20 Burge to Coolidge, April 8, 1924. *Ibid.*
21 Tabulation in the files of the Secretary of Agriculture, 1924.
22 American Farm Bureau Federation, *Weekly News Letter,* Vol. IV (May 8, 1924), 1.

There is no reasonable doubt but that by 1924, Peek's ratio-price idea had caught the imagination of farmers all the way from Illinois to Oregon. To be sure, some of the support was artificially manufactured. It was exaggerated by farm leaders for effect, and therefore must be discounted. Any poll distributed by farm journals and organizations must be used cautiously, since the questionnaires were frequently "loaded" to get a particular result. This was true of both those who favored and those who opposed the bill. Yet, there is every reason to believe that farmers had set their eyes on equality for agriculture—on parity. The significant point was that more and more farmers had come to accept the idea that only the federal government could put agriculture on an equality with other industries.

Most of those who favored the McNary-Haugen bill appealed for support on the basis of economic justice and fair play. A few, however, voiced political threats and warned that farmers could not be held in the Republican column unless substantial agricultural relief was forthcoming. A Republican state committeeman from Utah wrote to President Coolidge that his county would not go Republican unless the McNary-Haugen or some other effective measure was passed. Governor N. E. Kendall of Iowa wired Coolidge: "Iowa is strongly for McNary-Haugen bill. We believe its enactment is vital to Republican success."[23] Another Iowan and lifelong Republican wrote that unless farm relief legislation was enacted before Congress adjourned, "Coolidge may bid farewell to Washington after next March, for there are thousands of us fellows who will support no man for that office who chums with Hoover and Meyer."[24]

Many letters from Minnesota Republicans carried ominous political warnings to the President. A. O. Moreaux wired that Republicans in his state were looking to Congress "to save state from radicals in coming elections by immediate passage of satisfactory agricultural relief legislation."[25] C. F. Porter of South Dakota declared that effective farm relief was necessary "for the salvation of the Republican party in South Dakota."[26]

23 Kendall to Coolidge, June 5, 1924. Files of the Secretary of Agriculture.
24 F. Coddington to H. C. Wallace, May 15, 1924. *Ibid.*
25 Moreaux to Coolidge, June 2, 1924. *Ibid.*
26 Porter to Bascom Slemp, June 5, 1924. *Ibid.*

President Coolidge evidently decided there was sufficient smoke to investigate the possibility of political fire. He asked Frank App, a member of the executive committee of the Farm Bureau from New Jersey, to report on conditions in the Midwest. Writing from Des Moines, App said that the agricultural press, farmers, and farm leaders were "almost unanimous" in expressing friendship for the President. Yet, he warned that agricultural relief was looming as a big issue. "Illinois and Iowa will be satisfied with nothing less than some form of the McNary-Haugen measure. In these states it could be made a major political issue."[27]

Political threats and disorganized support for farm relief, however widespread, were not likely to accomplish much in themselves. It was not even enough to have loyal friends on Capitol Hill like McNary, Norris, Norbeck, Haugen, L. J. Dickinson, and a few others. Someone had to organize, finance, and guide a powerful farm lobby which would cut across party and agricultural organization lines. Only then could Congress be forced to act. It was George Peek who was about to emerge as the recognized leader of the movement for agricultural equality.

During the first Congressional fight between January and June, however, Peek spent only about two weeks in Washington. Although he lent force and influence to this initial skirmish, he was mainly preoccupied during the spring of 1924 with a fight to maintain control of the Moline Plow Company. His forced retirement as president of the firm and the bitter and acrimonious quarrel with his friend Hugh Johnson were some of the most pathetic and unhappy aspects of George Peek's life.

As previously indicated, the Moline Plow Company had been in a very bad financial condition when Peek became president in 1919. It would have taken a miracle to save the sprawling farm-machine empire, which was fast crumbling. Under the circumstances which Peek found the company, there were limitations on what even the best management could do. The farm depression added to the difficulties, and Peek made at least one bad business decision. The Moline firm manufactured the Universal Tractor. Before all of the "bugs" were out of it, Peek put it on the market. Its failure brought repercussions to the entire company from farmers, dealers, and jobbers.

[27] App to Coolidge, March 8, 1924. *Ibid.*

American Farm Bureau Federation Weekly News Letter

Alexander's "Ears That Hear Not Eyes That See Not"
There was a time when the farmer's voice didn't carry very far

After 1920 some retrenchment had taken place. Part of the company's assets had been sold to raise sufficient money to continue operations. Yet, the company tried to carry what was known in the implement business as a full line. Besides plows, it sold drills, wagons, manure spreaders, and other kinds of farm machinery. Peek had grown up in the industry at a time when it was popular for the major implement companies to do a full-line business. However, by 1923 the Moline Plow Company was in such bad shape financially that some of the creditors and members of the board of directors concluded that the entire firm must be liquidated, or that its operations must be reduced and restricted to a so-called tillage line, principally plows. Johnson estimated that about one million dollars in cash could be obtained to reorganize and strengthen the company's remaining activities if the tractor, harvester, drill, and some other lines were liquidated. In May, 1924, the Universal Tractor plant at Rock Island was sold.

At first Johnson opposed liquidation to the tillage line, but by late 1923, he had concluded that there was no other suitable course. On February 25, 1924, he wrote a long memorandum setting forth his views, which he had stated earlier to Peek and some of the directors. Matters were made worse when the directors canceled the management contract with Peek and his associates on September 6, 1923.

Despite the difficult outlook for the firm's future, Peek believed that the solution of the company's worst problems was in sight. He was convinced that the debt could be reduced to manageable size and ultimately liquidated through operations. Peek never admitted that he was licked. Moreover, he argued that it was bad business to retrench. Dealers and jobbers required a full line, he said, and the big companies would drive a smaller, single-line firm out of business. Peek did not think a tillage company could succeed. Therefore, to form one would be tantamount to complete liquidation. "More than anything else in the world," Peek said, he wanted to make the Moline Plow Company a success. He felt that reducing the firm to only a tillage company would discredit him throughout the farm machine industry.

Peek took Johnson's disagreement with him as a personal affront and as disloyalty. He was a man accustomed to command. When Johnson joined a group of bankers and directors who opposed Peek's ideas, he felt that it was rank betrayal. Johnson said it was only a difference of opinion. Peek said it was deception and trickery. He charged that Johnson and other lawyers simply wanted the job of liquidation for what they could make out of it. Although Peek did not seem to realize it, what he really resented was the tendency toward banker control and the removal of experienced industrialists like himself from management. After the liquidation and reorganization, Johnson became vice-president of the new company. Here was a lawyer, a man whom Peek scorned as never having "sold a dollars worth of implements in his life," being promoted to a high position in management.

On February 14, while at the Blackstone Hotel in Chicago, Peek penned some of his innermost thoughts. He revealed his belief that the idea of cutting back the firm's operations was "only a subterfuge to get rid of me." He confided to the privacy of hotel stationery that he must keep fighting against the liquidators and for the business on account of the "men who have followed me." Then he wrote that if General Johnson wanted to go into the liquidating business, he should not "make me the first victim."

In February and March of 1924 these two former friends carried on a long and bitter correspondence. Peek attacked Johnson's motives and even accused him of making decisions while under the influence of "booze." Johnson had betrayed him, had sold him out, he said. In reply Johnson held to the correctness of his position, all the while expressing a deep and heartfelt sorrow over their differences. These two strong-willed, bullheaded, aggressive men could not settle their disputes amicably, despite their deep affection for each other. Each was bluff and blustery to friends and supporters, but in private they experienced untold agony as the bitter feud continued.

It seemed as though perhaps the breach would be healed when Peek called at Johnson's office on June 5, 1924. There they had talked in "a friendly and confidential way." This conference Johnson confided, was one of the finest things that had ever happened to him. Although still maintaining his views on company policy, he confessed that no one could "ever know how my heart has suffered." This did not sound like the "Old Iron Pants" of the future Blue Eagle days, and it was an aspect of Johnson's character which most people never knew. Yet, Peek did not completely forgive

Johnson, although time wore away some of the bitterness. To the last he believed that Johnson betrayed him, as he put it, "into the hands of my enemies."[28]

On June 2, 1924, Peek resigned. Later in the year, he, Frank W. Edlin, and Charles B. Rose sued the Moline Plow Company for a million dollars, charging that their management contract had been violated. They won a settlement of $280,000 in November.[29]

After this Johnson dropped out of the farm relief fight. But Peek now turned his full attention to the campaign, and before the summer was over he had assumed command of the fight for agricultural equality.

[28] Johnson to Peek, February 1 and 25, March 30, and June 5, 1924, and January, 1925; Peek to Johnson, February 12 and 25, March 2, and December 21, 1924, and February 1, 1925. Peek Papers.
[29] Moline *Daily Dispatch*, November 19, 1924.

Chapter V

Opposition and Defeat

SCARCELY any legislation before Congress in the spring of 1924 received as much attention and publicity as the McNary-Haugen bill. Newspapers, popular magazines, trade journals, and government publications all carried extensive accounts describing the proposed legislation. Farm relief debate filled hundreds of pages in the *Congressional Record* as proponents and opponents aired their views in long-winded speeches.

As the measure became better known, a wave of opposition arose which was to smother it in defeat. The arguments and positions taken against the original bill in the spring of 1924 were typical of those expressed throughout most of the 1920's.

Standing in the forefront of those who opposed trying to lift farm prices by government action was the little man from Vermont, Calvin Coolidge, who had become president in August, 1923. It was well known that Coolidge held no brief for new or unconventional economic ideas. The "business of the United States is business," he had said. In a vague way this meant that business should be positively assisted by high tariffs and, in some instances, by outright government subsidies, as well as by reduced taxes and a minimum of government regulation or interference. He positively opposed any government aid or support to agriculture and labor. Subscribing to the "percolator" or "trickle down" theory of economics, he believed that these groups would benefit if industry were prosperous. Coolidge thought there was danger in "mistaken government activity" and considered government planning as the worst sort of economic heresy.

The President emphatically stated his position on agricultural problems in his first annual message, which was delivered about the same time the first McNary-Haugen bill was being written. "No complicated scheme of relief, no plan for government fixing of prices, no resort to the public treasury will be of any permanent value in establishing agriculture," he said. Cheers followed his statement that "simple and direct methods put into operation by the farmer himself are the only real sources for restoration." Coolidge declared that he favored lower taxes, reduced freight rates, cheaper fertilizers, diversification, and farm organization. Then turning specifically to the wheat problem, the President added: "The acreage of wheat is too large. Unless we can meet the world price at a profit, we must stop raising for export." Continuing his reference to wheat, Coolidge said, "I do not favor the permanent interference of government in this problem." The War Finance Corporation, however, might help some in financing exports, he concluded.[1]

Coolidge had left no doubt about his views. The farmer, for the most part, must work out his own salvation. Senator Pat Harrison wryly remarked that the section of the President's message which he liked the best was where he told the farmers to go to hell! In any event, it was clear from the beginning that the McNary-Haugenites would have to contend with presidential opposition. Senator Norbeck called at the White House in October, 1923, and suggested to Coolidge that he support surplus-control legislation. "I got nowhere," Norbeck wrote. The following January, Congressman Scott Leavitt of Montana, and Chester C. Davis visited Coolidge in a vain attempt to interest him in the new farm relief proposal.

More open and active opposition, however, came from other quarters. With relatively few exceptions, the business community, especially millers, speculators, elevator operators, brokers, commission merchants, and others connected with the grain trade were violently opposed to surplus-control legislation. More than any other group, they spearheaded the opposition drive.

No individual in the United States was more critical of the bill than Julius Barnes, one of the country's largest grain exporters. The antagonism of the milling industry was best expressed by A. P. Husband, secretary of the Millers National Federation. Hus-

[1] *Cong. Rec.*, 68 Cong., 1 sess., December 6, 1923, p. 100.

band wrote that the "application of public funds for the benefit of any particular industry is wrong in principle." He said that the bill was "un-American" because it placed the government in business, that it would benefit foreign consumers at the expense of the American public, that American flour exports would suffer, and that the bill was an administrative monstrosity.

It was argued that futures-trading and other normal practices of the grain business would be ruined. Millers particularly feared that, if the bill were passed, flour exports would drop and more wheat would be exported. This would materially hurt their business. Brand conferred with representatives of the industry on November 2, 1923, when he was working on the original bill. The millers present were unanimous in their demand that if the government did buy wheat, it "should be exported in the form of flour." When Husband testified before the House Agriculture Committee, Chairman Haugen suggested some amendments for the milling industry. But Husband was adamant. "I do not think the millers or any other industry . . . would favor the government entering into its business," he said.[2] The milling industry also objected strenuously to the section in the bill which conferred power upon the corporation, if necessary, to lease, acquire, and operate plants for processing farm products. The packers joined the millers in fighting the measure on this score.

The *Grain Dealers Journal* condemned the bill in nearly every issue between February and June. "It is absolutely impossible either from a farmers or from a grain dealers standpoint. The radicals have simply run wild," complained the editor. A later issue declared that no one favored the bill except "a few loud mouthed agitators. . . . The real beneficiaries would be the Washington bureaucrats and agitators who would have one more chance to get their fingers in a fat pie."[3] L. E. Moses, president of the Southwestern Millers League of Kansas City, was one of the few prominent grain men who did not oppose the measure.

The millers distributed a leaflet to congressmen and senators which declared that the McNary-Haugen bill was "paternalism

[2] *McNary-Haugen Bill,* Hearings before the House Agriculture Committee, 68 Cong., 1 sess., 1924, pp. 667–69 and 690.
[3] The *Grain Dealers Journal,* Vol. LII (February 25 and March 10, 1924), 224 and 291–96.

run wild." "The measure is a deliberate attempt to defeat the law of supply and demand. . . ," they profoundly observed! Declaring that the bill would set a precedent for the "nationalization of all industry," the writer concluded, "It means compulsory communism for the individualistic American farmer." The New York Produce Exchange said it was "class legislation," "price-fixing," and "vicious in principle, un-American and undemocratic in thought."[4]

As favorable sentiment continued to develop for the McNary-Haugen bill, the millers and grain dealers lashed out even more wildly. Husband wrote Coolidge that it "set aside the immutable law of supply and demand," that it was "deceptive in character and purpose," that it violated "age-old fundamental economic laws," and was "impractical and wholly un-American."[5] Representatives of the grain industry relied more on scare tactics than on economic argument and analysis, but they were nonetheless effective. The most common charges were that the measure was radical, economically unsound, unworkable, socialistic, communistic, and class legislation. Such was the tone and character of the opposition registered by the grain trade. It reflected more emotion than reason, more blind opposition than fairness in trying to help solve the farm problem.

The grain-trade lobby was well manned and adequately financed. The secretary of the National Grain Dealers' Association described how his organization functioned: "Grain men gave freely of their time, and we had from 5 to 15 men in Washington all through the danger period. We met in the morning and each man was assigned to see certain congressmen. In the evening each man reported the results of his interview."[6] Individual members of the grain fraternity sent out literature, entertained members of Congress, and used every other means to defeat the bill. The Chicago Board of Trade flooded the corn belt with anti-McNary-Haugen propaganda. A Marshalltown, Iowa, citizen reported that merchants were being told that if the bill passed, large elevator terminals would be closed and there would be no market for grain.

[4] Leaflet in the McNary Papers; and New York Producers Exchange to Arthur Capper, March 24, 1924. McNary Papers.
[5] Husband to Coolidge, April 28, 1924. Files of the Secretary of Agriculture.
[6] Quoted by Senator Burton K. Wheeler in the *Cong. Rec.*, 69 Cong., 2 sess., February 9, 1927, p. 3347.

This type of economic pressure was reminiscent of that used against William Jennings Bryan in the presidential campaign of 1896.

Other important business groups were equally active. Although many bankers in distressed rural areas favored surplus-control legislation, the executive council of the American Bankers Association instructed its federal legislative committee to oppose the McNary-Haugen bill. The United States Chamber of Commerce also expressed violent opposition to "any proposal for buying, selling, manufacturing or other handling of agricultural products by government agencies."

The frightening epithets undoubtedly had their effect. But there were more practical objections. Higher farm prices would likely mean increased grocery costs, and opponents of McNary-Haugenism held up the prospect of rising living expenses to millions of wage earners and white-collar workers. The Chicago *Tribune* quoted grain men as saying that a probable increase of 10 to 15 per cent would result if the bill passed.[7] The *Wall Street Journal* said there were many objections to the measure, but that higher commodity prices was the worst.[8] A Chicago citizen wired President Coolidge: "Don't forget that the consuming public is much greater than the farmers and if any legislation goes through which hurts them there will be nothing left of the Republican party at the next election."[9] The editor of the Washington *Post* asked if "the consumers of the country shall be taxed for the 'relief' of farmers?"[10]

Metropolitan newspaper opposition was not confined to the possibility of higher food prices. The Chicago *Tribune* editorialized, "Shall we communize the farms?" After scorching the measure unmercifully, the editor concluded, "That is nothing more than Communism, and Communism imposed upon the farmer by Congress."[11] On May 3, the *Literary Digest,* in a biased article, entitled "A Bill to Raise the Price of Wheat," quoted critical remarks from several large newspapers including the New York

[7] Chicago *Tribune,* March 8, 1924.
[8] *Wall Street Journal,* March 10, 1924.
[9] John F. Barrett to Coolidge, May 12, 1924. Files of the Secretary of Agriculture.
[10] Washington *Post,* May 13, 1924.
[11] Chicago *Tribune,* March 11, 1924.

World, St. Louis *Globe-Democrat,* Cleveland *Plain Dealer,* and the Philadelphia *Public Ledger.* The latter said, "This bill is one of the most vicious pieces of farm legislation ever seriously considered."

Some of the economic objections to the McNary-Haugen bill were conveniently summarized in the minority report of the House Agriculture Committee. One of the leading arguments against the bill was that it was price-fixing, a frightening prospect to many legislators. If the government raised the price of wheat, it was maintained that those with wheat on hand would profit from the advance. Thus a "colossal gift" would accrue to nonproducers. Furthermore, determination of a ratio-price would be next to impossible, the critics said, and the equalization fee was condemned as a tax levied for the benefit of a few.

The minority members of the committee also warned against higher living cost and they ventured "a guess" that it might not be "less than $1,500,000,000 per year." This sounded like a strange argument for those who were trying to help farmers. Other charges against the bill were that it would establish "an army of officials, agents, and employees"; that it would weaken the commodity co-operatives; that foreign governments would resent American dumping and retaliate against United States products; that American manufacturers would be handicapped by having to pay higher prices for raw materials; and that it would increase production and aggravate the surplus problem.[12]

This latter position was also well stated outside the halls of Congress. The Minneapolis Civic and Commerce Association declared: "The McNary-Haugen bill is a sedative and will not cure the trouble, which is overproduction. If it increases profits, that will lead to greater production and wipe out the profits. Dumping wheat abroad will bring retaliation. Price-fixing is wrong in principle." The *Wall Street Journal* insisted that if the McNary-Haugen bill became law, the "American people will pay dearly for an unwise experiment in socialism and government price fixing." Retaliation to dumping, said the editor, "is as certain as the rising sun."[13]

Those who opposed the bill also had the support of most pro-

[12] 68 Cong., 1 sess., *H. Rep. No. 631,* pt. II.
[13] *Wall Street Journal,* February 9, and May 7, 1924.

fessional economists. For example, Eric Englund, of Kansas State College, published an article in the *Journal of Farm Economics* in April, 1923, entitled "Fallacies of a Plan to Fix Prices of Farm Products by Government Control of the Exportable Surplus." Even the so-called "liberal" economists doubted if, at best, the ratio-price plan could work for any length of time. Thus, with few exceptions, businessmen and politicians who opposed the McNary-Haugen bill could dignify their arguments by quoting recognized professional economists.

Many critics of the ratio-price plan held that the farm problem could best be solved by letting nature take its course. Great emphasis was placed on so-called "natural laws," and the "law of supply and demand." "Economic law if given free play will accomplish an equitable readjustment," said a writer for the National City Bank of New York. John H. Rich of the Federal Reserve Bank of Minneapolis said that northwestern agriculture was undergoing "a drastic purging process involving the elimination of the unfit, the deflation of excessive land values, the collapse of credits built on an unsound basis, [and] the wiping out of farming operations on marginal lands."[14]

William Jardine, president of Kansas State College, who was soon to become secretary of agriculture, stated this position most clearly. Kansas farmers, he said, just wanted to be left alone. "We will work ourselves out of the hole we are in," he wrote. But Jardine, as early as May, 1924, advised farmers to curtail production so that it would not exceed domestic demand. He argued that the McNary-Haugen bill "might create an artificially high price for wheat for one year. But . . . the guaranteed high price would bring in all the marginal acreage; our exportable surplus would double and treble, and the structure would come toppling down of its own weight."[15]

One of the most blistering and effective attacks against the original McNary-Haugen bill was delivered by Congressman Sydney Anderson in a letter to C. G. Selvig, of Crookston, Minnesota. The force of Anderson's blow was enhanced by his reputation in farm matters, which had come from serving as chairman of the

[14] John H. Rich, "Not To Be Cured By Political or Legislative Processes," *Journal of the American Bankers Association,* Vol. XVI (January, 1924), 407–09.
[15] Washington *Post,* May 15, 1924.

Joint Commission of Agricultural Inquiry and the National Agricultural Conference. Moreover, he came from Minnesota, a supposed hotbed of McNary-Haugenism. Anderson declared that the measure was economically unsound, unworkable, and a danger to farmers because it would upset normal marketing procedures. The letter received wide distribution by opposition congressmen and grain dealers, and Secretary Wallace had to admit that it "will have much effect."

The assault was so damaging that Jewett and Brand urged Chester Davis, Montana's commissioner of agriculture, to answer Anderson. Davis was already active in the farm fight, having helped to form the Montana Export Corporation League in the fall of 1923. At the request of Secretary Wallace, he had served as an unofficial liaison between the Department of Agriculture and members of Congress and farm leaders during January and February, 1924. Before long he was to become second only to Peek as a leader in the battle for farm parity.

Born on a Dallas County, Iowa, farm in 1887, Davis was graduated from Grinnell College in 1911. Shortly afterward, he went to Redfield, South Dakota, where for a brief time he worked on a newspaper. Then he moved to Montana and became city editor of the Miles City *Star,* and in 1913 he accepted the editorship of the Bozeman *Weekly Courier*. While in Bozeman, he became well acquainted with M. L. Wilson, of Montana State College, who probably had a better understanding of Montana farming than any other man. Together they worked to improve the state's agriculture, and Davis stressed agricultural problems in his paper. In 1917 he was made editor of the *Montana Farmer* published at Great Falls. Davis was also active in various farm organizations, being instrumental in forming the Montana Hereford Breeders Association and other livestock groups. At one time he served as vice-president of the Cascade County Farm Bureau.

Firsthand experience and unusual study had given Chester Davis an intimate knowledge of agriculture and its problems. In 1921, when he was only thirty-four years old, Governor Joseph N. Dixon appointed him commissioner of agriculture and labor. For the first time, according to one agricultural editor, Montana had a "real department of agriculture." Davis completely revitalized the work and services of his department and won the praise and confidence of the state's dirt farmers. He possessed rare executive and administrative ability and had a keen, analytical mind. Much of the brains for the McNary-Haugen fight between 1924 and 1928 was furnished by Chester Davis. He was a tough and skillful antagonist in debate and argument. With several years of newspaper work to his credit, he knew the art of propaganda and publicity. It would have been hard to find a more valuable or effective recruit for the agricultural crusade.

In a five-page letter to Anderson dated March 15, Davis argued that parity—a term which he used—was both desirable and feasible. He accused Anderson of not wanting higher farm prices, and particularly considered Anderson's charge that the McNary-Haugen bill would lead to overproduction and that farmers should adjust their output to domestic requirements. Davis said that regardless of how wheat prices were raised, either by cutting acreage or through the McNary-Haugen bill, production would probably be stimulated. But the equalization fee, he declared, "would serve as a brake against overproduction." It is not likely, however, that the fee would have been an adequate "brake" against growing surpluses in the event of higher prices.

Nonetheless, Davis touched the heart of an important point. Throughout the 1920's, opponents of surplus-marketing legislation harped on the theme that farmers should cut their production and thus eliminate price-depressing surpluses. The implication was that prices would then rise. But this was offered more as a blind by those who wanted no government aid to agriculture than as a positive, achievable remedy. As will be shown later, it was well known that farmers would not and could not voluntarily reduce their production in an orderly manner. There were too many of them scattered over a large area. Indeed, forced co-operation by levying an equalization fee on the benefited crops was one of the strongest points of the Peek scheme.

Voluntary acreage-reduction campaigns had been especially common in the cotton belt, where a short crop often brought more money than a large one, but they had been without much success. Thus it was obvious that most of those in the reduced-production school simply did not want higher agricultural prices. Had they advocated some kind of forced production control, their position might have been accepted at its face value.

Davis's letter was generously circulated by friends of the Mc-Nary-Haugen movement, but it did not adequately counteract the harm done by Anderson. Peek and Johnson were so disturbed that they published a pamphlet entitled *An Answer to Representative Sydney Anderson Regarding the McNary-Haugen Bill.* They employed ridicule, sarcasm, and economic argument to blunt Anderson's attack, all with little effect.

Republicans in higher echelons were even more destructive to the bill's success. President Coolidge took every opportunity to crack the administration whip over those who looked favorably at the measure. He also sought to lighten criticism of official Republican policy by raising the tariff on wheat. An increase of 12 cents a bushel became effective on April 7, bringing the rate to 42 cents. Secretary Hoover also used his vast influence and popularity against the bill.

Prominent Democrats were about as active in the fight against the measure as Republicans. Former Secretary of Agriculture David F. Houston strongly opposed the bill and told Senator Thomas J. Walsh that it "would in the long run be detrimental to farmers." Walsh, who had at first favored the Peek plan, changed his mind by April and fought it because of the flexible tariff provision. Since he had previously worked against this tariff mechanism, to support it now, he said, would place him "in a wholly untenable position before my colleagues."[16]

But it was Democrat Henry T. Rainey, a congressman from Illinois, who struck some of the most telling blows at the first McNary-Haugen bill. Rainey jumped into the national limelight when, on March 12, he wrote Sam H. Thompson, refusing to support the bill and hotly denouncing the political pressure being exerted by the Illinois Agricultural Association. He told the association's president that he had received letters from county Farm Bureaus in Illinois "couched practically in the same language." Rainey said he would not be influenced by that type of "propaganda."[17]

Rainey declared that the measure was "unworkable and impractical," and would be like administering poison to a dying

[16] Houston to Walsh, May 29, 1924; and Walsh to M. L. Wilson, April 1, 1924. Walsh Papers.
[17] Rainey to Thompson, March 12 and April 9, 1924. Rainey Papers.

man. He wrote to Donald R. Murphy of *Wallace's Farmer* on April 13 that he considered it "the most dangerous legislation ever suggested since the Constitution." The *Modern Miller,* published in Chicago, reported that Rainey's argument "rips the proposed bill into remnants," and that the proposal had been "sandbagged in a masterly way."

Thompson's reply to Rainey was prepared by Peek and the entire correspondence was printed in the *Congressional Record.* Rainey became the darling of those who opposed the plan, and copies of his letters were scattered far and wide. Opposing farm journals like Dante Pierce's *Iowa Homestead* and *Wisconsin Farmer,* reprinted Rainey's caustic attack in full. Large headlines in the *Iowa Homestead* on March 27, 1924, read, "Rainey Dissects McNary-Haugen Bill." Businessmen, particularly grain dealers, requested copies of the Rainey letters and distributed them in franked envelopes. Let it be said, however, that within two years the farm lobby was sufficiently potent to bring Rainey into the McNary-Haugen camp. Later he did yeoman service in the farm cause, but in 1924 he did irreparable damage.

Other farm relief bills before Congress early in 1924 also greatly handicapped the drive for surplus-control legislation. Lack of unity among the farm forces provided an opportunity for their opponents to divide and conquer. The principal measures under consideration were the Norris-Sinclair, Curtis-Aswell, Norbeck-Burtness, and Capper-Williams bills. Peek was strongly opposed to all of these measures and he urged his supporters to fight them. He feared that they would divert attention from the basic problems of ratio-prices, surplus control, and tariff effectiveness for agricultural commodities. Peek did not maintain that the McNary-Haugen bill was the only plan that could help agriculture. But from the beginning he held that any legislation must achieve the principle of ratio-prices for the farmer through an effective protective tariff. Anything short of this, he denounced with all his strength.

Prior to the introduction of the McNary-Haugen bill the Norris-Sinclair measure had the most farm support. Farmers had confidence in Senator Norris, who already had earned a reputation among forgotten men. Norris hoped to improve farm income by reducing the spread between the producer and consumer. He believed that farmers could be helped by eliminating private commissions and charges of middlemen. The Norris bill proposed to establish a government corporation which could buy or lease storage and processing facilities, and sell manufactured or raw farm products. It was believed that a government agency could reduce marketing costs and institute savings not enjoyed by farmers who had to sell through private agencies. While the bill did not anticipate fixing farm prices, many followers were won by the expectation that the corporation would pay cost of production for agricultural commodities. The corporation was to be capitalized at $100,000,000, with authority to issue additional tax-free bonds.

The Norris proposal received a cold reception from Secretary Wallace. In fact, Wallace's correspondence reveals that he was indifferent, or actually opposed, to most of the farm relief measures except the McNary-Haugen bill. Like Peek, he believed they would not bring genuine relief to agriculture. To reduce handling charges, Wallace maintained, was not enough to help farmers materially, even assuming this could be accomplished.[18] Politically the bill was weak in that it was not aimed at immediate price rises. Senator Norris himself admitted that it would be several years before any benefits could be felt. Yet, he believed it would bring permanent relief. But farmers wanted help at once. By March, Norris was admitting that most influential farmers favored the McNary-Haugen measure over his bill.[19]

The Norbeck-Burtness bill was introduced in late 1923 to help meet the growing political unrest in the northwestern spring-wheat area of the Dakotas and Montana. To some extent it was planned to draw attention from McNary-Haugenism. The proposal was developed by John Lee Coulter, president of North Dakota Agricultural College, with the idea of increasing farm income through diversification. Coulter and others held that over-specialization in wheat had left farmers the victims of a single low-priced crop. The bill provided for a federal agricultural diversification commission and called for a government appropriation of $50,000,000. Loans not exceeding $1,000 were to be made

18 Wallace to J. H. Sinclair, February 18, 1924. Files of the Secretary of Agriculture.
19 Norris to Sam W. Teagarden, March 1, 1924. Norris Papers.

to farmers to buy pigs, chickens, and particularly dairy cows. Essentially, the measure was designed to change spring-wheat raisers into dairymen.

President Coolidge favored the bill and gave it public endorsement by calling a northwestern agricultural conference in February, 1924. Meeting in Washington, the conference, made up mostly of nonfarmers, gave official support to the plan. A minority group, however, representing actual dirt farmers, pledged themselves to back surplus-control legislation of the McNary-Haugen variety. On March 13, the Senate defeated the measure 41 to 32, and the McNary-Haugenites shed no tears. "The defeat . . . of the Norbeck-Burtness bill failed to cause even a ripple of disappointment among the farmers. Their eyes are on the McNary-Haugen bill," wrote Chester Davis from Montana.[20]

The Curtis-Aswell bill was drawn chiefly to divide and divert farm support away from the McNary-Haugen bill. It was just another co-operative marketing measure of which many were introduced during the 1920's. The measure had two important features. First, it provided for the government to loan $10,000,000 to stimulate and perfect co-operative marketing associations. This was to be administered by an interstate farm marketing association. Secondly, the association was to advise farmers on production, and to tell them when to increase or decrease their output of particular crops in order to receive the most profitable prices. The promoters of this scheme hoped to organize co-operatives sufficiently strong so that they could determine agricultural prices. The plan was developed by B. F. Yoakum, a New York businessman who had devoted considerable time and money to farm problems.

Actually, it had little merit. Laws already had been passed legalizing and encouraging the formation of farm co-operatives. Although lack of funds had handicapped the development of some co-operative organizations, that was not the main problem. A more fundamental difficulty arose when the co-operatives withheld stocks from the market at the expense of members in an attempt to influence prices. This helped nonmembers more than members and caused the failure of many co-operatives. Representative Aswell wrote to Rainey in April that it was rumored

20 Davis to George Peek, March 15, 1924. Peek Papers.

President Coolidge might soon announce that all farm relief proposals were "too paternalistic and socialistic," except the Curtis-Aswell bill.[21] But when Coolidge took no action, the bill came to nothing. The Capper-Williams bill was another co-operative marketing measure which commanded relatively little support in 1924.

Besides the various agricultural relief plans which kept friends of the farmers working at cross purposes, the first McNary-Haugen campaign was weakened by opposition from within the ranks of co-operative marketing organizations. Many of the commodity groups feared that surplus-control legislation would ruin them. It was obvious that if producers of a particular commodity were promised a ratio-price under the McNary-Haugen bill, they would find little advantage in joining a traditional co-operative. Chester Davis reported to Peek that "certain co-operatives" were opposing the measure, and this, he wrote, gave "the hidden opponents of the bill [McNary-Haugen] a weapon to hit it over the head with."

On February 21, the Oklahoma Wheat Growers Association passed a resolution opposing the bill. It stated, "We regard this bill as an attempt to create a government piece of machinery which will destroy the commodity marketing associations of the United States, particularly those of recent origin." C. H. Hyde of the Oklahoma Farmers Union declared, however, that the meeting had been dominated by the Enid grain dealers and that actual dirt farmers had not attended the meeting which condemned the bill. By April, Hyde could report that most of the anti-McNary-Haugen directors of the association had been "eliminated."[22] This is an excellent example of the results of local grass-roots pressure when supporters of the McNary-Haugen bill began to turn on the political heat. Nonetheless, action by the Oklahoma organization was publicized widely by critics of McNary-Haugenism. The Executive Committee of the Kansas Wheat Growers Association also objected to the bill.

One of the most prominent and respected men in agricultural circles who at first refused to support the McNary-Haugen bill was Frank Lowden of Illinois. Independently wealthy, a former congressman and governor, and a presidential aspirant in 1920, Low-

[21] Aswell to Rainey, April 17, 1924. Rainey Papers.
[22] Hyde to McNary, April 4, 1924. McNary Papers.

den had a large following in farm ranks. He was president of the American Dairy Federation, and viewed co-operative marketing as the "most important movement for stabilizing agriculture and putting farming upon [a] modern business basis that has come in my time."[23]

Peek did everything in his power during the spring of 1924 to win Lowden's support. "I can think of no greater political blunder that you could make than to remain associated with an organization opposing this bill which is sweeping the country like a prairie fire," Peek warned. He asked his Illinois neighbor to "issue a statement in favor of the bill and calling upon the administration to get actively behind it." Lowden replied, however, that although he would not oppose the measure, he preferred to confine his efforts to co-operative marketing.[24] As long as important leaders like Lowden were indifferent or opposed to the McNary-Haugen bill, its chances of success were slight. More conversions were needed before surplus-control legislation could be passed.

Thus by the spring of 1924, a majority of the business interests, the Coolidge administration, many powerful Democrats, most professional economists, the metropolitan press, numerous farm journals and country papers, those who favored other agricultural relief plans, most co-operative marketing advocates, and a number of important farm leaders made up a formidable array of opposition to the McNary-Haugenites. Indeed, was there any hope at all? And as if this were not enough, the radical farm organizations also fought the measure. Benjamin C. Marsh, director of the Farmers National Council which represented groups like the Nonpartisan League, the Farm-Labor Union of America, and the Oklahoma Farm-Labor Union, told members of the Senate that the plan would be ineffective and unworkable, and that it had been "cleverly designed to discredit government activity."

When the House of Representatives began debating the bill in May, there was little left to be said on either side. Yet the plight of agriculture was discussed by speaker after speaker in tiresome repetition. The tone of Congressional debate was that something must be done for the poor unfortunate farmer. Apparently every-

---

[23] Lowden to Julius Rosenwald, March 18, 1924. Lowden Papers.
[24] Peek to Lowden, March 1, and Lowden to Peek, March 5, 1924. Peek Papers.

one loved the horney-handed son of the soil. To hear congressmen talk, mostly for home consumption, farmers were the salt of the earth, the epitome of virtue, the preservers of democracy, and the source of all wealth. Most of the speakers admitted that Congress had some responsibility to help agriculture in the emergency, but critics said that the McNary-Haugen bill was not the answer.

Opponents of the measure had a powerful combination of speakers to denounce it. Edward S. Voigt of Wisconsin, James B. Aswell of Louisiana, Henry T. Rainey of Illinois, Robert Luce of Massachusetts, and David H. Kincheloe of Kentucky were among the foremost critics of the measure in the House. These men represented both parties.

Voigt was a particularly effective antagonist because he was a member of the House Agriculture Committee and came from the Northwest, a section in distress. On May 20 he flayed the bill on the grounds that it was unworkable, and that it would increase surpluses and raise consumer prices. He received hearty applause when he condemned artificial price-fixing and said the bill was economically unsound. Voigt also made the important point that Coolidge would not sign such a bill, and therefore Congress should work out something which would gain presidential approval. But even Voigt said he would vote for the bill if it were limited to wheat.[25]

Democrat Aswell was even more emphatic. This bill, he said, would set "the precedent of socializing and nationalizing the industry of agriculture, which would lead inevitably to the nationalization of all industry . . . overriding economic law by statutory laws and thus place our government squarely in the class of the bolshevistic government of Russia." After months of study, Aswell had concluded that the bill was "unsound, unworkable, full of Bolshevism, purely socialistic, indefensibly communistic." In historical perspective such exaggerated charges seem ridiculous, but in 1924 they carried considerable weight.

Other southern Democrats, while opposing the bill, took the opportunity to chide the northwestern Republicans. Those who were now crying loudest for agricultural relief, said Tom Connally of Texas, were the same individuals who had voted for the

[25] *Cong. Rec.*, 68 Cong., 1 sess., May 20, 1924, p. 9052.

Fordney-McCumber tariff, which had raised nonagricultural prices and hurt the farmer.

Haugen, Thomas L. Rubey of Missouri, F. S. Purnell of Indiana, and J. N. Tincher of Kansas took the lead in defending and promoting the bill. Brand in the Department of Agriculture prepared much of the material for congressmen and senators favoring the measure. Rubey reminded his colleagues that Voigt was evidently not too shocked at the idea of price-fixing, because he had introduced his own bill in April to fix the price of wheat at $1.65 a bushel. Tincher showed other inconsistencies in the position of the opposition. The two main arguments against the bill, he said, were that it would raise the cost of living and would ruin the farmer. Tincher could not reconcile how the farmer would be ruined by higher prices! Purnell frankly admitted that the bill was not perfect but said it "was the only constructive thing presented to this House that offers the American farmer immediate relief."[26]

Friends of the measure did everything possible to win support, and fought hard right down to the final roll call. But on June 3 the House defeated it by a vote of 223 to 155. A few days later Congress adjourned, ending the possibility of getting farm relief at that session.

The bill was defeated by a combination of eastern Republicans and southern Democrats. Congressmen from the South Atlantic and East South-Central states voted 66 to 14 against it. There was only 1 yea vote from New England, and in the Middle Atlantic states the vote was 64 to 9 against the measure. The stronghold of McNary-Haugenism was in the West North-Central, Mountain, and Pacific Northwest states, where the favorable vote was 74 to 10. Representatives of the Mountain states cast only 1 vote against the measure. A key area for possible future support was the East North-Central states, where thirty-three congressmen voted against the bill.

"The grain trade's bugaboo is killed," jubilantly announced the editor of the *Grain Dealers Journal* on June 10. "We will not be threatened with more fool legislation for at least six months," and the editor added, "Our whole business world would

26 *Ibid.*, May 22, pp. 9197-98, 9200-02, and 9211-12.

have been overjoyed if the Congress had adjourned for six years." He was pleased that the McNary-Haugen bill was "as dead as a smelt."

The McNary-Haugen bill, however, was by no means "as dead as a smelt." In fact, only the preliminary skirmish had been lost. The real battle lay ahead. The Ohio Farm Bureau Federation *News,* which had not supported the measure, admitted in July that the bill "probably had as much backing as any piece of farm legislation ever offered." And the ratio-price supporters were anything but ready to surrender.

Plans were already underway to improve and strengthen the farm lobby. One of the most effective techniques was to dub anyone who opposed the McNary-Haugen bill an enemy of farm relief. Representative Aswell attempted to stymie this trend when he announced that congressmen did not have to vote for the McNary-Haugen bill, or nothing. There was legislation of "the proper kind," he said, which could receive both Republican and Democratic support. Nonetheless, those who opposed the bill were increasingly classed as opponents of farm relief, a development which finally brought many recalcitrant legislators into line.

Chapter VI

Mobilizing a Farm Lobby

THE Congressional fight over the first McNary-Haugen bill had made two things abundantly clear. The agricultural forces must get better organized; and somehow they must enlist southern support.

The chances of picking up backers in the cotton belt did not look bright in the summer of 1924. The farm price of cotton had been over 30 cents a pound in December, 1923, when much of the crop had gone to market. During the following months it had declined, but was still bringing over 20 cents, which was above the ratio-price. The favorable cotton situation was due to three successive short crops from 1921 to 1923, to decreased foreign production, and to improved demand by American industry. It was no wonder that southerners did not jump on the McNary-Haugen band wagon.

In fact, most farm prices had risen markedly from the depression levels of 1921 and 1922. Wheat, which had suffered so severely following 1920, was bringing considerably over one dollar a bushel in the summer of 1924. Secretary Wallace emphasized in his annual report that, while problems still remained, "the wheat situation has greatly improved." Corn-hog producers were still in bad shape, but their condition was better. Sheepmen were actually enjoying prosperity. It was the cattlemen who continued to be hardest hit. In August, 1924, good beef steers sold in Chicago at prices below those for the corresponding months of 1922 and 1923. Considering the whole agricultural picture, however, there was cause for optimism. Farmers had not reached economic parity with other groups, but they were in a better position than at any time since 1920. By November, 1924, the ratio of all farm prices to those of nonagricultural goods was 86.

The Republican party was counting heavily on improved agricultural conditions, plus vague promises, to quiet the clamor for government relief. At their national convention in Cleveland, the Republicans drew up an agricultural plank which pledged "the party to take whatever steps are necessary to bring back a balanced condition between agriculture, industry, and labor." They proposed to achieve this objective by encouraging co-operative marketing, maintaining the protective tariff, and stimulating exports "without putting the government in business." Attempting to frighten the Old Guard, Senator Norbeck told a platform subcommittee that unless agriculture got some genuine concessions the party might look forward to a La Follette surge comparable to a "Kansas cyclone." But the Republican high command was not worried. The attitude of the entire convention, Norbeck said, was to "praise Coolidge and say the Lord be thanked for the wonderful little man in the White House."[1]

The Democrats and La Follette progressives went further in their promises to agriculture, hoping to woo some of the restless Republican farmers. The Democratic platform called for the "establishment of an export marketing corporation or commission in order that the exportable surplus may not establish the price of the whole crop." This seemed to be an outright endorsement of the Peek principles. Baruch had worked on the Democratic platform, which probably accounts for this part of the farm plank.[2] The La Follette group proposed to call a special session of Congress "to pass legislation for relief of American agriculture."[3]

But without widespread agitation and concentrated political pressure, it was unlikely that any substantial farm relief would be enacted, regardless of which party won the fall elections. Therefore, the leaders of the crusade for agricultural equality set out to correct one of their major weaknesses—lack of organization. They planned to organize a powerful farm lobby, centrally directed and adequately manned and financed. It had to be strong enough to reward and punish senators and representatives on the agricul-

[1] Norbeck to C. M. Henry, June 9, 1924. Norbeck Papers.
[2] Baruch to Peek, June 21, 1924. Baruch Papers.
[3] Kirk Porter, *National Party Platforms* (New York, 1924), 476ff.

tural issue alone. A good example of what they needed could be found in the old antisaloon league headed by Wayne Wheeler. In the drive for prohibition a few years before, Wheeler had made only one test for legislators. They had to vote dry. A potent farm lobby with the same singleness of purpose was the aim of the Mc-Nary-Haugen group. It must be organized without regard to party or farm organizations.

Even before the first McNary-Haugen bill was defeated, friends of the measure were planning just such an organization. George C. Jewett, Peek, Frank W. Murphy, R. A. Cowles, Charles E. Hearst, William Hirth, and others had discussed forming a national agricultural body which could speak "with one powerful and united voice for all concerned" on surplus-control legislation. About the time Congress adjourned early in June, Jewett was directed to call a great farm conference.

On June 16 he sent a special letter to about 60 farm leaders. The next day he mailed an invitation to 1,250 farmers, farm organization officials, and friends of surplus-control legislation, asking them to meet in St. Paul on July 11 and 12. The purpose of the conference, he said, was to form "a temporary organization to have charge of a national campaign to secure enactment into law of the basic principles of the McNary-Haugen bill."[4]

Since there was no formal agenda, several farm leaders met on July 9 to work out a program in advance. Jewett, Peek, Henry A. Wallace, Hirth, and Murphy were among those who played leading roles. Chester Davis, who normally would have had a key part in any deliberations, was unable to attend the St. Paul meeting because of illness in his family. As early as the summer of 1924, the front ranks in the farm battle had been filled.

Besides Peek and Davis, Frank W. Murphy, of Wheaton, Minnesota, and Hirth, head of the Missouri Farmers Association and editor of the *Missouri Farmer,* were the most important. But the yeoman service of Hearst, Thompson, Cowles, Earl Smith, W. H. Settle, and others cannot be overlooked. There was no more vigorous fighter for agricultural parity than Murphy. A small-town lawyer and owner of numerous farms in Minnesota's rich southwestern section, he had become convinced that farmers could be

4 Jewett to "You As a Worker for the McNary-Haugen Bill," June 16; and to "Farmers and Farm Organizations," June 17, 1924. Peek Papers.

saved only by surplus-control legislation of the Peek variety. During the winter of 1923–24, he had spent five months in Washington at his own expense, doing what he called "my everlasting best to get votes for the McNary-Haugen bill." Hirth, while a friend of the co-operative movement, was also militant in his support of the McNary-Haugen bill. Through his *Missouri Farmer* he funneled farm relief propaganda to the grass roots. Skillful at overemphasis, his forcefulness made him sound much more radical than he really was.

Among the 150 men present when the conference opened on July 11, 78 delegates were accredited. Peek attended as a representative of the Rock Island County Farm Bureau. The three big farm organizations—Farm Bureau, Grange, and Farmers Union—were all represented either by state or national officers. C. H. Hyde, vice-president of the Farmers Union spoke for that organization, Gray Silver for the Farm Bureau, and E. K. Eckert for the Grange. The large number of associations represented at the conference from the spring-wheat area indicates that much of the pressure for the McNary-Haugen bill was still coming from that section.

The conference voted to form a new farm organization to be called the "American Council of Agriculture." The council was not to replace any of the current farm groups but to supplement those already in existence. It was to be sort of a super organization among the farm organizations. The council had only one aim. "Its chief object," read the declaration of purpose, "shall be to make it possible for the existing agricultural organizations of whatever character to speak with one voice thru a united leadership wherever and whenever the general well being of agriculture is concerned." This meant to do whatever was "necessary and advisable to secure the enactment . . . of legislation embodying the principles of the McNary-Haugen bill and thus secure for American agriculture equality with industry and labor." After the St. Paul conference, the McNary-Haugen bill and equality for agriculture became synonymous terms in the minds of most farm leaders.

Although the McNary-Haugenites wanted to keep the agricultural question out of partisan politics, it was obvious that they must apply political pressure to achieve results. Therefore the conference declared, "In the coming national election we recommend rewarding those who supported the McNary-Haugen bill in Congress without the slightest regard to the party label." All candidates for the House and Senate were asked to pledge: "In the event of my nomination and election, I hereby pledge myself to vote for and faithfully support legislation that will give agriculture equality with industry and labor, in line with the spirit of the McNary-Haugen bill."

The same weakness appeared in the St. Paul meeting that had been evident in the Congressional fight: there was no southern support. Not a single delegate represented southern agriculture, unless Hyde of Oklahoma or Hirth of Missouri could be placed in that category. Recognizing this, the council decided to "give special consideration to the problems surrounding the cotton producers and to this end invite friendship and co-operation."

To head the American Council of Agriculture and direct the mounting pressure for farm relief legislation, the conference unanimously chose George Peek. Jewett and Murphy were also nominated, but withdrew when Peek indicated that he would accept the post. Peek was becoming the driving force behind the entire movement, and everyone knew it. His election as president of the council was only a formal recognition of existing facts. Other officers were Carl Gunderson of the South Dakota Wheat Growers Association, vice-president; R. A. Cowles, secretary of the Illinois Agricultural Association, secretary; and J. R. Mitchell of St. Paul, treasurer.[5]

Under the circumstances, Peek was the logical choice to head the farm fight. In the first place, he had worked out and popularized the idea of making the tariff effective and achieving ratio-prices. His name was coming to be automatically associated with agricultural equality. Moreover, he was a businessman and had personal contacts not generally open to ordinary farm leaders. Besides Baruch, there were Charles G. Dawes, Alex Legge, and many others. The fact that a well-to-do businessman proposed a sharp departure from accepted ideas of agricultural relief somehow made them seem less radical and dangerous.

Furthermore, Peek had no official connections with any of the large farm organizations, thereby obviating any suspicion or

[5] "Report and Record, Agricultural Conference, July 11 and 12, 1924." Mimeographed copy. *Ibid.*

jealousy among the Farmers Union, Grange, and Farm Bureau. For one of the major farm groups to originate and sponsor a particular piece of legislation in the 1920's was almost certain to bring indifference, if not outright hostility, from the others. The Mc-Nary-Haugen legislation was not a farm organization bill. It had come from completely outside their ranks, although, from the beginning, the Farm Bureau was most closely associated with the measure.

Other conditions added to Peek's effectiveness as a generalissimo in the farm relief battle. Being independently wealthy, he was not forced to depend on outside financial support for expenses incidental to his activities in Washington and elsewhere. He could and did provide his own travel, publicity, living, and other expenses, and, in some instances, supplied money to other farm leaders. Peek never kept any record of the money that he spent in connection with his farm relief work, but it amounted to many thousands of dollars. Writing in 1931, William Hirth declared, "Certainly no half dozen men have spent so much of their own money in trying to save agriculture from the collapse which now confronts it."[6] And since Peek accepted no other job after resigning from the Moline Plow Company, he was free to devote whatever time was necessary to the farm cause. His only business responsibility was looking after a couple of farms in Colorado and his stock investments.

Peek had other offers from industry, but he decided to devote all of his time to farm relief. Here was a cause bigger than himself and more important than private interests. There was a certain religious fervor about his crusade for agricultural equality. He felt a personal responsibility for preserving and rehabilitating a crippled agriculture.

Not only did Peek give freely of his time and money, but more than anyone else he contributed the enthusiasm and dogged determination to see the fight through. Motivated by a deep sense of urgency and a belief in the justness of his cause, he constantly thought and talked farm relief. And his earnestness and sincerity were contagious. Chester Davis first met Peek early in March, 1924, when he was on his way from Washington to Montana. He stopped off at Moline and went to visit Peek. Peek was so earnest and in-

[6] Hirth to William E. Borah, March 16, 1931. *Ibid.*

terested in farm parity that Davis could scarcely get away. In fact, before he left he sat down at a typewriter and hammered out some material which Peek could use in a speech to be delivered a few days later. Peek preached equality for agriculture in the spirit of a Dwight L. Moody or a Billy Sunday. He told one skeptic of the McNary-Haugen bill, "I believe it is just as impossible to stop this movement as it would be to undertake to flag a cyclone with a pocket handkerchief."[7]

"I know of no man in America who is better qualified to give militant direction to this campaign than yourself," Chester Davis told Peek.[8] Baruch said that he was "overjoyed" at Peek's selection to head the American Council of Agriculture. Peek could count on his full support to "work out something," Baruch wrote. "If you cannot do it nobody can."[9]

Thus, beginning in July, 1924, Peek assumed command, marshaled the farm relief forces into an effective battalion, and maintained the head position until after Hoover's election in 1928. Despite his prominent position in the fight for farm parity, Peek made every effort to keep in the background. He wanted it to appear as though the recognized farm leaders were promoting the movement. Such an impression was more likely to influence members of Congress. Peek furnished ideas and information for the farm representatives who did most of the testifying before Congressional committees. He often acted more like an observer than a promoter. Yet he was the real kingpin of the campaign, and found that he could not remain entirely inconspicuous.

With the formation of the American Council of Agriculture, the farmers at last had an organization through which they could speak and work. The main thing was to get co-operation among the sometimes jealous and always individualistic agricultural leaders. The growing militancy of at least some McNary-Haugen supporters was reflected in Frank Murphy's keynote address at the St. Paul meeting when he said:

> We are here today to give notice that no man or group of men—
> no interest or group of interests—no political party or com-

7 Peek to H. H. Cleveland, March 15, 1924. *Ibid.*
8 Davis to Peek, July 14, 1924. *Ibid.*
9 Baruch to Peek, September 26, 1924. *Ibid.*

bination of parties—no power on God's earth can keep in economic bondage—can submerge and reduce to a peasantry more than one-third of the population of the United States. . . . This is the hour of mobilization. All of our siege guns are to be moved to position. We are to go forward under one command. There is no doubt about our objective. We are no longer to be charged with not knowing what we want. All of the farm organizations of America are to be bridged with other forces in a common offensive.[10]

The St. Paul gathering infused new life into the farm fight at a time when it otherwise might have languished or been submerged by events surrounding the presidential election. A. R. Sykes of Iowa said during the conference, "The greatest fight ever inaugurated in behalf of farm legislation is now being made and will continue to a glorious finish."[11] Peek claimed that the council represented 2,500,000 farmers.

George Peek never did anything half way. He jumped into the work of directing the farm relief fight with his usual vigor. Within a few weeks central offices were established at 1200 Transportation Building in Chicago. He sent out hundreds of letters written on the council's new stationery, with its impressive list of officers and directors. He distributed pamphlets by the thousand, telling of the council's objectives and explaining the McNary-Haugen bill.

He accepted almost every opportunity to speak on the agricultural problem. On Farm Bureau Day at the Iowa State Fair in Des Moines he told a large crowd that "American agriculture is on trial for its life." In considerable detail he outlined farm needs and argued that the only practical remedy was to include the farmer in the protective system. "Agriculture," he said, "has remained unorganized, individualistic, fighting its battles with nature and accepting the inequalities forced upon it by the influence of other groups. The time has come when in order to preserve its very existence, agriculture must rise and assert itself." Peek could make a good speech and he drew large audiences.

[10] American Council of Agriculture, *A Plea For Permanent Economic Equality for Agriculture With Industry and Labor* (September, 1924). A pamphlet.

[11] Minneapolis *Morning Tribune*, July 12, 1924.

About a fortnight after the St. Paul conclave, Peek wrote to President Coolidge advising him of the council's formation and outlining its objectives. He asked the President to instruct the Secretary of Agriculture to appoint an extraordinary farm conference to study agricultural problems. He insisted, however, that members of the commission should not be inimical to the principles of getting equality for agriculture.[12] This letter, editorialized the St. Paul *Dispatch,* "was the voice of the farmer. It issued from the soil. It enunciated the platform of agriculture."[13]

In his acceptance speech on August 14, Coolidge said he planned to appoint a committee to investigate and report to Congress on desirable farm legislation. However, as had been true before, Coolidge made it clear that he did not favor any of the surplus-control bills of the Peek brand. The fundamental remedy, he said, was "not so much through the enactment of legislative laws as through the working out of economic laws." What was needed, Coolidge declared, was "more organization, co-operation, and diversification."[14]

Coolidge never replied to Peek's letter of July 31, but finally on August 29, the President's secretary, Bascom Slemp, assured Peek that Coolidge planned to appoint members to a special farm conference. This did not satisfy Peek, as he had requested that the Secretary of Agriculture select the personnel of the commission. To him there was a great deal of difference between having Wallace or Coolidge name such a group.

When Baruch heard about a possible conference, he wrote Peek asking if he approved Coolidge's suggestion. Baruch said that both the friends and enemies of agriculture knew the problems, and that the proposal of another conference "is nothing but a sop to keep the farmer quiet, so, that if it [farm vote] does not go to La Follette, at least it will not go to Davis." Baruch remarked that his interest would decrease considerably if Peek accepted Coolidge's plan.[15]

It is not clear just how much influence Baruch may have had, but a week later Peek withdrew the council's request for the ap-

---

12 Peek to Coolidge, July 31, 1924. Peek Papers.
13 St. Paul *Dispatch,* August 15, 1924.
14 *New York Times,* August 15, 1924.
15 Baruch to Peek, September 29, 1924. Baruch Papers.

pointment of an agricultural commission. The council, Peek said, had concluded that Coolidge was relying on Hoover rather than on Wallace for farm advice, intimating that the President could not be trusted to appoint a friendly commission.

The council's executive committee met in Chicago on October 6 to work out future plans. With the election only a month away, it was decided to ask each presidential candidate, if elected, to call a special session of Congress "for the express purpose of passing farm legislation." Peek sent letters to each of the contestants, and Davis and La Follette agreed, that if they should win, they would call a special session. But Slemp said only that "the President would at all times take every reasonable Government action to promote the welfare of agriculture."[16]

The tremendous Coolidge landslide was a sharp setback for the farm reliefers, although La Follette did make heavy inroads on Republican strength in parts of the upper Midwest. Chester Davis analyzed the Montana situation by saying, "The chief difficulty as I see it . . . lies in the fact that the wheat price has been fairly satisfactory throughout the west with the result that the farmers as a whole have traveled along with the conservative or the reactionary surge." Quite a percentage of the farmers voted for La Follette as a protest, Davis added, but there was "an overwhelming nonpartisan support for Coolidge particularly in the towns."[17]

George Jewett wrote Senator McNary that in some sections farmers would probably be "lulled to sleep through the favorable prices for wheat and corn." When Frederic W. Wile asked E. B. Reid, acting Washington representative of the Farm Bureau, why the agricultural West went almost solidly for Coolidge, Reid replied, "Because the American farmer is at heart a conservative and not a radical."[18]

Most of the supporters of the McNary-Haugen bill voted for Coolidge despite his well-known stand against such legislation. The St. Paul *Dispatch* and the Des Moines *Register* both backed the Republican nominee, largely because of his promises and the

[16] Quoted in *Agricultural Relief,* Hearings before the House Agriculture Committee, 68 Cong., 2 sess., 1925, p. 447ff.

[17] Davis to George Peek, November 8, 1924. Peek Papers.

[18] Quoted in the *Farm Journal,* Vol. XLVIII (December, 1924), 13.

party platform. On August 15, the day after Coolidge's acceptance speech, the *Dispatch,* a strong organ of McNary-Haugenism,
declared: "Mr. Coolidge has made the problem of agriculture his
problem. He has struck an alliance with the farmer." After the
election the editor said that no farm group should press legislation until the President's conference had acted. "To make any
move in advance of the administration's evidently sincere program would, it seems to us, be proof of bad leadership."[19] This
was obviously a reference to Peek and the American Council of
Agriculture. Harvey Ingham, editor of the Des Moines *Register,*
visited Coolidge, who told him "that something must be done."
Ingham apparently had confidence in Coolidge, but at the same
time he must have had some mental reservations. He explained
to Frank Lowden that the President would need a lot of guidance
on farm problems![20]

Peek did not reveal how he voted in 1924 until about eight
years later. A Congressional committee tried to ferret out his
political stand, but he claimed that "even my wife does not know
how I voted." However, he forsook his lifelong Republicanism
and quietly voted for Davis. He could already see that Coolidge
was a major stumbling block in the drive for farm parity.

19 St. Paul *Dispatch,* December 3, 1924.
20 Ingham to Lowden, September 16 and November 13, 1924. Lowden
Papers.

Chapter VII

At Dead Center

THE ELECTION of Coolidge was a hard blow, but no particular surprise to Peek and his group. The death of Secretary Wallace on October 25, 1924, however, was an entirely unexpected shock which shook the campaign for farm relief to its very foundation. The farmers, said Charles J. Brand, had lost their "last line of contact with government." Henry C. Taylor recalled that it "was paralyzing news. . . . Our leader whom we could always count on was gone and we were stunned."[1] This accident of fate opened the way for Coolidge to appoint a department head opposed to surplus-control legislation. Brand, Taylor, and others in the department who were tainted with McNary-Haugenism soon left voluntarily or were forced out. Writing to Peek in November, Brand predicted that Coolidge would do nothing worth-while for the farmers. In fact, he was already looking for another job. Being a "consulting specialist," he wrote, "when we need some honest to god work is getting too much for my conscience."[2]

In keeping with his campaign promise, Coolidge appointed a special nine-man agricultural conference on November 7. The personnel of the conference indicated that it would not favor legislation demanded by Peek and the American Council of Agriculture. Four of the nine appointees—Chairman Robert D. Carey, former governor of Wyoming; Fred H. Bixby, president of the American National Livestock Association; Ralph Merritt, president of the Sun-Maid Raisin Growers of California; and William

[1] Quoted in Russell Lord, *The Wallaces of Iowa* (Boston, 1947), 257.
[2] Brand to Peek, November 18, 1924. Peek Papers.

M. Jardine, president of Kansas State College—were known opponents of the McNary-Haugen bill. The other five members—O. E. Bradfute; R. M. Thatcher; W. C. Coffey; C. S. Barrett; and L. J. Taber—were either strong co-operative marketing advocates, or only mild backers of surplus-control legislation.

To the McNary-Haugenites the conference looked like a "deliberate dud." Many Midwesterners viewed it as "a lullaby for the farmer and an alibi for the President." Yet, the American Council of Agriculture was in a most embarrassing position. Bradfute, Taber, and Barrett, national presidents of the Farm Bureau, Grange, and Farmer's Union respectively, were not only members of the conference, but were also on the council's executive committee.

On December 1 about fifty farm leaders met in Chicago to discuss ways to further the McNary-Haugen bill. Peek, Hearst, Murphy, Hyde, Henry A. Wallace, Milo Reno, Hirth, Davis, along with economist Edwin G. Nourse, were there. Peek warned his friends to beware of currently better agricultural prices. If the emergency had passed, he said, the "cause of the late depression" was still present. He declared that the American Council of Agriculture wanted to "work in entire harmony" with the President's conference, but he added, "it is the plain duty of this Council to respectfully make known its position to the commission, and to affirm its position before the country, and to Congress, on the pressing special need for legislation that shall admit the farmer to a place in the American protective system." In light of the party platforms, he declared, "the farmer is coming back to the corridors of Congress next month in the role of a ruthless collector of promissory notes."[3]

The council members present voted unanimously to continue their fight for a farmer's export corporation to remove surpluses from the domestic market. About two weeks later, Peek sent Chairman Carey a twenty-six-page memorandum, outlining the position of those favoring an export corporation.[4]

Meanwhile, Chester Davis had arrived in Chicago to revise the old McNary-Haugen bill. From late in November until nearly Christmas, when he returned to Montana, he worked in the coun-

3 Remarks by George N. Peek, December 1, 1924. Typescript. *Ibid.*
4 Peek to Carey, December 17, 1924. *Ibid.*

cil's Chicago office attempting to draw up a less objectionable measure, but one which would accomplish the same results. Peek and Brand had agreed right after the election that some "revised proposition" would have to be presented, if it were ever to pass Congress.

Peek believed first of all that they must eliminate the idea of the government in business. He suggested changing the name to Farmers' Export Corporation, which "would make it appear as a farmers' corporation." Peek told Frank W. Murphy: "I think we should forget, if we can, the McNary-Haugen bill which was drawn as emergency legislation. The emergency has passed for the time being on most of the products covered therein, and it seems to me that our job is now to prevent a recurrence which is sure to occur when the world again produces normal crops."[5]

Thus, Peek and Davis developed a new bill in December of 1924. They dropped the ratio-price feature, hoping to avoid the charge of price-fixing. Their revised measure would simply give farmers the world price, plus the tariff. Peek explained later that "we switched from a ratio price basis to world price plus the tariff for political reasons. . . . Chester and I will have to assume the responsibility for that."[6] Peek was never really satisfied with this change, as current farm prices plus the tariff often did not equal the ratio-price or parity price. According to him, nothing less than parity was fair. In any event, he did not see how Republican protectionists could logically oppose giving farmers the full benefit of the tariff. However, he underestimated the mental flexibility of those who could argue the economic soundness of tariff protection for industry, but who, with a straight face, denied the same thing to agriculture.

When President Coolidge sent his annual message to Congress on December 2, it was obvious that his farm views had not changed. Although he conceded the Peek theory that agriculture should be placed "on a sound and equal basis with other industries," he declared that "the government can not successfully insure prosperity or fix prices by legislative fiat." Increased prices and decreased costs, the President said, had nearly brought the farmer "to a parity with the rest of the nation." He assured Congress that his special

[5] Peek to Murphy, December 17, 1924. Davis Papers.
[6] Peek to R. E. Brown, November 22, 1932. Peek Papers.

agricultural conference would soon recommend specific and helpful legislation.

By this time Peek had decided to move to Washington. He arranged to close his Moline house and arrived with Mrs. Peek in the nation's capital on January 3, 1925. The Peeks rented an apartment at the Roosevelt Hotel at Sixteenth and V streets. From there the "Man from Moline" settled down to the task of directing the continuing fight for farm relief. He was determined to see the matter through.

However, Peek did not devote all of his time to farm relief. He kept up his lively interest in golf. Together with Mrs. Peek, he regularly attended plays and concerts, or enjoyed dinner with Washington friends. But these were only minor diversions. His main interest was the round of meetings, conferences, and strategy sessions which went on constantly at the Peek apartment. Sometimes only two or three of the McNary-Haugen crowd would be in Washington; on other occasions ten or a dozen, or more, might be there. They always conferred with Peek. Conferences with Davis, Murphy, Hirth, Hearst, and others would often last far into the night.

Georgia Peek was as interested as her husband in the farm fight, and never seemed to tire of the interruptions and infringements on their privacy. She was a great force in George's life, and he was unusually devoted to her. An utterly charming woman, she was described by one of her friends as an aristocrat to her fingertips, dainty, pert, trim-figured, with greying hair. She was gracious, hospitable, and never impatient as she did her part in making the farm leaders comfortable when they were around her apartment and home. Georgia Peek wrote some of the best propaganda literature of the campaign, which was circulated under the name "Peter Nelson." She literally gave her life to Peek and his "cause."

While Peek was waiting for the President's conference to report, he conferred on the farm problem with a number of leading businessmen and financiers. Vice-President Elect Charles G. Dawes, who had originally opposed the ratio-price plan, now helped Peek by writing letters of introduction to some of his friends. Dawes still did not openly favor the scheme, but he believed it should be fully considered. Dawes explained to Owen D. Young that Peek had been "largely responsible for keeping the agricultural question . . . out of the realm of demagoguery. I have a sincere admiration for his force and strength of character, and regard him as a friend of years standing." Peek and Mark Woods, of Lincoln, Nebraska, visited Young who, according to Peek, "expressed himself as being in full sympathy with our purpose." Then Young called Dwight D. Morrow of J. P. Morgan and Company, and they explained surplus-control legislation to him.[7] As mentioned before, Peek's business background gave him many contacts not open to ordinary farm leaders.

The President's Agricultural Conference made its first report on January 14, covering just the cattle situation. This was the only part of the farm industry in which the President believed an emergency existed. It emphasized the fact that cattle raisers were hard hit, but suggested only more liberal credit facilities, lower transportation rates, higher tariffs on hides and meats, and better management as the answer to cattlemen's problems. The McNary-Haugenites had been watching the conference's activities with a careful, if somewhat critical eye, and now decided they must take direct action.

On January 20, Peek and other officers of the American Council of Agriculture appeared before the conference to argue their case. Peek emphatically declared that his organization would not be satisfied with any bill that did not prevent the "tyranny of the surplus from determining the price of domestic requirements as well as the price of the surplus itself." Prematurely enthusiastic, Peek wrote, "Our crowd made a great impression. There is no doubt but that we have started something."[8]

The next evening, representatives of the council were invited to testify before the joint agriculture committees of the House and Senate. Peek, Murphy, Thompson, Hirth, and Hearst all appeared. Peek explained that their new bill should eliminate most of the objections to the 1924 version. The ratio-price feature had been dropped, he said, and farm prices would be raised by "relying upon the activities of an export corporation to go into the market and buy . . . until the price rises to the height of the existing tariff wall."[9]

[7] Charles G. Dawes to Owen D. Young, December 31, 1924; and Peek to Dawes, January 3, 1925. *Ibid.*

[8] Peek to Chester Davis, January 26, 1925. *Ibid.*

Peek pointed out that the new bill would establish a farmers export corporation and include wheat, corn, rice, cotton, beef, and pork. Cotton was put back in this second bill, and rice, another southern crop, was also added in hopes of winning southern backing, which so far had been conspicuously lacking. Sheep and wool were not included, because the tariff was already effective on them. The equalization fee, a most vital part of the proposal in the eyes of farmers and farm leaders, was still included. Again it was argued that farmers should pay for the losses on exports if they received a higher price for that part of their crop sold at home.

On February 3, Senator McNary introduced a bill, S. 4206, which incorporated the revised Peek and Davis principles. Representative Haugen did not get the companion measure, H.R. 12390, before the House until February 23. Both bills were reported favorably by the respective agriculture committees on February 26. This date was apparently too late for Congress to take any action at that session.

But as a last-ditch stand, Senator Robert B. Howell of Nebraska introduced the measure as an amendment to the naval omnibus bill on the last day of the session. The Senate rejected his amendment 69 to 17, a vote which was no real indication of the bill's support. Only a few tried and tested advocates of federal aid to agriculture such as McNary, Norris, Norbeck, Brookhart, Frazier, Shipstead, Ladd, and Howell voted for it. These were the men whom Senator Moses later was to dub the "sons of the wild Jackass."

Meanwhile, on January 28, the President's Agricultural Conference issued its main report. After declaring that "agriculture is the most important industry of America," the report stated that farmers should have the full benefit of the tariff. However, it added that the problems of agriculture were highly complex, and "do not lend themselves to any one remedy or any specific piece of legislation." But any program which stimulated production, the report said, could not be countenanced. "There must, therefore, be a balanced production by which production is kept in step with the demand of domestic markets and with only such foreign markets as may be profitable."

9 *McNary-Haugen Bill*, Joint Hearings before the Senate and House Agriculture Committees, 68 Cong., 2 sess., 1925, p. 3.

Having stated the philosophy of restricted production, the conference recommended government aid to co-operative marketing as agriculture's brightest hope. Additional farm credits, reduction in freight rates, and higher tariffs on certain dairy and animal products were also offered as helpful suggestions. The entire report reflected the strong influence of President Coolidge, who recommended that the report "be embraced in suitable legislation at the earliest possible date."[10]

The conference wanted legislation along the line of the Williams bill, which had received some consideration in the previous session. On January 28, Williams introduced a new bill authorizing the creation of a federal marketing board empowered to register co-operative marketing associations and terminal associations handling farm commodities, and to assist in correlating all marketing activity of co-operative groups. The board could also inspect and audit the books of the registered co-operatives. A $500,-000 appropriation was requested for the first year.

Actually, the bill proposed little more than putting a special department of the federal government at the disposal of farm marketing associations to advise them on more efficient and economical methods of distribution. Hoover admitted partial authorship, and the Democrats charged that it had been drawn in his office. Finis J. Garrett of Tennessee may have been right when he said it had been conceived in partisan politics, and was not designed to put farmers on a parity with other groups. It was framed, said Garrett, to meet "an embarrassing political situation" into which the President had projected his party during the campaign.[11]

The recommendations of the President's conference and the Williams bill fell with a dull thud on the ears of aggressive McNary-Haugenites. R. A. Cowles, secretary of the American Council of Agriculture, wrote to many farm organization officials on January 29, telling them to express their displeasure immediately. Administration forces, however, pushed ahead. Early in February the Capper-Haugen bill was substituted for the Williams measure, although the same principles were retained. But it was doomed to defeat from the beginning. The McNary-Haugen crowd descended

[10] 68 Cong., 2 sess., *Senate Doc. No. 190,* January 28, 1925.
[11] *Cong. Rec.,* 68 Cong., 2 sess., February 21, 1925 p. 4337.

on Washington and loudly denounced it as meaningless. To them it smacked of giving three cheers for the farmers and forgetting about them. Although they did not condemn co-operative marketing as such, they did everything possible to defeat the bill. Representatives of the large co-operative marketing associations were even more vocal in their criticism.

Grass-roots farmers who were looking for government price-lifting legislation had little or no faith in co-operative marketing. It is true that they had a mild interest in co-operative marketing as a means of furnishing possible help at some future time, but few farmers considered it an answer to their immediate problems of price. D. E. Stephens, director of the Oregon Agricultural Experiment Station at Moro and a good friend of Jardine's, wrote that the Saprio commodity co-operatives had "ended in dismal failure." He wanted "Dear Will," as a member of the President's conference to understand "that the Northwest farmers, nearly 100 per cent strong, are in favor of passing legislation embodying the essential features of the McNary-Haugen bill."[12]

Outside of active administration support, a few politicians, city editors, and a sprinkling of sidewalk farmers, very few recognized spokesmen for agriculture insisted on the measure's passage. Many supporters of the McNary-Haugen legislation in Congress favored the Capper-Haugen bill, but not because they thought it would do much good. They did not want to go home without passing something that could be called farm relief.

Peek kept a sharp eye on Congressional proceedings and religiously attended the hearings every day for over two weeks during February. Testifying on February 16, he made a strong plea for his revised surplus-control bill, although it was not under consideration. Peek said that co-operative marketing would not materially help the farmer and, especially, it would not meet the emergency. If Congress were to pass a co-operative marketing bill in the guise of agricultural relief, he asserted, it had better do nothing at all.

When asked if he opposed co-operative marketing legislation, Peek replied that he favored it if the co-operatives wanted such a bill. This was a clever way of opposing the measure without ap-

12 Stephens to Jardine, December 30, 1924. Files of the Secretary of Agriculture.

pearing in the role of an obstructionist. The co-operatives themselves were fighting the measure tooth and nail, and it was clear that the bill could be passed only over their violent protest. Peek was willing for the marketing groups to take the blame from the administration while he put in some solid licks for his export bill.

Representative Tincher of Kansas, a supporter of the first McNary-Haugen bill, was Peek's sharpest questioner. The presidential election had convinced Tincher that it was futile to buck the administration on the farm issue. He favored some kind of a compromise. He challenged the tactics and authority of Peek and the American Council of Agriculture, saying that, by electing Coolidge, the farmers had "clearly turned you down." "Don't you think," he asked, "that you strike the death knell to the Haugen bill [export corporation] in view of the President's position and your attitude?" "No," Peek replied.[13]

Peek charged that the recommendations of the agricultural conference were vague, and that nothing specific had been suggested to achieve even those uncertain objectives. For example, the report said that the farmer should receive the benefit of the protective tariff, but it was silent on how this might be done. Farmers wanted and needed a domestic price maintained by the protective tariff on that portion of the crop consumed at home, he argued, but Congress was going to give them co-operative marketing. To Peek this was like saying that a patient needed a particular medicine, and then prescribing something else.

Other supporters of the McNary-Haugen bill echoed Peek's sentiments. They discounted the beneficial effect of co-operative marketing and damned it by indirection. At the same time, they made it clear that they were supporting surplus-control legislation and following Peek rather than the President on agricultural matters. The constant injection of the McNary-Haugen bill into the hearings annoyed several congressmen. Once Tincher declared, "we are not going to debate the McNary-Haugen bill all through the hearing." Tincher, along with some Democrats, also accused the export coporation supporters of ignoring political realities. To push a bill which the President bitterly opposed was impractical, they said. Tincher asked if the McNary-Haugen

13 *Agricultural Relief,* Hearings before the House Agriculture Committee, 68 Cong., 2 sess., 1925, pp. 447–515.

William M. Jardine
secretary of agriculture, 1925–29

crowd expected the committee to "follow Mr. Peek and some of these men that are for the McNary-Haugen bill," or support a program which the President would approve. Peek, confronted by such questions, always replied that he would like to work with the administration but said, "I am for agriculture first."[14]

Representatives of the cotton, tobacco, milk, and other co-operatives attacked the Capper-Haugen bill more directly and vigorously. They opposed having the government control or restrict their operations by any licensing system. Walton Peteet, secretary of the National Council of Farmers' Co-operatives, came out strongly against the conference's recommendations even before they were made public. Peteet said that the co-operatives just wanted to be left alone. Charles W. Holman, Washington representative of the National Milk Producers Federation; Carl Williams, president of the Cotton Growers' Exchange; and officers of the Burley Tobacco Growers' Co-operative Association, all condemned the bill. Representative Kincheloe of Kentucky declared, "Of course, the farmers do not want this thing, but it has been determined to inject them with a little administration virus whether they want it or not."[15]

During the hearings, Congressman Dickinson of Iowa introduced his own co-operative marketing bill. It was entirely innocuous and simply provided for a board in the Department of Agriculture to advise and assist co-operatives. No registration or inspection of books was provided. On February 26, the House voted 203 to 175 to substitute the Dickinson for the Capper-Haugen bill.[16] This was a direct slap at the administration, as members of the President's conference had repeatedly said that the Dickinson substitute did not meet their recommendations. Jardine testified that he did not think the Department of Agriculture was suited to advise on problems of co-operative marketing. Nonetheless, the amended bill then passed the House 285 to 95. Everyone knew the measure was of little or no fundamental importance. Yet by voting for it, one could give the impression of favoring farm relief. The Senate, however, took no action and farm relief became a dead issue for that session.

14 *Ibid.*, 431 and 448.
15 New York *World*, February 26, 1925.
16 *Cong. Rec.*, 68 Cong., 2 sess., February 26, 1925, p. 4745.

Failure to achieve satisfactory agricultural legislation was not the greatest disappointment to Peek and his friends. They had not believed that Congress would pass their bill during the early part of 1925. However, they bitterly resented Coolidge's dogged opposition to their plans, particularly as it was reflected in the appointment of William M. Jardine as secretary of agriculture.

The President nominated Jardine on February 15, when the Senate and House committees were considering co-operative marketing legislation. He was confirmed by the Senate four days later. Born forty-six years before in Utah, Jardine had spent his first seventeen years on his father's ranch. He was graduated from Utah State College in 1904, and for a short time managed a large farm company which tilled thousands of acres in Utah. From 1907 to 1910, he served as assistant cerealist in the United States Department of Agriculture. But in the latter year he went to Kansas State College as professor of agronomy, and in 1918 became the institution's president.

Jardine was a capable and successful administrator. More important to Coolidge, however, was Jardine's strong opposition to McNary-Haugenism or any other government program to lift agricultural prices. Coolidge wanted a man who was not the least bit contaminated by Peekian principles, and one who would end the friction between the Department of Agriculture and the Department of Commerce.

Jardine had vigorously opposed the surplus-control bills in 1924, and had repeatedly expressed his confidence in co-operative marketing as the solution to farm problems. There had never been any question about his devotion to the Coolidge economic theories in regard to the government's relation to agriculture. "I firmly believe that in the long run co-operative marketing is a thing that is going to put agriculture on a permanent basis," he told members of the House Agriculture Committee a few days before he became secretary.[17] After studying the McNary-Haugen bill critically and openmindedly, he declared, "I think it would raise Ned with the farmer." In advocating co-operation, he said that he was preaching "the soundest doctrine I know."[18]

McNary-Haugen opponents praised the Jardine appointment.

[17] *Agricultural Relief*, Hearings before the House Agriculture Committee, 68 Cong., 2 sess., 1925, p. 238.

It was "a victory for sense" said the Chicago *Journal of Commerce*,[19] and the Washington *Star* considered his stand on Mc-Nary-Haugenism as his most noted qualification.[20] The *New York Times* heartily approved the selection. "The government may be able to help a little here and there," said the editor, "but the farmers must work out their own salvation."[21] This was exactly Jardine's position. There were two thousand miles between the New York editor on Manhattan Island and William Jardine in Manhattan, Kansas, but there was no difference in basic philosophy regarding how agricultural problems should be solved. One might conclude that Times Square farmers and those working in the Kansas wheat fields held about the same views.

Jardine's appointment was a direct affront to Peek and the farm groups supporting surplus-control legislation. It completed a solid administration phalanx against the demands of the so-called western radicals. Coolidge, Hoover, and now Jardine made up a powerful trinity of opposition. And whereas Wallace and Hoover had frequently clashed over the work and jurisdiction of their departments, the breach would now be healed. Chester Davis was right when he wrote, "It means we are outsiders at the Department of Agriculture probably for the next four years."[22]

Yet, Peek and his supporters had made more of an impression than their opponents would openly admit. The day after Peek appeared before the House Committee, Governor Carey wrote to W. C. Coffey: "As to the McNary-Haugen crowd, we will have to give their matter every consideration . . . I wish there was some way to come to an understanding." Carey denied that "their principle is right or that their proposed remedy is workable," but he concluded: "I know that every time there is a surplus of wheat in the country, the demand for an export corporation will be made. In fact, I believe that sooner or later some election will be won or lost on this basis."[23] Even Secretary Jardine expressed the hope that he would "have a suggestion or two . . . that might do some-

18 Jardine to B. L. French, April 15, 1925. Files of the Secretary of Agriculture.
19 Chicago *Journal of Commerce*, February 17, 1925.
20 Washington *Star*, February 15, 1925.
21 *New York Times*, February 17, 1925.
22 Davis to Peek, February, 1925. Peek Papers.
23 Carey to Coffey, February 17, 1925. Files of the Secretary of Agriculture.

thing to satisfy the supporters of the McNary-Haugen idea."[24]

If Coolidge was depending upon time and better agricultural prices to weaken the demands for government farm relief, he was badly mistaken. Memorials from six state legislatures—Oregon, Montana, South Dakota, Minnesota, Iowa, and Missouri—were passed early in 1925 and forwarded to members of Congress. Others followed later. And even a few southerners were beginning to weaken. When the revised export corporation bill was under consideration in January, Representative H. P. Fulmer turned to Peek and said: "I want to say . . . that our people fully realize that if we can do something to help you people in the west to increase your purchasing power, that will naturally help out people in the South, because it will create a demand for our cotton. Therefore we are willing to go to the last ditch unless there is something in the bill that will work against our people."[25] Here was a spark of hope, a spark that might ignite a flame uniting the West and South.

On March 3, the day Congress adjourned, Senator Frazier sounded a prophetic warning. The farmers, he said, were "anticipating some remedial legislation from the United States Congress. They are entitled to it. Whether it shall come under a Republican administration or under a Democratic administration, or what not, it is going to come. The farmers are going to keep fighting until they get a square deal."[26] And indeed they were.

[24] Jardine to Carey, April 27, 1925. *Ibid.*

[25] *McNary-Haugen Bill*, Joint Hearings before the Senate and House Agriculture Committees, 68 Cong., 2 sess., 1925, p. 41.

[26] *Cong. Rec.*, 68 Cong., 2 sess., March 3, 1925, p. 5309.

Chapter V I I I

"Shall We Industrialize America
at the Expense of Agriculture?"

AFTER REVIEWING the agricultural scene, the editor of the *New York Times* wrote on February 17, 1925, "The agricultural price fixers and government crop buyers and sellers are still heard occasionally in congress and have their doctrinaire bureaucrats in the Department of Commerce, but the demand for expensive and dangerous quackeries is now largely spent." This statement expressed hope, not fact, wishful thinking rather than reality. The real fight for agricultural relief was still ahead. No other issue in national politics was to plague the Coolidge administration as much during the next three years.

At this point some interesting questions should be raised. What prompted farmers and their spokesmen to continue demanding federal aid for agriculture? Why, after the emergency period of 1921 to 1923, did farmers still look to the government for help? Even Peek admitted privately that the "emergency" had passed. Why did farmers refuse to accept the preachings of Coolidge, Hoover, and Jardine that they could work out their own salvation, that "economic law" would solve their problems? Did the campaign for federal farm aid after 1925 run on the momentum already generated? Was it purely emotional or was there something deeper and more significant behind the struggle?

Before attempting to answer these questions, one should look at the social and economic condition of American agriculture in the middle 1920's. Without trying to analyze all of the economic aspects of the subject, even a casual look at agricultural statistics indicates that farmers were not descending to the level of European peasants, as some agricultural leaders insisted. So far as farm prices were concerned, the purchasing power of many products was higher than in the so-called golden era before 1914. After 1921 the prices of nonagricultural goods generally dropped, and the prices of most farm products gradually increased. Professor John D. Black figured that the ratio of farm prices to wholesale prices of nonagricultural goods rose from a low of 69 in 1921 to 89 in 1925. By 1928 it reached 91.[1]

Considering farm income as a whole, the Department of Agriculture estimated that the money income per farm family in 1925–26 was 81 per cent of what it had been in the inflationary period of 1919–20. By 1925, gross farm income reached $12,043,000,000.

Standards of living for considerably over half of the farmers were actually better than in the 1905–14 period, and agricultural labor was rapidly being lightened by the use of tractors, motor trucks, and electricity. By 1925 there were 505,000 tractors on American farms. In Iowa over 16 per cent of the farmers owned tractors, and by 1930 this percentage had increased to 29 per cent. Between 1920 and 1930 the number of farms reporting tractors increased from 3.6 to 13.5 per cent. This development increased efficiency and reduced much of the burden of farm work.

Motor trucks were also in much wider use. In the decade after 1920 the number of trucks on farms increased from 139,169 to 900,385. More farm work was being done by electric motors, and electric lights were becoming increasingly common. Moreover, by 1930, 34 per cent of the farmers had telephones, and 58 per cent of them owned automobiles.[2] When 90 per cent of Iowa's farmers drove to town in motor cars, as was the case in 1930, it did not seem as though they were rapidly heading toward serfdom—unless it was subserviency to auto dealers! More than one critic of farm relief legislation in the 1920's credited the farmer's trouble to his excessive use of the automobile.

Surface conditions then seemed to indicate that agriculture was "out of the woods." President Coolidge pointed to current agricultural income in the middle twenties, and repeatedly assured farmers that everything was, or soon would be, satisfactory.

[1] John D. Black, "Progress of Farm Relief," *American Economic Review*, Vol. XVIII (June, 1928), 255–58.

[2] Bureau of the Census, *Fifteenth Census of the United States*, 1930. Agriculture IV (Washington, 1932), 532.

"Industrialize . . . at the Expense of Agriculture?"

Looking at the question superficially, this appeared to be true. Current income statements appeared quite favorable, but the long-range balance sheet was something else. There were fundamental problems and underlying conditions which bred discontent and prompted farmers to demand government aid to increase their real income.

One of the problems was that while the per-capita real income of farmers was as good in 1925–26 as before World War I, much more of that income was going to pay mortgage interest and higher taxes. These expenditures left less money for living expenses. Consequently, farmers were pressed to maintain the higher standards of living which had become particularly noticeable about 1917, with wartime prosperity. Despite postwar financial distress, farmers attempted to continue a better living standard which was reflected in the purchase of automobiles, radios, water systems, electric appliances, furnaces, and telephones. But this was only part of the story. Greater commercialization and a higher degree of mechanization required additional expenditures and caused a hardship on farmers already pinched for cash. The only way farmers could maintain a decent living standard and meet the ordinary expenses of operation was to take it out of mortgage-interest payments, perhaps postpone their children's higher education, or go further into debt.

Farmers in the 1920's were not in revolt because they did not live as well as their fathers. The fact was that most of them lived much better. If farm families had been willing to live no better than before World War I, there probably would have been no cry for equality, parity, or government relief. The editor of the *Indiana Farmer's Guide* caught this point when he wrote on May 14, 1927:

> One reason the farmer of today feels himself less fortunately situated than his father was, or than he himself was fifteen or twenty years ago, is that he has acquired a new standard of living. The farmer of today is not willing to work the long hours his father worked, put up with the same privations, live the same frugal and comfort denying life. He demands for himself and his family any number of things which his father never dreamed of having. He requires more money both to run

his business and to provide for his living. He demands that his farming give him larger profits, bring him in more money than farming used to bring. . . . Farmers are unwilling to keep on working harder than other business men and getting less pay for it.

What farmers bitterly resented was the fact that they were not participating equally in the expanding prosperity enjoyed by other major groups in the economy between 1923 and 1929. One authority has figured that the purchasing power of urban factory workers in 1925–26 was actually 16 per cent *higher* than in the inflationary period of 1919–20. But farmers' purchasing power was 19 per cent *less*.[3] Farmers read about the increasing number of millionaires in trade, industry, utilities, and other nonagricultural fields, while they fought a losing battle to preserve their already inferior living standard. In other words, farmers argued that they did not get the reward to which they were entitled.

Farmers also suffered from declining land values. It might be expected that most of the foreclosures would have occurred during the worst of the depression in 1921 and 1922. This, however, was not the case. A study of farm foreclosures in thirty-one counties in southern Iowa showed that there were 587 farmers who lost their farms in 1922; 633 in 1923; 724 in 1924; and 746 in 1925. When it finally became clear that a farmer could not become financially solvent under current economic conditions, he was forced to turn his assets over to his creditors. The increasing number of foreclosures after 1922 was a delayed reaction to farm ills which were first felt in 1920.

But the underlying, fundamental force behind the McNary-Haugen movement was something even deeper than the matter of living standards, incomes, or farm foreclosures. Basically, it was a conflict between agrarian and industrial capitalism. In the 1920's farmers were making a last-ditch stand against industrial and commercial domination. A generation earlier William Jennings Bryan had fought a losing battle against the onrushing tide of industrialism personified by Mark Hanna and William McKinley. In attempting to win Senator Thomas J. Walsh's support

[3] John D. Black, "Agriculture Now?," *Journal of Farm Economics*, Vol. IX (April, 1927), 160–61.

to the McNary-Haugen bill, George Fort Milton declared that it was "the same fight we have had throughout our American political and economic history, a conflict between the industrial east and agricultural west."[4] Peek explained to Baruch that "the agricultural South and . . . West is the natural alliance to protect agriculture against the aggressions of an industrial East."[5]

The relatively prosperous prewar and war years had blunted the attack of the disgruntled agrarian hordes which had followed Bryan. At least this was true except in a few local areas such as North Dakota, where prosperity declined and the Nonpartisan League gained control. But farmers were reawakened to their condition of inequality by the depression of 1920–21, and they struck back with all the power at their command. The McNary-Haugen bill, like free silver in 1896, was more symbol than substance. Its supporters were not just after higher prices; they were seeking to place agriculture on an equality with industry and commerce in political, social, and economic affairs. McNary-Haugenites resented the subordination and position of inferiority to which they believed agriculture was being subjected.

Time and again the McNary-Haugen crowd said they would not permit the country to be industrialized at the expense of agriculture. They apparently did not recognize it, but their worst fears already had been realized; agriculture already had become subordinated to industry. Nevertheless, it was this attitude which was responsible for the farmers' desperate mood and vigorous action, even after economic conditions improved in the middle twenties.

In 1926, a substantial western farmer declared in Washington that the fight behind the McNary-Haugen bill was a "deadly struggle between financial and industrial America, determined to make the American farmer a peasant, and 35,000,000 farmers—freemen—who were determined to live as full a life as other Americans on just as high a level, and who would never be peasants, with hat in hand, bent of knee and bowed of back."[6] A. R. Sykes of Iowa testified before a Congressional committee: "I wish on

4 Milton to Walsh, July 30, 1926. Walsh Papers.
5 Peek to Baruch, September 27, 1924. Peek Papers.
6 Quoted in Theodore M. Knappen, "The Spreading Farm Vote—What Does It Portend?" *Magazine of Wall Street,* Vol. XXXVIII (June 19, 1926), 309.

behalf of my people to protest against industrializing this country. . . . I believe that primarily God intended this to be an agricultural country."[7]

The idea of complete industrial preponderance in the political and economic life of the nation was bitterly opposed by leaders of the McNary-Haugen movement. They were prompted by
a deep distrust of urbanites, and by their Jeffersonian faith in the
virtues and political trustworthiness of an independent land-
owning yeomanry. As early as 1922, Peek declared: "Some of the
countries of Europe made their choice, electing to become industrial rather than agricultural, thus relegating their agriculture to
a system of peasantry. The political results speak for themselves."[8]

It will be recalled that in his first brief on the agricultural
problem, Peek had emphasized the danger of industrial predominance to political democracy and self-government. He distrusted
the teeming masses of the cities. He repeated this theme in nearly
every speech before farm groups. "Shall agriculture longer continue to be a basic industry?" he asked a big crowd in Des Moines.
"Shall it attract your sons to a life of wholesome and fairly paid
endeavor? Shall it keep your towns and villages alive? Or shall agriculture exist merely to feed the mouth of industry?"

Other McNary-Haugen leaders echoed these views. In addressing the American Council of Agriculture at its organization meeting, Frank W. Murphy praised farmers for their political stability.
"If you would understand the soul of America," he asserted, "if
you would catch the fire of that great spiritual force that keeps
the flame of patriotism burning in this land of ours—if you would
know the source from which flows that great current of fine purposes, high resolves, courageous, clean, Christian citizenship, visit
the shrines of American farm homes, and there you will find it
all."

Holding to the same theme, the American Council of Agriculture's declaration of purpose stated that, throughout history,
the well-being of agriculture had been synonymous with the well-
being of civilization. Nations had risen and fallen, the declaration continued, not because of armies or lack of them, but "as

[7] *Agricultural Relief,* Hearings before the House Agriculture Committee,
68 Cong., 2 sess., 1925, p. 433.
[8] Peek to Frederick Wells, February 27, 1922. Peek Papers.

those who tilled the soil were happy and frugally prosperous, or as they became victims of economic wrong, neglect, and discontent."

William Hirth explained to Representative Clarence Cannon of Missouri that agriculture was "dying," and that "radicalism" and "socialism" were becoming dangerous in American cities. Unless people at the "crossroads" were happy and contented, he said, "then instead of our myriad farm homes continuing to be the great bulwark against this ever-increasing tide of radicalism," farmers would be striving to destroy our "venerable institutions."[9]

Were these the mouthings of harebrained blatherskites who had come under the influence of Populist or Nonpartisan League orators? Not at all. Had not that popular tribune of the people, Theodore Roosevelt, expressed the same view? In 1908 he had written: "No nation has ever achieved permanent greatness unless this greatness was based on the well-being of the great farmer class, the men who live on the soil; for it is upon their welfare, material and moral, that the welfare of the nation ultimately rests."

Such sentiments came from all over the farm belt. John P. Wallace declared, "we are at the parting of the ways. Either we will go on making agriculture a business, placing it on a parity with other industries having the same consideration at the hands of our lawmaking bodies, or we will have a peasant class of farm folks."[10] Time and again Peek repeated: "The question is, shall we industrialize America at the expense of agriculture, or shall we retain the American tradition of the independent, landowning farmer? It is the most profound question the nation has faced since the Civil War."[11]

It took more than distressed agricultural conditions to keep the farm fight alive. So far as the leaders of the movement were concerned, they were influenced by a deep philosophical motive. They had a sense of urgency which made them think they were saving the country by saving agriculture.

In the eyes of militant farm leaders, Herbert Hoover came to

9 Hirth to Cannon, March 27, 1924. Davis Papers.

10 *Agricultural Relief*, Hearings before the House Agriculture Committee, 69 Cong., 1 sess., 1926, p. 32.

11 George N. Peek, "Why the Farmers Need An Export Corporation," *Prairie Farmer*, Vol. XCVII (August 15, 1925).

personify what they considered to be the unfair and destructive policies of fostering industry at the expense of agriculture. Under the Hoover influence, they charged, the federal government was being used as an engine of aggrandizement for the industrial, financial, and commercial interests.

Hoover had first become unpopular among farmers as food administrator during World War I. On August 30, 1917, President Wilson had set the minimum price of No. 1 wheat in Chicago at $2.20 a bushel. This price had been recommended by a committee headed by Dr. H. A. Garfield. Four days earlier, Congressman George M. Young of North Dakota said that if Hoover should have his way the price would be set at only $1.65. Although President Wilson stated that "Mr. Hoover, at his express wish, has taken no part in the deliberations of the committee," Hoover was soon coming under attack from farm groups. Through his power as food administrator, he was able to make the minimum price the maximum price. At one time Hoover admitted that without controls wheat might have gone to $5.00 or more a bushel. When President Wilson established the $2.20 figure, wheat was selling above $2.75 in Kansas City. Thus farmers and their spokesmen came bitterly to resent the government's program, especially when nonfarm prices were not controlled. And they laid most of the blame on Hoover.

The feeling in farm circles did not improve when the price for 1918 wheat was set at only $2.00 a bushel. More and more the charge was repeated that Hoover had cheated wheat farmers out of millions of dollars. Although some of the accusations rested on rather flimsy evidence, it is true that Hoover did not want extraordinarily high food prices. He had a responsibility to all citizens, most of whom were primarily consumers. Nonetheless, the idea that Hoover was an enemy of a prosperous agriculture persisted.

The wheat situation was only part of the story. In November, 1917, J. P. Cotton of the Food Administration, announced that, as far as possible, the Food Administration would try to maintain a ratio-price of thirteen-to-one for hogs farrowed in the spring of 1918. To farmers this meant that the price of hogs per hundred pounds would equal the value of thirteen bushels of corn. The purpose, of course, was to encourage hog production to meet the pressing war needs for pork and fats. Various circumstances in the fall of 1918, however, caused the Food Administration to abandon all pretense of maintaining the thirteen-to-one ratio.[12] Consequently, bitter indignation at Hoover developed in the corn belt. Chief among his critics were Henry C. and Henry A. Wallace. Hoover did his best, with the help of numerous friends, to justify his actions and policies, but no excuses or explanations could clear him in the minds of most American farmers.

The unpleasant memories which farmers had of Hoover's wartime activity were still fresh in mind when an administrative quarrel between him and Secretary Wallace was made public. On October 20, 1921, Hoover had written to Walter F. Brown, head of President Harding's government reorganization committee, that "the functions of the Department of Agriculture should end when production on the farm is complete and movement therefrom starts, and at that point the activities of the Department of Commerce should begin." Then he continued, "Broadly speaking, the functions of the Department of Agriculture relating to soil production should end when the grain, fruit, or animal moves from the farm and the tree moves from the forest, and the Department of Commerce should take up its activities when manufacturing, transportation, and distribution begins." Hoover specifically mentioned the work of the Bureau of Markets. He said that it had been expanding under enlarged appropriations and increased powers until there had developed a "clear duplication of functions as between the Department of Commerce and the Department of Agriculture." This duplication, he said, should be "obviated by imposing the performance of duties mentioned upon one department to the exclusion of the other." Then he added, "The Department of Agriculture should tell the farmer what he can best produce, based on soil, climatic and cultural conditions, and the Department of Commerce should tell him how best to dispose of it."[13]

Wallace said he knew nothing of the Hoover letter before December, 1922, but on January 16, 1923, he sent a long letter to Brown, sharply attacking the Hoover position. It was indefensible,

[12] Walter T. Borg, "Food Administration Experience With Hogs, 1917–19," *Journal of Farm Economics*, Vol. XXV (May, 1943), 444–57.

[13] Hoover to Brown, October 20, 1921. Files of the Secretary of Agriculture.

he declared, for the Agriculture Department's work to stop with production as Hoover suggested. He admitted that some duplication existed, but said it had grown "out of the persistent encroachment by the Department of Commerce upon the fields properly belonging to the Department of Agriculture."[14]

When the fight became public, farmers and farm leaders rallied to Wallace's support. They showered Hoover with blistering attacks, which continued even after Wallace's death. Peek and other officers of the American Council of Agriculture needled Hoover and distributed anti-Hoover propaganda far and wide. Hoover wrote to Howard M. Gore, Wallace's successor, that the American Council of Agriculture proposed "to have a go at the Department of Commerce for activities in which it has never been engaged. . . . I mention this as one of the movements being broadcast in the country which emphasizes the necessity for early action."[15]

Despite Hoover's many denials, there can be no reasonable doubt about his original intentions. The language of his first letter to Brown is too clear to permit misunderstanding. It was only after strong pressure from Wallace and the farm organizations that he retreated and pretended that his ideas had been misconstrued. In any event, this seemed like another Hoover "trick," an unfriendly gesture toward agriculture. And what angered farmers more than anything else was that both Harding and Coolidge seemed to rely more on Hoover than on their secretaries of agriculture for farm advice.

Peek and the McNary-Haugenites heartily disliked Hoover, not only for his past record, but because of his active opposition to surplus-control legislation. After 1921, Hoover was the subject of bellicose attacks at nearly every farm conference or meeting of agrarian leaders. When Congressional hearings were held on various agricultural bills, it was unusual if some of the witnesses did not denounce Hoover and picture him as the foremost enemy of agriculture.

The aspect of Hoover's policies to which agricultural spokesmen took the greatest exception was his suggestion that farmers solve their problems by cutting production. When he had been

[14] Wallace to Brown, January 16, 1923. *Ibid.*
[15] Hoover to Howard M. Gore, November 26, 1924. *Ibid.*

asked to state his views to the President's Agricultural Conference in 1925, he declared, "Generally, the fundamental need is balancing of agricultural production to our home demand." In its report the conference restated this principle in almost identical language, recommending that "a balanced American agriculture be established by which production is kept in step with the demand of domestic markets and with only such foreign markets as may be profitable."[16] To farm leaders this seemed like direct evidence of Hoover's unfortunate influence on agricultural policy, a policy to which they were violently opposed.

Peek, Hearst, Murphy, Hirth, and other agricultural leaders charged that this was a conscious attempt to submerge agriculture under industrial domination. Protesting heatedly before the House Agriculture Committee, Peek declared: "I can only conclude that it [restriction] means that agriculture must stop exporting, that cotton, tobacco, wheat, corn, rice, and livestock production must be restricted to domestic requirements, while industry, . . . is permitted to continue in the exporting business, selling its surpluses in the world market at world prices independent of the portion used in America."[17] Such a policy, he argued, would not benefit the American farmers. To restrict production to American demands, he said, would starve out many producers and ultimately result in an expansion of industry and the contraction of agriculture. Peek charged that if the government did its duty, it would develop a plan to expand farm exports rather than preach restricted output.

Mark Sullivan caught the spirit of this basic conflict between the agrarians and industrialists. Where would the farmers end, he wrote, if they produced only enough for domestic requirements, while industry was urged to flood the world markets with manufactured goods. "Definite subordination of farming to other industries must be the ultimate outcome of these two policies running parallel," he concluded, "the policy of non-export for the farmer and aggressive export for the manufacturer."[18]

Emphasizing this same point, one of the farm groups told its

16 68 Cong., 2 sess., *Sen. Doc. No. 190*, (January 28, 1925).

17 *Agricultural Relief*, Hearings before the House Agriculture Committee, 68 Cong., 2 sess., 1925, p. 455.

18 Mark Sullivan, "The Waning Influence of the Farmer," *World's Work*, Vol. LI (April, 1926), 657–61.

backers: "If the Mellon-Hoover policy of expanding industrial exports, no matter at what cost to other groups means anything at all, it means the definite submergency of agriculture. These men and their policies say in substance that American farmers must provide the food and raw materials for American industry and labor at prices no higher than foreign manufacturers and labor pay. Why? In order that American industry may export manufactured goods in competition with Europe."[19] Summing up recent Republican farm policy in 1928, Peek said, "The whole effect of the policies of the last two administrations has been to hasten the industrialization of America at the expense of agriculture."

This basic concern of protecting agriculture and the country from industrial domination was what gave militancy to the farm relief campaign in the 1920's. Without such a philosophical basis, the drive would have been impotent and without real foundation. Not to recognize this is to miss the true significance of the Mc-Nary-Haugen movement.

Hoover became the whipping boy in the Coolidge administration for the discontented agrarians. In much of the farm mind he personified industry and big business, which was crushing the life out of a struggling agriculture. The louder one denounced Hoover and his agricultural views, the more certain it seemed that one was a true friend of the American farmer. The "arch-enemy" of agriculture, farm relief advocates were calling him by 1927.

Of course, Hoover was only one of many who favored some kind of production control in the 1920's. In fact, the idea had much wider acceptance during that period than has been generally recognized. Only occasionally was it suggested that farm acreage might be reduced by law, but the idea of voluntary restriction by individuals and groups of farmers was frequently stated.

The overproduction thesis went back as far as seventeenth-century colonial America. In Virginia and Maryland attempts had been made to restrict tobacco production during periods of low prices. Although the idea that prices could be increased by cutting production appeared from time to time afterwards, it received little serious attention until the twentieth century. So long as

[19] North Central States Agricultural Conference *Bulletin No. 17,* October 6, 1927. Davis Papers.

foreign demand continued strong for American farm products, as was true in the nineteenth century, capacity production seemed like the most sensible policy.

But when foreign markets for several leading commodities began to decline after 1900, there were frequent demands to cut production. This was especially true in the cotton belt. Between 1905 and 1908, in 1914, and again in the winter of 1921–22, campaigns had been launched to induce farmers to decrease their cotton acreage on a voluntary basis by as much as 25 per cent. However, all of these campaigns failed or had only meager results.

In the early 1920's, Henry A. Wallace, who succeeded his father as editor of *Wallace's Farmer,* and Harry N. Owen, editor of *Farm, Stock and Home* at St. Paul, were among the leading advocates of controlled output. During the winter of 1921–22, Wallace carried on a vigorous campaign through the columns of his paper, urging farmers to cut their corn acreage. "There is such a thing as over-production," he warned, "and if the farmers of the corn belt don't believe it, they can soon convince themselves . . . if they continue to produce 3,000,000,000-bushel corn crops year after year."[20] Wallace soon discovered, however, what southerners had already learned: it was easier to talk about acreage reduction than to achieve it. He believed that his agitation had helped cause Iowa farmers to reduce their corn acreage by 287,000 acres in 1922, but he lamented that acreage restriction campaigns were "a rather thankless task."

Speaking before the Farm Economics Association in December, 1922, Wallace explained his ideas in more detail. He argued that there was nothing sacred about food production and that farmers should cut their output in times of low prices. Yet, he said, farmers could not safely adopt this as a national policy unless the federal government was "willing to step in and safeguard their production by national crop insurance and price stabilization schemes with the object of relieving the farming business of its peculiar hazards." The big question was not the farmers' right to control production, but the practicability of such a policy, he said. Wallace recommended that continued educational campaigns should be carried on looking toward controlling farm output. He concluded by saying that unless the federal government

20 *Wallace's Farmer,* Vol. XLVII (February 25, 1922), 253.

could aid agriculture in expanding export markets, it should help fit production to domestic requirements, particularly in the case of corn, hogs, and wheat.[21]

On this issue, Henry A. Wallace's thinking was ten years ahead of that of most of his contemporaries. But he was not alone. L. L. Sharp of the Washington Farm Bureau, for example, wrote that farmers must see that supply is no greater than demand. "There is nothing un-American in this doctrine," he declared, "as it is the rule in practically every other line of business."[22]

The move to restrict acreage even had the limited support of Henry C. Wallace. He told Henry A. that "we should cut down production to our own needs, or a little more."[23] A year later, in 1923, the Secretary wrote in his official report that, in light of market prospects, "the production of wheat should be gradually placed on a domestic basis." W. J. Spillman of Wallace's Department recommended the same thing. "We have got to become independent to Europe as a market for wheat if our wheat growers are ever to get a fair price," he said in 1924.[24]

Harry N. Owen was one of the most vigorous proponents of production control. Early in 1922, when Wallace was discussing the corn problem, Owen was advising farmers to plant fewer acres, grow more per acre, and decrease total production. To concentrate on marketing and distribution, he said, was all wrong. Owen declared that limiting production, along the lines followed by business, was the best solution to farm problems. He even reprinted Roger Babson's bold statement that "too many farmers are in the business and . . . about ten per cent should be carpenters, plasterers, and common laborers." While favoring the principle of production control, Owen, like most others, was extremely vague as to how it might be accomplished. He did suggest that there should be a provision in any export corporation bill which would not permit the corporation to maintain farm prices if acreage was more than enough, on a twenty- to thirty-year average, to furnish sufficient crops for domestic consumption. He thought

[21] Henry A. Wallace, "Controlling Agricultural Output," *Journal of Farm Economics,* Vol. V (January, 1923), 16–27.

[22] Sharp to H. C. Wallace, April 9, 1921. Files of the Secretary of Agriculture.

[23] Henry C. Wallace to Henry A. Wallace, September 18, 1922. *Ibid.*

[24] Quoted in the *Farm Journal,* Vol. XLVIII (May, 1924), 92.

such an amendment would deter expanded output which would probably come with higher prices.[25]

There was a good deal of miscellaneous support for production control. The editor of the Texas edition of the *Progressive Farmer* reported, early in 1924, that any plan to raise farm prices would fail in the long run unless the government also controlled production. An editorial in the Wichita *Eagle* stated that eventually farmers would have to get so well organized that they could limit acreage if there was overproduction and low prices. "It is unfortunate that restriction of acreage should have to be resorted to while there are in the world people who are starving for bread, but it is so."[26] And this was a decade before the New Deal!

The *Wall Street Journal,* Washington *Post,* and other metropolitan papers supported the idea of reduced production as a means of helping agriculture. The editor of the *Post* wrote on May 14, 1924, "The remedy is plain: Let American wheat growers quit trying to compete with cheap foreign wheat and cut their production down to home needs." Businessmen and elements in the financial community also gave lip service to the principle. Yet, when acreage restriction was seriously proposed by Henry A. Wallace in 1922, he met much opposition from the grain trade and financial interests. The editor of the *Country Gentleman,* who opposed any effective federal aid to agriculture, also sharply criticized Wallace. He even complained about the high price of corn!

Here was additional support for the charge that business interests were not really concerned with the welfare of the farmer. When a government price-lifting scheme like the McNary-Haugen bill was proposed, they fought it bitterly and told the farmer to solve his own problems by adjusting supply to demand. But when someone seriously suggested such a course, they pounced on it as dangerous and economically unsound. The farm relief leaders were absolutely right in one contention: business and industry did not want higher prices for food and raw materials, regardless of what might happen to the farmer.

[25] Owen to H. C. Wallace, May 2, 1924. Files of the Secretary of Agriculture; and *Farm, Stock and Home,* Vol. XXXVIII (January 1 and 18, and February 1, 1922).

[26] Quoted in *The Southwest Wheat Grower,* Vol. I (March 14, 1923), 4.

Jardine, like Hoover, was a strong advocate of voluntary acreage adjustment and argued that eventually farmers could be educated to it. "This is all educational," he explained. Jardine said that it would be better to import some wheat occasionally rather than produce a constant surplus which would depress prices. But he was careful to add: "We can not have a law to cover that. We must keep on educating them." The Secretary proposed that co-operative marketing associations "advocate sensible production programs."[27] Indeed, one of the leading arguments advanced for strong co-operative marketing associations was that they could advise their members on production and thereby regulate output to a profitable level.

Jardine was not stupid—far from it. But he was stubborn and naïve. Even a casual look at recent agricultural history with which he was presumably familiar, would have told him that voluntary attempts at planned production had been dismal failures. Several important factors were responsible for this. In the first place, there was a conflict of interest between the individual farmer and the entire group of producers. For example, if cotton farmers as a whole would benefit from a smaller crop, which they usually did, it would be to each individual's advantage to increase his acreage, or to promote his production in some other manner. If a farmer thought his neighbors were going to cut acreage, he might benefit by increasing his in order to take advantage of possible price increases.

The pressure of public opinion on farmers was not greatly felt. They were isolated and did not mind ignoring restriction campaigns and being known as a "scab." Furthermore, many farms were occupied by tenants and sharecroppers who had little control over farm management. Absentee owners directed planting policies. And bankers who held mortgages and controlled credit sometimes insisted that a particular cash crop be planted. Sometimes low prices actually stimulated production. Farmers who needed a certain cash income to meet expenses and keep operating were virtually forced to plant more acres and grow more units in order to meet their money requirements. Thus it is clear that voluntary acreage restriction was not practical.

27 *Federal Co-operative Marketing Board,* Hearings before the Senate Agriculture Committee, 68 Cong., 2 sess., 1925, p. 25ff.

Moreover, it had become evident that co-operatives could not get control of a sufficient amount of the basic commodities like cotton, tobacco, and wheat to have any noticeable influence on price. In fact, nonmembers often got a higher price than members, causing the latter to become disgruntled and drop out of the organization. Many of the wheat, tobacco, and cotton co-operatives which had been organized amidst so much enthusiasm after 1920 had failed miserably within five years. In 1925, a manager of fifteen cotton farms in southwestern Oklahoma told Jardine that "there is nothing in co-operative marketing." He then related the sad experience of the Oklahoma Cotton Growers Association. Farmers were fighting among themselves, he said, and forty lawsuits were then pending in Tillman County alone to force those who had signed contracts to deliver their cotton through the co-operatives.

Jardine and Hoover knew all of these things as well or better than anyone. But they were trapped between their own philosophy of government and its functions, and how farmers really acted. Along with Coolidge and others, they proposed something which farmers would not generally accept; yet they refused to take the next logical step and advocate some type of forced co-operation which might permit a degree of planned production and marketing. They particularly opposed the equalization-fee provision of the McNary-Haugen bill, which was one method of making all farmers participate in a program. In light of later restriction programs adopted by the New Deal, it is interesting to record that most of those who advocated voluntary acreage reduction in the 1920's were Republicans.

Occasionally during that period, someone would suggest forced acreage reduction administered by the federal government. Congressman George M. Young of North Dakota expressed this view early in 1922. He discounted the probability that crop limitation could be achieved by voluntary co-operation. Higher prices and cost of production could be obtained "in times of peace as well as in times of war if the government will resolutely take hold of the problem and control the production."[28] About a year later he wrote a constituent, "the time has come when farmers throughout the entire country should limit production to a point within the

28 *Cong. Rec.*, 67 Cong., 2 sess., January 12, 1922, pp. 1142–44.

requirements of our own country. . . . We should adopt as a permanent policy that we will not export wheat at any time at below the cost of production, plus a reasonable profit. This can be done by crop limitation."[29]

F. A. Farmer of Kansas made even more specific suggestions. He said that the federal government should control agricultural production and hold surpluses for a "rainy day." Here was the concept of Henry A. Wallace's ever-normal granary instituted about a dozen years later. Then he would have had the local tax assessor obtain information on how much each man intended to plant. This data would be sent to the secretary of agriculture, who would determine how much of a particular commodity was needed, and apportion back to farmers through county organizations their prorata share. On the amount produced, he said, the government should maintain the full prewar ratio price, or parity.[30]

President Coolidge probably never saw this letter addressed to him, but if he read it, astonishment and disbelief must have fastened itself upon his pinched, uncomfortable looking face. Certainly no sane man could seriously propose such bureaucratic control over American agriculture. What preposterous economic foolishness. He had never heard of such heresies in safe and sane New England. This must be the idea of some crackpot who had stood bareheaded too long under a scorching Kansas sun. Thus, Coolidge may have reasoned!

But, as previously mentioned, most farmers and their leaders refused to accept the philosophy of restricted acreage and reduced production. This was partly due to the long history of freedom, independence, and individualism experienced by the American farmer. Furthermore, it was argued that there were too many other factors in production besides acreage. Weather, pests, output per acre, and other things were all important. Therefore, farmers claimed that acreage limitation was not a safe and accurate regulator of production.

In the hearings before the Senate Agriculture Committee in January, 1925, Senator Norris sparred sharply with Jardine on this point. And Congressman Tincher told Governor Carey that any

[29] Quoted in *The Southwest Wheat Grower,* Vol. I (February 14, 1923), 7.
[30] F. A. Farmer to Coolidge, May 19, 1924. Files of the Secretary of Agriculture.

legislation which looked toward restricting production would be rejected by the House of Representatives. He predicted that not 30 per cent of the membership would favor such a policy. Nonetheless, the Coolidge administration continued to push the idea of restricted production through voluntary acreage control, arousing bitter antagonisms among most farmers and their spokesmen.

Why was it that farm leaders became almost hysterical in their objections to acreage restriction when it was proposed by Coolidge or Hoover, but said nothing when one of the Wallaces advocated the same thing? Peek, for example, never criticized H. C. Wallace for urging a 15 per cent reduction in wheat acreage in 1923. To the farm leaders it was a difference in motive and ultimate result. They considered a temporary reduction of acreage entirely different from controlled production as a part of permanent national policy. Henry A. Wallace had emphasized that if acreage was to be restricted, the federal government must provide protection for farmers by crop insurance or some price stabilization plan. Leaders of the McNary-Haugen movement claimed that temporary acreage reduction might be helpful, but in the long run it was just another step in making agriculture subservient to an expanding industry.

Thus, the idea of economic scarcity for agriculture did not appeal to American farmers in the 1920's, and for that matter they never have happily accepted it. They wanted to produce capacity crops and get government aid to sell them at profitable prices. As yet farmers were chiefly concerned with marketing. They and their leaders were groping toward some method whereby, with government help, they could control the price of their products. But it is obvious that they were not ready to accept restricted production, which was an important element in permitting business to regulate prices. They criticized Coolidge, but in part, at least, farmers joined the President in support of laissez faire.

Unwilling to accept production control, farmers continued to fight for surplus-control legislation. The President might be adamant, but members of the Senate and House could be forced to act if public pressure became strong enough. Peek and his little band of followers must set the prairies on fire. They would save America from the awful political and economic consequences of a declining agriculture.

Chapter IX

Strengthening the Farm Lobby

To the casual observer it may have appeared that McNary-Haugenism was a dead issue in the spring of 1925. The most that its supporters had been able to accomplish was to defeat palliative administration substitutes. Yet there was no sign of discouragement in the surplus-control camp. George Peek was stubborn. He had faith in the eventual triumph of right. And he believed that he was right.

On March 4, Peek and a number of other farm leaders met in the office of Congressman L. J. Dickinson to devise future strategy. The emphasis which the Coolidge administration was placing on co-operative marketing was beginning to have its influence on the McNary-Haugen group. At the March 4 conference, it was decided to draw up a new bill, providing for a federal farm board which would carry on surplus-control operations through the commodity co-operatives. As in previous measures, an equalization fee was to be levied to distribute the costs of handling surpluses proportionately among producers. The move to utilize the co-operatives in handling surpluses was designed to help reduce administration opposition, as well as to win the support of additional commodity co-operatives. A new Dickinson bill was formulated incorporating these principles. A month later, on April 4, the American Council of Agriculture called a meeting in Chicago, where the farm leaders endorsed it.

On May 12 the farm relief campaign got a strong boost when the Grain Belt Federation of Farm Organizations was formed in Des Moines. The Farmers Union sponsored the first meeting, which was attended by representatives of such organizations as the Iowa Farmers Union, Grange, and Farm Bureau, the Missouri Farmers Association, the National Corn Growers Association, and the American Council of Agriculture. There were twenty-three charter-member organizations affiliated with the new movement, but the principal promoters were Milo Reno, militant president of the Iowa Farmers Union, and Hirth of Missouri. According to its constitution, the object of the new organization was to secure "equal rights and privileges" for American agriculture.

The delegates passed a resolution asking Congress to establish an export corporation to handle farm surpluses. They added, however, that the national government would be expected to maintain it only until the farm organizations, through their co-operative agencies, could assume the burden of surplus control. Here was another bid to the commodity co-operatives to enter the fight, principally the cotton and tobacco groups, which had been cool to all appeals by corn belt missionaries. It was hoped that the suggestion of helping co-operatives to become strong enough to deal effectively with surpluses would strike a responsive chord among the commodity groups. Southern backing was also solicited by directly inviting cotton growers to join grain-belt farmers "to the end that henceforward we may fight our common battle standing shoulder to shoulder."[1]

Farmers Union influence at the Des Moines gathering was clearly evident in the demand for cost of production "based on the American standard of living." This had been an aim of a large group within the union for several years. In 1922, Peek had recognized cost of production as reasonable and fair, but he never insisted upon it during his fight for farm relief. The constitution of the Grain Belt Federation, however, provided for a permanent cost-of-production committee which was directed to work for this principle. The new organization was popularly known as the Corn Belt Committee.

Farmers now had another organization, like the American Council of Agriculture, which cut across party and farm-organization lines. The Corn Belt Committee, headed by Hirth, was directed to carry the fight to Washington. Congressmen and sena-

[1] "Constitution of the Grain Belt Federation." Davis Papers; Resolutions of the Corn Belt Federation, adopted at Des Moines, May 12, 1925. Peek Papers.

tors, as well as the administration, could look forward to increasing pressure from the grass roots.

Since Congress was not in session, Peek found little reason to remain in Washington. So he returned to Illinois and divided his time between his home in Moline and the office of the American Council of Agriculture in Chicago.

On June 5, he and the council's other executive officers met with representatives of the commodity co-operatives to consider legislation which would meet with the approval of those groups. Frank Lowden, having been greatly influenced by Peek and W. H. Settle of the Indiana Farm Bureau, had paved the way for these meetings among the co-operative leaders. Other co-operative officials present were R. W. Bingham, of Louisville, and Carl Williams, of Oklahoma City. Dan Wallace, Chester Davis, and Hirth were also there. A second meeting was held on July 10. These conferences were highly important preliminary moves in getting the cotton and tobacco co-operatives into the fight for the McNary-Haugen bill.

Leadership of the legislative battle was strengthened in April when Chester Davis left Montana and became grain marketing director for the Illinois Agricultural Association, with offices in Chicago. Now on the premises, he devoted much more time working with Peek and other leaders. Since the Illinois Agricultural Association was one of the most vigorous proponents of the McNary-Haugen bill, its officers did not begrudge whatever time Davis spent helping to lay the groundwork for the fight in the next session.

While Peek was at Fairacres in Moline during the summer, he was joined by E. C. Alvord and Glenn McHugh, and, together, they worked on problems relating to a revised bill. Alvord was assistant legislative counsel for the House of Representatives, and later became an eminently successful lawyer. He had worked on previous legislation, and Peek depended heavily upon him. McHugh, assistant legislative counsel for the Senate, helped to draft new bills, later married Peek's niece, and finally became a vice-president of the Equitable Life Assurance Society of New York. Every morning for several weeks, Peek and his younger associates worked over every angle and detail of surplus-control legislation. In the afternoons they played golf at the Rock Island Arsenal Golf Club.

Following an early evening dinner, Peek would have them all busy again until midnight, or past, going over charts, analyzing data, and preparing arguments.

Meanwhile, Peek kept appealing to Lowden. The importance of winning Lowden's public approval of the McNary-Haugen bill at this juncture can hardly be overestimated. A highly respected leader in the co-operative movement, his open endorsement would undoubtedly bring important additional support. Moreover, since he was wealthy and had many business friends, his backing would greatly help to give the plan added economic and political respectability. He might even contribute to the depleted treasury of the farm lobby.

Lowden, however, was cautious. He did not commit himself publicly until late in 1925. After holding conferences with him in May, Peek reported, "It now looks as though we might expect the co-operation of his organization of co-operatives in the cotton and tobacco districts from which we have not had a great deal of support in the past."[2] It was not until January, 1926, however, that Lowden came out strongly for the Peek farm relief principles. In addressing the annual meeting of the National Council of Co-operative Marketing Associations in Washington, he made it plain that some method must be devised to handle farm surpluses.

Peek did not confine his activities within the four walls of an office. During the summer and early fall of 1925, he traveled over the Midwest speaking before numerous farm groups. On Farm Bureau Day at the Minnesota State Fair in September, he spared neither the opponents of the McNary-Haugen bill nor those persons who proposed substitute measures. He blistered Hoover and his influence on American agricultural policy, and pleaded for a solid front among farmers at the next session of Congress. Peek's incessant attacks on Hoover apparently pricked him in a tender spot. Copies of Peek's Minneapolis address were distributed by the thousands, one of which found its way to Hoover's desk. After looking over it, he mailed it to Jardine with the comment: "In case you have not seen it, I send you herewith one of Mr. Peek's recent effusions."[3]

2 Peek to Owen D. Young, May 24, 1925. *Ibid.*
3 Hoover to Jardine, September 22, 1925. Files of the Secretary of Agriculture.

Despite the efforts of Peek and his followers, there was nothing to indicate that the administration's opposition to the McNary-Haugen bill had at all weakened. Coolidge and his appointees were still singing the song of co-operative marketing. And increased farm prices in the summer of 1925 seemed to confirm the President's contention that the situation would cure itself. After studying conditions, Chester Davis wrote to Peek, "Current index figures on the major farm crops—cotton, corn, wheat, beef cattle, and hogs—are very favorable to the farmer." Consequently, he warned, that as farm leaders they must "guard against becoming committed to a line of familiar dogmatic argument." Unless they checked their statements against current conditions and existing facts, he said, they could not expect to command respect among those who "look to us for agricultural leadership."[4]

On December 7, President Coolidge was in Chicago to address the annual meeting of the American Farm Bureau Federation. His coming had been enthusiastically publicized, and the grand ballroom of the Sherman Hotel was jammed with delegates and visitors. The crowd waited tensely as the President began to speak. "I propose actively and energetically to assist the farmers to promote their welfare through co-operative marketing," he said. Following other remarks on this problem, he warned farmers against overproduction, and expressed the hope that consumption would eventually catch up with production.

"His words fell on the audience like a wet blanket," wrote O. M. Kile, historian of the Farm Bureau. "As the presidential party left the room the applause was notably slight and the atmosphere chilly and barely respectful." The majority of representatives were disgusted. Two days later they defied the President by adopting a resolution demanding "the creation of an agency with broad powers for the purpose of so handling the surplus of farm crops that the American producer may receive an American price in the domestic market."[5]

Coolidge had closed his speech by saying, "the future of agriculture looks to be exceedingly secure." Commenting on this, humorist Will Rogers quipped that agriculture was indeed se-

---

[4] Davis to Peek, August 1, 1925. Davis Papers.

[5] O. M. Kile, *The Farm Bureau Through Three Decades* (Baltimore, 1948), 134–36.

cured—most of it by at least two mortgages! Rogers defined co-operative marketing as a scheme "whereby, if your stuff is not bringing as much as it costs you to raise it, why you all go in together and take it to town. Then when you sell it you can be together to cheer each other up." Coolidge "diagnosed the case but left no medicine," Will concluded![6] At least it was not the cure demanded by militant midwesterners.

Coolidge's indirect slap at those who favored surplus-control legislation helped to produce sharp reverberations within the Farm Bureau. For several months leaders such as Hearst and Thompson had indicated that they wanted a president who would carry on an aggressive fight for the McNary-Haugen bill. President Bradfute was continuing to support the co-operative marketing faction. Thus, those who were following Peek, with some southern backing led by Ed O'Neal of Alabama, ousted Bradfute and elected Sam H. Thompson. Thompson had been in the forefront of the legislative fights of 1924 and 1925.

Coolidge, however, was not without supporters. The Washington *Star* said editorially that the difference between the President and the "professional friends of the farmer is that the President bares realities . . . and talks sense," while the McNary-Haugenites "produce a pipe with an invitation to smoke up and dream dreams."[7] An editorial in the *Pacific Rural Press* praised Coolidge and promised that there would be "no paternalistic legislation for farmers" so long as he was in the White House.

The key to much of Coolidge's popularity, and the grip which he held on the imagination of so many Americans is well reflected in additional comment by the editor of this West Coast farm journal. Referring to the President's annual message, he said: "Jazz-maniacs will find his new message dull; the whoop-'em up boys will think it slow; and the panacea evangels will call it old-fashioned. And it is old-fashioned. Calvin Coolidge is an old-fashioned man. He believes in old-fashioned virtues such as economy, sobriety, reverence, and hard work."[8]

People in the "roaring twenties" who lived beyond their means, considered reverence childish or naïve, drank bootleg liquor, and

6 Washington *Post*, December 20, 1925.
7 Washington *Star*, January 6, 1926.
8 *Pacific Rural Press*, Vol. CX (December 19, 1925), 668.

profited from speculative stocks without turning a hand; men and women who had none of the "old-fashioned" virtues attributed to Coolidge felt nonetheless comforted to know that he was in the White House. This confidence in Coolidge blocked badly needed economic and social reform, and, more pertinent to the farm parity movement, blunted the attack of the farm leaders more than can be imagined.

If Coolidge was obstinate and uncompromising, so were proponents of surplus-control legislation. On December 22, representatives of twenty-three farm organizations, including the Corn Belt Committee and the American Council of Agriculture, met in Des Moines to lay plans for the current session of Congress. The delegates assailed Secretary Jardine's "makeshift plan of quieting the farmer by furnishing him with facts," and demanded the organization of an export corporation to handle surplus crops. The delegates angrily condemned "anyone who thwarts a constructive agricultural program evolved by farmers," and said that a fair price, not advice, was what farmers needed.[9] A joint legislative committee of twelve was created, six each from the Corn Belt Committee and the American Council of Agriculture. Frank W. Murphy was appointed chairman.

Meanwhile, one of the most significant developments in the drive for farm parity was taking place in Iowa. On December 4, 1925, the Agricultural Committee of the Iowa Bankers Association sent out a questionnaire to 1,700 Iowa bankers, asking them what course should be followed in handling farm problems, especially those relating to corn. Of the 893 replies, 504 favored establishing an export corporation to deal with surpluses under government supervision.

On December 16, representatives of the Agricultural Committee and the Council of Administration of the Iowa Bankers Association met at Ames. There it was decided to hold a state-wide meeting in Des Moines under the sponsorship of the Bankers Association. The governor, state secretary of agriculture, superintendent of banks, businessmen, farm journal editors, agricultural organization officials, congressmen, and senators were to be invited. It was suggested that these representatives should then develop a national marketing plan for the corn belt designed to control

[9] Des Moines *Register,* December 23, 1925, and January 8, 1926.

surplus crops. Representatives from ten states besides Iowa were to be invited, including men from Illinois, Indiana, Michigan, Missouri, Minnesota, Ohio, South Dakota, Nebraska, Kansas, and Wisconsin. The bankers believed that Iowa should take the lead because its problems were fairly typical of those in the entire corn-hog region.[10]

The "All Iowa" agricultural marketing conference was held at the Hotel Fort Des Moines on December 29. At the same time Peek, Murphy, Hirth, and other leaders of the American Council of Agriculture and the Corn Belt Committee also met in Des Moines. They were on hand to give advice and proper guidance to the fledgling movement sponsored by the bankers.

Farmers, agricultural leaders, college professors, bankers, and politicians were among the 1,100 people present. The banker element, sitting separately, passed a resolution offering its "wholehearted support and faithful co-operation to aid in working out in every way we can, some constructive plan that will help stabilize the farming industry in this state and help to get the farmer a return for his commodities to which he is justly entitled." All businessmen of the state were urged to join in achieving this objective.

The full conference then adopted resolutions calling for the creation of an export corporation. It pledged political support to those who were working for agricultural parity; the governor was urged to appoint an "All Iowa" advisory committee which would work with him in sponsoring an "All Corn Area" conference within the next thirty days; and the advisory committee was asked to appoint a legislative committee to work in Washington. Copies of these resolutions and intentions were sent to the President, members of his cabinet, and national legislators.

Before adjourning, the delegates took the following pledge: "Recognizing that this problem, notwithstanding its magnitude and complexity, is vitally important to the well-being of all of us, we vigorously pledge ourselves here today, . . . to lend all of our support and aid unstintingly and in the spirit of faithful teamwork and co-operation that our farming industry may become entitled to their just rewards for which they heretofore alone have been so valiantly and courageously fighting. In this work we an-

10 Iowa Bankers Association, "An All Iowa Agricultural Conference, December 21, 1925." Printed letter in Davis Papers.

nounce that we MEAN BUSINESS and shall see it through."[11] This pledge was not drawn up and taken by wild-eyed, bankrupt farmers, but by conservative, Coolidge-voting bankers. Because of the nature of their business, they understood better than most business men the interrelationship between agricultural and industrial prosperity.

Within a few days Governor John Hammill appointed a fifty-man advisory committee which held its first meeting in the Governor's office on January 8, 1926. This group recommended passing surplus-control legislation of the McNary-Haugen type, and then invited the governors of nine other states to call similar agricultural marketing conferences. The executive committee or their representatives could then meet with the Iowa and Nebraska committees sometime before February 1. Governor Adam McMullen of Nebraska had already appointed a committee in his state. The Iowa group subscribed $1,600 to carry on the work, and an "All Corn Area" meeting was scheduled for January 28. The next day Governor Hammill telegraphed the governors of ten states, inviting them "to join in helping to organize the agricultural area of the Mississippi Valley in particular so that we can all unite on a sane, practical, sound and constructive farm-marketing plan."

The "All Agricultural Area" Marketing Conference met as scheduled on January 28, 1926. This was an important day in the drive for farm parity. The air in Des Moines was charged with excitement as representatives from eleven states met to lay down their objectives and map out strategy for the fight ahead. Each state had from three to twenty delegates, and at least four governors were present. The McNary-Haugen leaders were there en masse—Peek, Hirth, Hearst, Murphy, and Senator Dickinson.

The convention agreed to form an organization for the purpose of making cost-of-production studies, and to devise a method of orderly marketing. As about everyone expected, the Dickinson bill, which had been developed at the close of the previous session, was endorsed. The idea of creating a farm export corporation held the center of the entire meeting. Next the delegates instructed Governor Hammill to appoint a committee composed of two members from each of the eleven states—and North Dakota was asked

11 Resolutions Adopted at the All Agricultural Area Marketing Conference, January 28, 1926. Davis Papers.

Senator Charles L. McNary of Oregon
chairman of the Senate Committee on Agriculture and Forestry
1927–33

to join the movement—which was to present the agricultural demands to Congress, the President, and the Secretary of Agriculture. "Our executive committee must under no consideration surrender the principles of our agricultural platform" the delegates promised. And they all agreed to work toward putting "agriculture upon a parity with all other business enterprises."

Before the end of the day, Hammill appointed the Executive Committee of 22. No one was surprised when he named Peek chairman. At 5:45 P.M. this group met in the Governor's office where Peek was authorized to select an even smaller committee to direct the work in Washington. He explained that it would be too cumbersome to call twenty-two men together every time a major decision had to be made. He chose Ballard Dunn, editor of the Omaha *Bee* and C. V. Truax, of the Ohio Farm Bureau as vice-chairmen, and Walfred Lindstrom, of Indiana, as treasurer. The Executive Committee of 22 added immeasurable strength to the farm lobby by channeling special business support behind the McNary-Haugen bill. Peek could now claim that he spoke not only for the farmers, but also for business in the Midwest.

In order to unite all of the special groups which were backing the McNary-Haugen bill, Peek asked that Frank W. Murphy, chairman of the executive committee of the American Council of Agriculture, and William Hirth, chairman of the Corn Belt Committee, be permitted to have voting power in the Executive Committee of 22. This would completely integrate the work of the principal farm lobby organizations, he said. His motion was approved without discussion.

The next morning, Peek's executive committee met again. He emphasized the need of close co-operation among the Executive Committee of 22, the American Council of Agriculture—of which he was still president—and the Corn Belt Committee. He suggested that joint headquarters be established in Chicago with a branch in Washington. Peek was of such dominant importance in the whole movement, that his suggestions were automatically approved. That afternoon he met with officers of the Corn Belt Committee and the council, and they agreed to present a united front in Washington. The American Council of Agriculture already had an office at 523 Transportation Building in Chicago, and the only change was that now all three of the lobby groups would utilize and maintain it.

No time was lost applying additional pressure to Congress and the President. Peek announced that midwestern farm organizations and businessmen were now united as never before to carry on the fight for surplus-control legislation. Ballard Dunn warned one of Jardine's assistants that he hoped "the administration will realize the tremendous earnestness of this movement in the middle-west." He went on to say that the farm fight was yet in conservative hands, but it could become radical.[12]

On February 8, Peek took up the matter of raising sufficient money to finance an all-out farm lobby. He also urged that moves be made to enlist southern support. He warned that this latter problem "required extreme caution and must be approached with every care in order to keep partisan politics out of the movement."

A week later it was agreed to try to raise a war chest of $150,000. This amount was to be prorated among eleven states on the basis of their bank resources. The figure allotted to each state varied from $1,950 for South Dakota to $39,000 for Illinois. Peek and his associates hoped that large contributions could be obtained from businessmen and bankers thus reducing collection costs.

Previous attempts to raise funds to finance a farm campaign had been most discouraging. The American Council of Agriculture had been disappointed when it was able to collect only $9,-926.19 between July, 1924, and December, 1925. Peek had been responsible for getting most of this. Baruch had given $5,000, and an unidentified donor—probably Alex Legge of International Harvester Company—another $2,500. The Illinois Agricultural Association had paid in $1,000, the Missouri Farmers Association, $500, and the Washington and South Dakota Wheat Growers Associations had each given $250.[13] Without Peek's personal contributions, and that of Baruch, it would have been impossible to keep any kind of an organized lobby in Washington during 1924 and 1925. The largest item of expense, $2,681, had been for printing, and $2,574 had gone to C. H. Zealand, who had been employed to solicit funds. But money came in slowly from grass-roots supporters, and Zealand was able to collect only $1,520 at a cost of $1,242!

12 Dunn to F. M. Russell, February 4, 1926. *Ibid.*
13 R. A. Cowles to Peek, April 9, 1926. *Ibid.*

Strengthening the Farm Lobby

It was obvious that more money—much more—must be collected if an effective farm lobby was to be established. The expense of maintaining two offices, one in Chicago and one in Washington, would be heavy. Besides the normal office and traveling expenses, there was the salary of Chester Davis. In February, 1926, shortly after Peek was appointed chairman of the Executive Committee of 22, he asked Davis to join him on a full-time basis. Peek promised to pay Davis $10,000 a year. This was a sizeable commitment in light of an empty treasury. However, Peek felt Davis's help was so vital that, if necessary, he was willing to personally underwrite his salary. Of course, Peek received no funds from any of the farm organizations and, besides, paid his own expenses.

More effective organization did not represent the only progress made by the McNary-Haugenites in 1925. Working through Vice-President Dawes, Peek and Davis were able to give surplus-control legislation a new look of economic merit by obtaining a qualified endorsement from the great English economist, Sir Josiah Stamp. Although Dawes never subscribed to the details of the various farm bills, he was more friendly to the farmers' cause than most other administration leaders. As Chester Davis recalled, "farm representatives were always welcome in the Vice-president's office. Many important meetings took place there, and many converts lined up with the farmers who would probably have been counted on the other side if it had not been for the air of economic respectability which our association with the Vice-president gave the farm bill and its proponents."[14]

On January 5, 1925, Dawes sent his friend Sir Josiah a copy of the Peek farm relief plan and asked for comment. This was the beginning of a correspondence which lasted until late in December. Peek and Davis presented the American case. Sir Josiah never completely agreed with them, but he did make one guarded endorsement of the principles. Writing of the operations of an export corporation, he said, "there seems to be no reason why this process [government buying and selling farm surpluses] should not be carried on until the domestic price is pushed to the point at which the return to the farmer will bring his economic position into favorable comparison with that of other producers."

Despite Stamp's apparent lack of enthusiasm for the Peek

14 *Finance*, Vol. XLIX (August 25, 1945). 40.

proposal, the farm forces quoted him widely to prove the sound-ness of their position. The correspondence was published in January, 1926, and thousands of copies were distributed by both the farm lobby and General Dawes.[15]

As the farm leaders again prepared to present their case to Congress early in 1926, their forces still had one vital weakness. They had not been able to enlist any significant southern support. Prospects of lining up some help south of the Mason and Dixon's line were getting brighter, however, and it was to this problem that Peek now turned his chief attention.

[15] G. N. Peek, C. C. Davis, Sir Josiah C. Stamp, *The Agricultural Problem of the Export Surplus* (January, 1926). A pamphlet. Davis Papers.

Chapter **X**

The Marriage of Corn and Cotton

THE CONFERENCES held by Peek and co-operative leaders in the summer of 1925 had been the beginning of a closer union between the corn and cotton belts. Although these meetings were only exploratory, co-operative officials had come to recognize the disposal of farm surpluses as one of agriculture's main problems. Besides Lowden, Walton Peteet, secretary of the National Council of Co-operative Marketing Associations, was conspicuous among this group.

The national council, however, was still under the Sapiro influence. When Sapiro learned that Peteet was leaning toward the McNary-Haugen bill, he sharply reminded him that the council had officially gone on record against all surplus-control legislation. He further explained that the council had given its word "to the President and Secretary Jardine that we would support co-operative legislation only, and that we were not going to support the so-called 'surplus' legislation."[1]

If any such deal had been arranged between co-operative leaders and the administration—and Peteet denied knowing anything about it—it partly explains the reluctance with which the co-operatives came to support the McNary-Haugen movement. The wheat co-operatives had given considerable backing to Peek's bills, but most of the cotton and tobacco men had remained aloof. But Sapiro was fighting a losing battle in his attempt to keep southern co-operative leaders out of the McNary-Haugen camp. Peteet maintained that he had a right to investigate surplus prob-

[1] Sapiro to Peteet, January 4, 1926. See Peteet-Sapiro correspondence in the *Cong. Rec.,* 69 Cong., 1 sess., March 29, 1926, p. 6502ff.

lems, even though his organization opposed the McNary-Haugen bill. He told President R. W. Bingham of the council that he was ready to resign.

It was heartening to hear Lowden and Peteet expressing open support of surplus-control legislation in late 1925 and early 1926. Lowden told the House Agriculture Committee in January, 1926, that the surplus must be handled by a federal farm board working through the co-operatives. Any losses, he said, should be paid by the producers themselves through an equalization fee. Equally encouraging was the friendly attitude of some of the state cotton co-operatives.

The time looked ripe for Peek and his followers to gain some active southern support. If a bill could be developed which would satisfy both the cotton and tobacco co-operatives, and the wheat and corn-hog producers, then farm leaders could present Congress and the President with a fairly united front. The Dickinson bill had called for disposing of surpluses through the co-operatives, but it had been drawn without consultation with, or approval of, the southern groups.

On March 19 and 20, Peek and William H. Settle, president of the Indiana Farm Bureau, met with directors of the American Cotton Growers Exchange in Memphis. Peek was in no mood to quibble. "We told the cotton people to write their own ticket," he said, "change the proposal in any way that they wanted to and that we would co-operate with them in getting what they wanted in return for their co-operation in helping us get what we want."[2] It was just that simple.

The problem up to that time had been to convince southerners that they needed help. But a slight drop in cotton prices had more effect on southern farm thinking than all of the economic arguments and propaganda which could be mustered by a dozen excited corn belt emissaries. In 1925 the South had produced 16,-105,000 bales of cotton. This large crop had not caused undue excitement or alarming price drops, but farmers were receiving considerably less for cotton in the winter of 1925–26 than during the previous year.

As Peek presented his case, the main question in the minds of cotton growers was the possible use and effect of the equalization

[2] Peek to Lowden, March 24, 1926. Davis Papers.

fee. The cotton situation was different from that of wheat or pork. Southerners did not propose to create a two-price system— one foreign and one domestic—by levying an equalization fee on every pound or bale in order to pay losses on exports. They simply favored orderly marketing of the world's largest cotton supply. If there were some agency to take part of the cotton off the market in years of bumper crops, the surplus would not depress the price. The theory was that it could then be marketed later when more favorable circumstances prevailed, perhaps in a period of low American or world output. If the co-operatives had sufficient financial backing, and if they could get all cotton growers in their organizations, they might handle the surpluses in years of heavy production. Peek argued that the fee would solve both of these problems. A small tax on each pound or bale would raise money for stabilization operations by the co-operatives, and also force all producers to bear their share of the cost.

Peek at last carried the day, and the directors of the American Cotton Growers Exchange agreed to meet him and other Mc-Nary-Haugen leaders in Washington on March 29. "We are expecting whole-hearted support and active co-operation here within the next few days," Peek wrote. Davis observed that, "the coming of the cotton people into the picture will upset the other people's calculations, if I am not mistaken."[3]

Meanwhile, Peek and Davis, backed by their chief supporters, had been planning their legislative strategy. Arriving in Washington on March 1, they set up headquarters in the Lee House. The next day they met with a special committee of congressmen and senators from the North-Central states to discuss general procedure. On March 3, Peek headed a delegation which presented recommendations for agricultural legislation to the President and Secretary Jardine. Coolidge scowled his disapproval but remained silent.

When Peek appeared before the House Agriculture Committee on March 4, he had a powerful group with him. Besides the regulars like Thompson, Hirth, Hearst, and Murphy, there was John Tromble, vice-president of the Farmers' Union, Governor Hammill, C. W. Croes, Mark Woods, and others. Between thirty-five and forty representatives of the various farm organizations

3 Peek to R. A. Cowles, March 22; and Davis to Cowles, March 25, 1926. *Ibid.*

were then in Washington helping to strengthen the farm lobby. When asked how many agricultural leaders would return the following day, Peek replied: "I do not know. . . . There are so many that I can not keep track of all of them."

There was no doubt but that George Peek was running the show. As usual, he attempted to stay in the background and let the authorized farm officials carry the burden of testimony and argument, but he called every behind-the-scenes play. Writing of Peek's generalship, Davis declared, "Peek is remarkable in his patience and force and keeps discord and elements together better than any man I ever saw."[4] There were times when he had "to use the big stick," as Davis called it, but he was usually able to make the farm groups appear determined and united. Not only was there a problem of maintaining a solid front among farm representatives, but a delicate situation existed within the House leadership. Dickinson and Haugen, both Iowans, were jealous of one another, and it took wisdom and skill to keep the farm issue from becoming the victim of personal differences.

Hearings before the House Agriculture Committee began on March 6, and continued daily until April 21. Although opponents of surplus-control legislation were heard—Jardine, Sydney Anderson, B. F. Yoakum and others—the testimony was in a sense "loaded." Most of the witnesses favored the Peek scheme. Peek did not testify himself, but he attended the hearings and proudly watched Hirth, Murphy, and Hearst state the case for his principles.

Corn belt representatives monopolized most of the hearings during the first month, or until early April. By that time the cotton people were in Washington ready to do battle. On March 25, the executive committee of the American Cotton Growers Exchange met in Washington to study the agricultural situation. A committee of five was appointed to stay on and help pass a surplus-control law. B. W. Kilgore, president, and C. L. Stealey, manager of the Oklahoma Cotton Growers Association, were the most important of this group.

As soon as the cotton representatives appeared in Washington, the farm relief forces agreed on a new bill, which was presented to the committee by Sam Thompson on March 29. A month

4 Davis to Cowles, March 4, 1926. *Ibid.*

later, April 27, the House Committee reported favorably another Haugen bill, H. R. 11603, commonly referred to as the third Mc-Nary-Haugen bill. It was based on the Dickinson bill, H. R. 6563, which had been introduced on January 4.

The revised measure called for setting up a federal farm board of twelve members to be appointed by the president. The board was to help all producers by encouraging orderly marketing of farm crops. In the case of basic commodities—including wheat, cotton, corn, butter, cattle, and swine—the board was to remove price-depressing surpluses from the market by contracting with co-operatives. If no co-operative association was capable of carrying out an agreement to control the surplus, then the board could contract with other agencies. The board was to guarantee the losses which co-operatives might incur in their attempt to remove surpluses from the domestic market. Butter was added to the basic commodity list to get the support of dairymen. The dairy interests had opposed the previous McNary-Haugen bills, because they were afraid that higher wheat and corn prices would increase their feed costs.

As in the earlier bills, an equalization fee was to be levied on each unit of a commodity sold. In the case of wheat, the fund would be used to pay the losses on exports while maintaining a higher domestic price behind the tariff wall. But in regard to cotton, money from the fee was to help co-operatives market the crop in a steady and orderly fashion. By levying a fee or tax, all producers would be forced to help finance any benefits which might come from orderly disposal of the crop.

In the first draft of the revised Haugen bill the equalization fee was to be deferred for two years. To replace the income from such a tax, a revolving fund of $375,000,000 was to be provided by the federal government. Of this amount, $100,000,000 was earmarked for cotton stabilization, $250,000,000 for other basic commodities, and $25,000,000 for loans to co-operatives dealing with other products. This version foreshadowed the principles ultimately incorporated in the Agricultural Marketing Act of 1929.

Before the House voted, however, the bill was amended so that the fee would be collected immediately on all basic commodities except cotton. It was deferred for two years on that crop and limited to $2.00 a bale. The revolving fund was cut to $175,000,-

ooo. During the hearings, several shifts were made on the question of levying an equalization fee. Each of them was designed to meet some particular objection, or to win new support. The changes were tactical moves by the farm lobby. Southerners argued that collection of the fee should not be started immediately on their crop because, unlike in the Midwest, producers were not yet sufficiently familiar with the idea.

In addition to directing the board to work through the co-operatives, another important modification was included in the 1926 bill. The original McNary-Haugen measure, it will be recalled, had asked for ratio-prices. In the 1925 version this concept was dropped and a world price, plus the tariff, was demanded. The new measure called for protecting "domestic markets against world prices and assure the maximum benefits of the tariff upon agricultural commodities." More specifically, the bill would not permit the board to underwrite losses incurred by co-operatives in handling surplus crops unless farmers had been paid a "fair and reasonable" price. This concept was taken from various laws dealing with business and industry, particularly the Interstate Commerce Act. The McNary-Haugenites believed that such a general objective could not be consistently attacked by the industrial interests. Moreover, they hoped to avoid the charge of price-fixing. On the whole, the McNary-Haugen group had made a sincere effort to modify their measure to meet some of the administration's most serious objections.

While the House Agriculture Committee had the Haugen bill under consideration, Peek had the farm lobby working at top speed. The editor of the *Grain Dealers Journal* bemoaned the fact that "farm agitators" had "descended in droves" upon congressmen and had so "befuddled" them that "they are in blackest doubt."[5] Representative Tincher charged that there was "vicious lobbying." He resented that amendments had been made to the bill at a meeting to which he had not been invited. But George Peek and Frank Murphy were there, he stormed. It was too bad, he said, that farm lobbyists were consulted instead of a member of the committee![6]

The Executive Committee of 22 under Peek's direction, pub-

[5] *Grain Dealers Journal,* Vol. LVI (March 24, 1926), 339.
[6] Atlanta *Constitution,* May 19, 1926.

lished a weekly bulletin, which was sent to thousands of local, state, and national farm and business leaders. Appeals were made to bombard congressmen and senators with letters and telegrams. The legislative maneuverings were traced in detail and drafts of the various bills were carefully explained. Propaganda favoring the Haugen bill was distributed in wholesale quantities under the franking privileges of friendly congressmen and senators. Almost every issue of the *Bulletin* carried the cry, "Congress must hear from home."[7]

In some instances a particular congressman or senator was singled out for special treatment by the farm forces. Davis reported in April that Representative Charles E. Fuller of Illinois was "entirely bad" on the McNary-Haugen bill. Writing to R. A. Cowles, he asked, "Will it be possible for you to see that a particularly warm fire is lighted under him in his own district?" And indeed the fire was lighted. Fuller voted for the bill, as did Rainey, who had effectively opposed a similar measure two years before. On another occasion Davis told Cowles, "The prairies can be set on fire most any time now, Bob."[8]

Davis also emphasized that pressure must be exerted on Coolidge and Jardine. The files of the Secretary of Agriculture show that hundreds of farmers bombarded the Chief Executive and his agricultural adviser with letters and telegrams. Expressing the theme that had been uppermost in many farm minds since 1920, one Illinois citizen wrote Jardine, "The face of the farmer of the Middle West is turned towards Washington."[9] Reaching Washington were hundreds of letters that were prepared by agricultural leaders and only signed by farmers. Peek had a mailing list of about 2,600 key people on whom he relied to arouse farmers at the grass roots.

Lack of money plagued Peek and his associates as they pressed Congress to pass the Haugen bill. Writing from the Chicago office on April 14, Cowles told Peek and Davis that funds would be exhausted by the end of the month.[10] Peek replied that the office

7 North Central States Agricultural Conference *Bulletin No. 6* (April 26, 1926) and *Bulletin No. 7* (April 30, 1926).

8 Davis to Cowles, April 7 and 15, 1926. Davis Papers.

9 D. S. Knight to Jardine, April 22, 1926. Files of the Secretary of Agriculture.

10 Cowles to Davis, April 14, 1926. Davis Papers.

must remain open and that no employees should be discharged. "I need them all at the present time," he said, "and will become personally responsible for the expenses incurred." A short while later Peek sent his personal check for $1,000 to pay the office expenses for a few more weeks.[11]

A little money dribbled in from farmers and country bankers, but it was not enough to pay the bills. Solicitors representing the American Council of Agriculture and the Executive Committee of 22 had only scant success. A fundraiser for the Executive Committee of 22 in Indiana reported that in May he had been able to collect only $581. Under these circumstances, Peek and his friends had to bear the real financial burden. On April 26, Mark Woods of Lincoln, Nebraska, donated $5,000. "This is a godsend at this particular time," Peek wrote, "because the battle is getting hot and as you know I have been spending a tremendous amount of money at least for me."[12]

Despite the increasing effectiveness of the farm lobby, criticism of the Haugen bill was as intense as ever. If some congressmen were being influenced by arguments, threats, or cajolery, there was no sign of weakening by administration leaders or certain business interests. While there was much outright obstruction, most of the opposition was more subtle. Not many opponents of the McNary-Haugen bill dared to say openly that they opposed any legislation which would raise farm prices. Yet they would not concede that the federal government had any real responsibility in getting better agricultural incomes. As in 1924 and 1925, critics proposed measures which they hoped would quiet the farm clamor and yet not be inconsistent with their economic philosophy.

It was interesting to watch the tactics employed by opponents of the McNary-Haugen bill. At first they attacked the equalization fee as a dangerous and undesirable tax to pay for export losses. Then when the McNary-Haugenites suggested postponing collection of the fee for two years and appropriating money from the federal treasury to pay the losses, the bill was criticized as a subsidy to agriculture. These positions indicated a complete lack of sincerity. Someone or somebody was going to have to pay the expense of handling surplus crops, unless production was cur-

[11] Peek to Cowles, April 17 and May 11, 1926. *Ibid.*
[12] *Ibid.*, April 27.

tailed. But administration leaders were counting heavily on the normal rural conservatism to keep the farm relief boat steady. "There is great conservative farm thought," wrote Jardine in February, 1926, "and this thought is mobilizing every day."[13]

The administration plan was incorporated in the Tincher bill, which was introduced on April 16. It included Secretary Jardine's suggestions, and Tincher claimed that the President "spoke very friendly about this bill." Later Coolidge gave it open support. The measure would have established a farm marketing commission with a revolving fund of $100,000,000 to loan to co-operatives. Jardine argued that farm prices could be stabilized if co-operatives had more liberal credit facilities to help them hold excess production. Jardine was careful to use the term "price stabilization." When Haugen asked him if he was "really for increasing the price," Jardine replied, "I am for stabilizing the price."[14] He never came out directly in favor of lifting farm prices by legislative action.

The Jardine-Tincher proposal was based on the idea that co-operatives needed more credit, and that if they could make more liberal advances to members, additional producers would join. The co-operatives, it was believed, could carry surpluses from one season to another and keep them from depressing prices. It is difficult to credit so intelligent a man as Jardine with sincerity in this matter, but his correspondence reveals that he believed the plan would actually work. He clung to his position despite devastating criticism by farmers who were or had been members of co-operatives, and by economists in his own department. He was apparently so fearful of government aid to agriculture that he got himself into a position of supporting a program foreordained to fail. Kansas farmers and others wrote him constantly, recalling the recent history of co-operatives in his own state. Andrew Shearer, a close Kansas friend, said, "you are making the mistake of your life. It is breaking my heart to see you disappoint your old farmer friends."[15]

13 Jardine to L. R. Clausen, February 16, 1926. Files of the Secretary of Agriculture.

14 *Agricultural Relief*, Hearings before the House Agriculture Committee, 69 Cong., 1 sess., 1926, p. 1344.

15 Shearer to Jardine, April 20 and May 5, 1926. Files of the Secretary of Agriculture.

Nils A. Olsen, assistant chief of the Bureau of Agricultural Economics, wrote a stinging memorandum to Secretary Jardine on April 24. He argued that the co-operatives could not handle farm surpluses because they did not control a sufficient amount of the commodities to exercise a determining factor upon price. Olsen claimed that to unload the surplus problem upon the co-operatives, surpluses produced by both members and nonmembers, would destroy the organizations. Members would not stand to be taxed while outsiders, who would receive the benefit of any higher price level, went free. Although the bill anticipated the formation of new co-operatives, Olsen indicated that the creation of mushroom organizations supported with government loans would not likely succeed. He emphasized what most co-operative men knew—you can not build successful co-operatives from the top down.

Peek and the McNary-Haugen proponents attacked the Tincher bill with fume and fury. No farmers or farm-organization leaders appeared in Washington to back it. Letters poured in from the grass roots condemning Jardine's "fake," "emasculated," and "ineffective" legislation. Ralph Snyder, president of the Kansas Farm Bureau, wired Jardine that Kansas farmers would rather have nothing than the Tincher bill. Hirth said Congress had better adjourn without doing anything if the Tincher bill was to be "rammed down our throats." Occasionally a political threat was heard. Shearer told Jardine that farmers wanted the Haugen bill and meant to get it. "The old farmers alliance wasn't a patching to this movement," he said.[16]

The Curtis-Aswell bill was also introduced to divert attention from surplus-control legislation. The measure had not been materially changed since 1925, and provided for a national farm marketing association to aid in forming co-operatives, to advise them on production and diversification, and to encourage the formation of interstate marketing organizations. A revolving fund of $10,000,000 was to be created to finance loans to co-operatives.

Another farm relief idea which won considerable support was the export-debenture plan. Professor Charles L. Stewart, agricultural economist at the University of Illinois, was its author; and the Grange, which had never been enthusiastic about the Mc-

16 *Ibid.*, May 5, 1926.

Nary-Haugen bill, gave it most active support among the farm organizations.

Stewart proposed to give exporters of basic agricultural products treasury certificates or debentures whose value would be determined by Congress. This was to represent the difference between the cost of production in the United States and abroad. The debentures were to be negotiable and could be used to pay import duties. It was the theory that exporters would be able to pay above world prices for exportable surpluses to the extent of the debenture. Twenty cents, or about half the amount of the tariff, was generally suggested as the amount of the debenture which should be paid on wheat. In effect, the plan was an export bounty. Senator William B. McKinley of Illinois introduced a bill incorporating the Stewart principles on January 7, 1926, and Representative Charles Adkins presented it to the House four days later. But it received only scant attention and was temporarily submerged in a sea of McNary-Haugenism.

Secretary Jardine must have winced when he read Stewart's analysis of the scheme and realized its economic and social implications. Stewart wrote: "In shifting a part of the economic burden of price enhancement to payers of federal income and other taxes . . . consumers are spared much more than the treasury is set back. . . . By letting federal taxpayers relieve the poor man somewhat a decided economic gain is accomplished for the public."[17] What kind of economic heresy was this!

On April 26, the House Agriculture Committee took the unusual step of reporting favorably the three principal farm relief measures, the Haugen, Tincher, and Aswell bills. The majority of the committee opposed the Tincher and Aswell measures, but there was no use taking a direct slap at the President by refusing to report Tincher's bill. House debate began on May 4. Backers of the Tincher and Aswell bills spent little time explaining or defending their own legislation. Their main purpose was to defeat the Haugen bill. Administration leaders recognized that the most they could do was to block favorable consideration of Haugen's legislation. There was no chance of aroused farm leaders permitting enactment of the Tincher bill.

Congressman Franklin W. Fort, president of the Lincoln Na-

17 Charles L. Stewart to Jardine, April 12, 1926. *Ibid.*

tional Bank of Newark, was in the front ranks of the opposition. He attacked the bill as price-fixing, as dangerous to the co-operatives, as economically unsound, and as a detriment to farmers, because higher prices would lead to decreased consumption. Although this kind of opposition was effective, a more serious trouble in getting any farm relief was the attitude of congressmen who kept asking what the bill would do for their constituents. Butler B. Hare of South Carolina wanted to know if the bill would really help cotton farmers. Bertrand H. Snell said that New York dairy farmers were not prosperous. "What is there in this bill that would be of aid and assistance to them," he asked? And Loring M. Black of Brooklyn asked Haugen, "Would it increase the price of food?"[18]

Haugen and other supporters of surplus-control legislation presented their case well, but, as is usually true, Congressional debate changed few votes. On May 21 the Haugen bill was defeated 167 to 212, with forty-eight congressmen not voting. Comparing the 1926 vote with that of two years earlier, those favoring the McNary-Haugen idea seemed to show relatively small gains. Only in the South Atlantic states was there a noticeable shift in favor of Peek's legislation. In that section 14 votes were gained. However, much more progress had been made than appeared on the surface. The move in the South toward McNary-Haugenism was beginning and was strong enough to be labeled a definite trend. A little more work in the South, or perhaps lower cotton prices, and it was probable that southerners would join midwesterners to make the marriage of corn and cotton complete. But the vote also revealed something else. Fewer Republicans voted for the Haugen bill in 1926 than in 1924, indicating that numerous congressmen were responding to the crack of the administration whip.

Defeat of the Haugen bill meant the death of surplus-control legislation at that session. Yet the farm lobby would not let the issue drop and announced that the legislation "will be pushed in the Senate." The Senate was over a month behind the House in considering farm relief. Hearings were held between March 29 and April 13. On the latter date the Senate Agriculture Committee voted to attach the Haugen bill to H.R. 7893, which had previously passed the House, and provided for setting up a division of

[18] *Cong. Rec.*, 69 Cong., 1 sess., May 4, 1926, p. 8699ff.

Representative Gilbert N. Haugen of Iowa
chairman of the House Agriculture Committee, 1919–31

co-operative marketing in the Department of Agriculture. It was known as the McNary bill.

Beginning debate on June 1, Senators repeated much of what had been already said in the House. However, some different aspects of the problem were considered, and emphasis shifted slightly. During the discussion, there was, for the first time, militant talk by midwestern Republicans about attacking the entire tariff system if Congress did not extend its benefits to surplus agricultural crops. For example, Senator Norbeck, a consistent protectionist who had never "waivered in the faith," declared that government policies had put industry and labor on economic "stilts," and that farmers deserved equal benefits. Unless they did get help, he said, "farmers will tear down the tariff structure. . . . Perhaps, he may, like Sampson of old, pull down the temple upon himself but desperate people will do desperate things."[19]

Low tariff Democrats, such as Carter Glass, Joseph T. Robinson, Oscar Underwood, and "Cotton Ed" Smith, were pleased to see midwestern Republicans threatening to kick over the tariff traces. However, they did not take the threats too seriously. Senator Robinson said he was always ready to join a coalition to break down tariff barriers. "I wonder if the Senator from South Dakota is ready," he remarked. Robinson added that the real reason so many Democrats opposed the McNary-Haugen bill was because "it is based . . . upon the perpetuation of a system admittedly unjust."[20] Of course, midwestern Republicans were only bluffing. Southern Democrats knew it, and so did the administration. Corn and wheat belt farmers were asking for a larger slice of the tariff pie for themselves; then they threatened to attack the whole system if they did not get it. This approach was weak from every political angle. Subsequent events showed that Henry A. Wallace was one of the very few midwestern farm leaders who actually made good his threat.

The only real excitement generated by the Senate debate was the publication of a letter on the farm problem by Treasury Secretary Andrew W. Mellon. It was one of the most significant documents published during the farm fight, because it clearly expressed the conflict between agrarian and industrial capitalism. No one

19 *Ibid.,* June 15, 1926, p. 11289.
20 *Ibid.,* p. 11357.

else in the 1920's stated so openly why industrialists opposed the McNary-Haugen bill and probable higher agricultural prices.

The effect of the bill, Mellon argued, "will be to increase the cost of living to every consumer of five basic agricultural commodities." Then, he continued, "we shall have the unusual spectacle of the American consuming public paying a bonus to the producers of five major agricultural commodities, with a resulting decrease in the purchasing power of wages, and at the same time contributing a subsidy to the foreign consumers, who under the proposed plan will secure American commodities at prices below the American level." Therefore, Mellon concluded, European labor could live more cheaply than American labor and foreign industrial costs would be less than those in the United States. Foreign competitors could then undersell American manufacturers in world and domestic markets.[21]

Here was a bold and frank admission from a high party spokesman, giving the real reason why the administration so violently opposed the McNary-Haugen bill. Coolidge and Hoover had been more tactful, more indirect. But Mellon laid his cards face upward. In effect he was saying that the McNary-Haugen bill was unsound, not because it would fail to raise farm prices, but because higher prices would injure industry. Regardless of what happened to American farmers, industry and labor must have cheap food and raw materials so as to compete favorably in the world's industrial markets. Indeed, if Mellon had his way, farmers were to be gardeners in a predominantly industrial society.

The Mellon letter brought a flood of recriminations and protests from Peek and other McNary-Haugen leaders. They pointed to it as positive proof that the administration had no real concern for agriculture and was willing to sacrifice farmers on the altar of industrialism. They damned the administration policy of giving legislative aids to industry, labor, and transportation while denying the same thing to farmers. And Democrats had a heyday. The New York *World* said that Mellon had seen the "mote that is in the farmers eye, but the beam in his own eye he has considered not." Senator Thomas J. Walsh presented evidence to show

[21] Mellon to Haugen, Dickinson, and Daniel R. Anthony, June 14, 1926. Reprinted in *Cong. Rec.*, 69 Cong., 1 sess., June 15, 1926, p. 11266.

that after the Fordney-McCumber tariff had become effective on September 22, 1922, Mellon's Aluminum Company of America increased the price of sheet aluminum 3 cents a pound within the next ten days! Mellon would champion profits influenced by legislative action so long as they went to himself or industry generally, Walsh declared, but he opposed any government aid to agriculture. But Walsh himself would not support the bill because of the tariff feature.

Hoover also threw his influence against the measure. He was more tactful than Mellon, but argued that his "Quaker conscience" would not permit him to support farm legislation which would subsidize the British Empire, put the government in the business of buying and selling farm products, or deliver the farmers over to government price-fixing. "I have another ten years to live," he concluded, "and I don't want to face the American farmers five years hence," and have to explain the results of such a measure.[22] He did face the farmers some six years later after his "economically sound" Agricultural Marketing Act had ended in dismal failure, and they helped to rush him from the presidency in ignominious defeat.

As the Senate vote approached, it looked like it might result in a tie which would have to be broken by Vice-President Dawes. Although, as mentioned before, Dawes had not publicly supported the measure, he had been most co-operative in helping to bring the bill to a vote. The farm relief forces thought they could depend on him. The night before the Senate was to vote, Peek and Davis called on Dawes at his room in the Metropolitan Club, which he sometimes used when his family was away from Washington. General Dawes was sitting at a table littered with sheets of paper, puffing furiously on his underslung pipe. "Well, boys do you know what I'm doing," he remarked as they entered the room. "I haven't the slightest idea," Peek replied. "It looks like there will be a tie tomorrow and I'll have to break it," Dawes said. "I'm writing a statement explaining why I voted *against* the bill." When George Peek recovered his breath, he shouted, "Why in hell are you going to do that?" Then Dawes explained that he could not approve exempting cotton from the equalization fee. It was a "cheap political trick" and he would have none of it. Peek

22 Hoover to Julian N. Friant, June 12, 1926. Peek Papers.

usually kept his temper, but not that night. Nothing he could do or say, however, could change Dawes's mind.

Dawes did not need to use his statement because the Senate defeated the measure on June 24 by a vote of 45 to 39. Then Coolidge and Jardine urged the Senate to pass the Fess amendment, which was identical with the defeated Tincher bill. According to one Washington correspondent, this was the first time the President had made a direct public appeal on the controversial farm issue. But Peek turned the pressure of the farm lobby against the administration proposal and the Fess bill was overwhelmed 54 to 26. Farmers had asked for bread and they would not accept what they considered a stone. A few days later the Senate approved the House bill to set up a bureau of co-operative marketing in the Department of Agriculture. Another session had ended with no significant farm legislation.

As had been true in the House, the Senate vote showed that more southern support must be obtained. Of the most prominent southern Democrats only Caraway, McKellar, and Simmons voted for the measure. Senator Glass even criticized his Democratic colleagues who voted for the bill. He censured Simmons, the "David of the tribe" who had set out to "slay the Goliath of high protection," for capitulating "to the Philistines."[23]

Following the defeat of the third McNary-Haugen bill, Representative Fort said that "legislation will come just as soon as the leaders of farm organizations are able and willing to set down with minds free from the hypnotic equalization fee doctrine and ready to discuss the subject on other and sounder lines."[24] The editor of the Washington *Star* observed on June 28 that the McNary-Haugen bill had "no chance in the future that is worth putting a bet on," and urged its supporters to turn to the Fess-Tincher bill.

Midwesterners and a growing number of southerners, however, were in no mood to take orders from easterners as to the proper kind of farm legislation. Peek absolutely refused to compromise on the equalization fee issue. And whether or not farmers and farm leaders understood all of its implications, most of

[23] *Cong. Rec.*, 69 Cong., 1 sess., June 22, 1926, p. 11736ff.
[24] Franklin Fort, "Why Farm Relief Failed," *American Bankers Association Journal*, Vol. XIX (July, 1926), 22.

them went along with him. In the minds of farm leaders failure to get their legislation at that session was not defeat, only delay. The editor of the *Dakota Farmer* warned that farmers were "jotting down" the actions of their senators and representatives, and were about ready to make "needed changes."[25]

Political threats came thick and fast out of the Midwest. On June 10 the Algona (Iowa) *Upper-Des Moines Republican* predicted that "Coolidge and his cohorts" would hear from the farm relief issue in the coming election. The editor conceded that Coolidge was probably sincere, but, he continued, "the farming west is in no mood to accept excuses." Dan W. Turner, temporary chairman of the Iowa State Republican Convention, told a large crowd in Des Moines that "we have just begun to fight." He warned opponents of the McNary-Haugen bill, "more in sorrow than in anger," that agriculture must have, and intended to get, government aid. A writer in the *Wheat Growers Journal* prophesied that the McNary-Haugen bill would "be a storm center in American politics unless and until it is finally disposed of by a smashing defeat at a general election."[26]

The political fulminations were not entirely without foundation. Senator McKinley of Illinois, a Coolidge supporter, was defeated for renomination in the spring of 1926. In 1920 he had won most downstate farm counties, but his opponent carried most of them six years later. In Iowa, the erratic and turbulent Brookhart, who had lost his senate seat temporarily, was renominated and later elected. Brookhart's victory "reflected the sentiment of the people of our State against the prevailing policy of the East toward the citizens of the West," said Charles Hearst.[27]

But was there any real danger that the "trans-Mississippi Grangers" might really get mad and start an electoral stampede? Would they refuse to be rounded up into the party herd for the fall elections? Could the administration stalwarts hypnotize their haymaker constituents into believing that they did not want the McNary-Haugen bill after all? Time would tell. But Coolidge did not seem afraid.

And what about the farm lobby? It had no intention of quit-

25 *Dakota Farmer*, Vol. XLVI (July 15, 1926), 684.
26 *Wheat Growers Journal*, Vol. VI (July 1, 1926), 12.
27 Hearst to Peek, June 9, 1926. Davis Papers.

ting. Peek was admittedly tired, and by June 20 he was preparing to leave Washington for a much needed vacation. He had been on the job almost constantly for two years, working, organizing, publicizing, and gradually exerting more and more pressure on Congress. "I am thoroughly worn out with all this fight," he wrote, "and want to take a few days rest before I try to think of anything else."[28] He would soon be back, however, and next time Congress would pass his McNary-Haugen bill.

[28] Peek to Hearst, June 30, 1926. *Ibid.*

Chapter XI

The McNary-Haugen Bill Passes Congress

EEK left Washington for Montana on July 4, 1926. He planned to fish, golf, avoid the torrid summertime heat of Washington, and, as he put it, just loaf. But he did not leave the farm fight completely behind. He could not do that. On his way west he attended a meeting of the Corn Belt Committee and the American Council of Agriculture in Des Moines. The delegates again defiantly shouted, "protection for all or protection for none." Farm representatives bitterly condemned Mellon's "shortsighted industrial policy," and warmly commended members of Congress who had "faithfully supported the farm relief bill."

While Peek enjoyed the vacation wonderlands of the great Northwest, Chester Davis sat through the sweltering heat of Chicago, busily building up support for the McNary-Haugen bill. He wrote to every member of the House and Senate who had voted for the measure, and also directed work in the distant provinces. Walton Peteet, who had quit the National Association of Co-operative Marketing Associations earlier in the year, was now working with the farm lobby. He spent several weeks during the summer in Tennessee and Texas "with good results." Senator Nye was doing additional work in North Dakota, and Frank Murphy was continuing the campaign "with extreme activity" in Minnesota. Congressman Charles Brand was "lighting some fires" in Ohio. Thus Davis reported to Peek.[1]

Davis was also scanning the horizon for completely new recruits. "What do you think of including tobacco in the next model bill?" he asked B. W. Kilgore. Kilgore replied that he favored

1 Davis to Peek, summer, 1926. Davis Papers.

trying "to interest . . . the tobacco people in the movement," and suggested that Davis contact J. C. Stone of Lexington, general manager of the Burley Tobacco Growers Association.[2] Following this lead, Davis soon had several tobacco co-operative officials hitched to the McNary-Haugen wagon.

The work of the farm lobby, however, got its biggest boost from a somewhat unexpected event—a sharp decline in cotton prices. A measure of backing in the cotton belt had been achieved in the spring of 1926, but the equalization-fee plan had not captured the imaginations of many dirt farmers in the South. As shown before, cotton co-operative officials had lent support to the campaign, but it was moderate, not militant.

By September the farm price of cotton had fallen to around 12 cents a pound, only a little more than half of what it had brought a year earlier. Large acreages and good yields were responsible for a record-breaking crop of 17,977,000 bales. Heavy carry-overs from 1925 on top of this tremendous output helped drive prices to ruinous levels. Millions of bales glutted the markets, and there was no provision for handling the surplus. Southern farmers and farm leaders now began to say that if the McNary-Haugen bill had been in operation, the calamity might have been avoided.

Although low cotton prices were unfortunate for southern farmers, it proved to be a godsend to the farm relief efforts. Cotton men, many of them previously lukewarm to McNary-Haugenism, now became vigorous champions of federal aid to agriculture. Traditional States-rightism was pushed into the background, and they demanded that their legislators get government assistance for their sagging industry. A New Mexico cotton farmer wrote that growers were finally "beginning to wake up."

And rice producers were also joining the farm relief team. C. E. Carnes, vice-president of the Rice Farmers' Credit Association of Crowley, Louisiana, explained to Davis: "Our rice people have never been so thoroughly convinced of the merits of any plan as that which is now proposed. . . . It is our intention to line up the entire rice interests of the three states [Louisiana, Arkansas, and Texas] for this measure." A month later Carnes was able to report that rice leaders "are preparing to support this measure with

2 Davis to Kilgore, July 23, 1926; and Kilgore to Davis, July 29, 1926. *Ibid.*

their entire strength."[3] The picture was looking immeasurably brighter for Peek and his associates.

The next tactical move was to bring representatives of the corn-hog, wheat, cotton, tobacco, and rice growers together. Then a united front could be presented to the next session of Congress. Such a conference had been considered during the summer, but, as Peek said, "for one reason or another the time . . . never seemed just right." Low cotton prices, and generally unsatisfactory returns for grain, however, seemed to make the time ripe by the fall of 1926. The general index of agricultural purchasing power had dropped from 93 in August, 1925, to 82 a year later.

The farm relief leaders gathered for a big conclave in St. Louis on November 16 and 17. Representatives from the West, Midwest, and South adopted resolutions already prepared by Peek and Davis, declaring that their common economic interests justified and required unified action. They approved the McNary-Haugen bill in principle and condemned production control as unworkable. Members of Congress who had supported surplus-control legislation were praised, regardless of party, and farmers were urged to hold their legislators strictly accountable. The approved declaration concluded by saying that farmers "recognize no sectional lines, no political differences, no commodity rivalry in planning for future co-operation."[4] Hearst told Davis that the best of harmony existed throughout the meeting. "I feel that wonderful progress was made in cementing the interests of the agriculture of our country," he added.[5]

It is doubtful if farm leaders in the United States had ever before demonstrated greater unanimity in their demands. The vast majority of authorized agricultural representatives had finally agreed on principles and objectives. Peek and a few others had worked hard and long to achieve this goal. It testifies to the determination and persistence for which Peek was so noted.

Many of those who opposed federal aid to agriculture in the 1920's excused themselves by saying that farmers were not united, that they did not know what they wanted. Of course, anyone who

---

[3] See Carnes to Peteet, October 16, 1926, Davis Papers; and Carnes to McNary, November 23, 1926, McNary Papers.

[4] "A Program of the South And West." A leaflet. Davis Papers.

[5] Hearst to Davis, November 23, 1926. *Ibid.*

asked all farmers to agree was only side-stepping the question. Businessmen did not support tariff legislation unanimously; yet that was not used as an argument against passing protective laws. It was also charged that leaders were really not representative of the ordinary dirt farmer, and, therefore, the demand for surplus-control legislation could be ignored. Farm leaders were accused of being promoters and of farming the farmers! Peek was subjected to more than one attack on this score.

These attitudes resulted from prejudice against the farm cause, and were designed to camouflage the issue. Admittedly, farm organizations were not models of democracy. Farm organization politics were sometimes ruthless and dictatorial. Yet farm groups were probably as democratic as the business and labor organizations of that period. Farmers resented other economic groups telling them what they should do and have, and they could not understand why the government did not heed their accredited spokesmen. Were not labor leaders consulted on legislation of interest to workers; did not the United States Chamber of Commerce and the National Association of Manufacturers speak for business? And on the matter of overemphasis, was it not the duty of farm leaders to breathe smoke and fire? In a government of groups and blocs, the faction that hit hardest was likely to get the best results. Farmers were slowly learning this vital fact.

Neither Peek nor Davis attended the St. Louis meeting, although they had planned the whole operation. They were in New York addressing a meeting of the Academy of Political Science. Peek considered the problem of agricultural equality, while Davis dealt with agriculture and the tariff. Peek told his learned audience that he was engaged in a battle to determine "whether an independent agriculture, enjoying the advantages and benefits of life on a level comparable with that prevailing in our cities and towns can be established and maintained." This could be accomplished, he argued, by proper legislation. A short time later, Lowden presented the farm cause before the American Economic Association. "I think we have elevated this question to a plane where it is being given serious consideration," he said.[6] In other words, Lowden felt that the McNary-Haugen bill had achieved a reasonable degree of economic respectability.

[6] Lowden to Peek, January 5, 1927. *Ibid.*

Arriving back in Washington late in November after an absence of about five months, the Peeks rented a furnished apartment at 2227 Twentieth Street, N. W. In October, Peek had undergone a minor operation to remove a slight impediment from his throat, but once again he felt ready to command the farm battle. A steady stream of farm leaders came and went from the Peek apartment as "Old George" laid plans for the approaching session of Congress. There was much more optimism in the farm camp, now that the cotton men were fighting shoulder to shoulder with the wheat and corn-hog growers. Besides the old regulars from the Midwest, new faces began appearing at the Peek household. There were C. O. Moser, B. W. Kilgore, and W. W. Pitts, legislative committee of the American Cotton Growers Exchange; Xenophon Caverno, president of the Missouri Cotton Growers Association; and J. N. Kehoe, vice-president of the Burley Tobacco Growers Co-operative Association.

During December, Peek and Davis developed a new bill. If possible, they wanted to revise their measure in order to reduce administration opposition. President Coolidge's remarks on agriculture in his annual message of December 7 indicated that he had not experienced a change of heart. Referring to the surplus question, he said that any policy must avoid price-fixing and putting the government in business.

The revised measure, like its predecessor, called for establishing a federal farm board which would work through the co-operatives in disposing of surplus crops. There was to be one member from each of the federal land bank districts. Basic crops included cotton, wheat, corn, rice, and hogs. During the Senate debate, the McKellar amendment adding tobacco to the list of basic commodities was approved. An equalization fee was to be levied on the sale of these products to raise funds to pay losses on exports, or to help the co-operatives hold surpluses for higher prices. A $250,000,000 appropriation was to be provided to bear the expenses until equalization fees could be collected.

The new bill contained some important changes. All reference to price was eliminated. It simply aimed at "orderly marketing of basic agricultural commodities" by controlling and disposing of surpluses. There was also a change in the basic commodity list. Cattle and butter were dropped and rice and tobacco were added.

Cattlemen did not want to be included. Equalization funds were renamed stabilization funds because of Secretary Jardine's constant talk about "stabilizing prices." Furthermore, the equalization fee was not to be collected from producers, but in the "transportation, processing or sale" of a commodity. Collection of the fee was not deferred on any basic commodity, as had been true in the previous bill.

A more important concession to the administration was a provision which restricted the board's operations. It could not begin functioning unless approved by advisory councils composed of representatives of farm organizations and co-operatives dealing in a particular commodity, or the members of the board representing the federal land-bank districts in which over 50 per cent of a crop was produced. In other words, if over 50 per cent of the cotton was grown in two federal land-bank districts, the board members from these areas would have to agree to start or end surplus-control activities. The board had much less authority than had been provided in earlier bills. Actually, it could not directly handle farm commodities at all. One important addition to the 1927 bill was an insurance feature proposed by O. F. Bledsoe of the Long Staple Cotton Association. This section permitted the board to "insure any co-operative marketing association against decline in the market price for the commodity at the time of sale by the association, from the market price for such commodity at the time of delivery to the association."[7]

The main difference between the Peek-Davis measure and the administration-sponsored Curtis-Crisp bill was the levying of an equalization fee. This was the crux of the matter, the heart of the covenant, as Senator Watson put it. Under no circumstances would the farm leaders compromise on this point. The administration bill called for a $250,000,000 revolving fund which could be loaned to co-operatives to handle surpluses. But the loans were not to be secured except by the commodities themselves. The McNary-Haugen supporters insisted that producers, not the United States Treasury, should through the fee pay the cost of any price-raising or stabilization operations. Moreover, they argued that the equalization fee would deter excessive production. It was recognized,

[7] *Agricultural Relief,* Hearings before the Senate Agriculture Committee, 69 Cong., 2 sess., 1927, p. 2ff.

of course, that increased prices would be passed on to consumers just as would a price increase from any other cause.

When Congress assembled in December, 1926, it was clear that over two years of work by the farm lobby had produced a marked change of feeling toward the McNary-Haugen bill. Despite continued opposition by administration spokesmen, an increasing number of legislators were announcing that they would vote for surplus-control legislation. "There does not seem to be any disposition toward any very long hearings in either the Senate or House," Davis wrote.[8] And he was right. Farm relief hearings in the House totaled only 163 pages, and in the Senate, 70 pages. Under the relentless pressure of the farm groups, decisions had already been reached by most representatives and senators. The story was told of Senator James Watson of Indiana, who voted for the bill after originally opposing it. One of Watson's friends said, "Jim, how come?" Watson replied, "Well, you know there comes a time in the life of every politician when he must rise above his principles."

McNary and Haugen introduced the Peek-Davis bill in December, and debate began a month later. From the outset it was obvious that the farm forces at last had the votes. Senator Moses of New Hampshire lamented that everyone knew the bill would pass. In an attitude of despair, opposition senators charged that it was unconstitutional, unworkable, radical, that it would "sovietize the United States," and that it would raise food prices. The metropolitan press frantically repeated all of these accusations. Almost every morning along with their breakfast, senators and representatives were treated to a bitter attack on the bill by the Washington *Post*. One ditty said: "The pigs are squealing for their swill, So hurry up the hoggin' bill."[9]

But there was no use engaging in lengthy debate. The farm lobby had the Congressional situation firmly under control, and the leaders were anxious for a show down. On February 11 the Senate passed the bill by a vote of 47 to 39. Congratulating Peek on his leadership, Frank Lowden declared, "It is a great fight you have made and you are entitled to all praise for the leading part you have played in it." Hearst wired Davis: "Our prayers are for

8 Davis to William Hirth, December 16, 1926. Davis Papers.
9 Washington *Post*, February 17, 1927.

you boys who are putting up such a good fight. . . . We are betting our last dollar on you."[10]

And the grip of the farm relief advocates was, if anything, more firm in the House. Democrat James O'Connor of New Orleans said it was useless to oppose the bill. "It is going through," he said, and any suggested changes would die "before a firing squad." Tincher, too, gave up hope of getting the bill amended. Dickinson, "the spokesman for Peek," would not permit it, he said. Aswell, who was hopelessly attempting to get his co-operative marketing bill accepted, claimed that many congressmen were going to vote for the McNary-Haugen measure against their better judgment. He quoted one colleague as saying, "I am for it; I have got to support it, because the crowd at home are on my trail."[11] The editor of the Wichita *Beacon* claimed that a majority was obtained "under the bludgeoning of one of the most persistent and skillful lobbies ever seen in Washington."[12]

For those who were watching the legislative situation in the House, February 17 was a memorable day. The galleries were packed. There was tense excitement as members milled around the chamber. Loud roars of "no" greeted every amendment or substitute as the McNary-Haugenites firmly held their lines. Representatives of the farm organizations were conspicuously present.[13] For the first time, the tobacco men were on hand "as full of

[10] Lowden to Peek, February 8; and Hearst to Davis, February 11, 1927. Davis Papers.

[11] *Cong. Rec.*, 69 Cong., 2 sess., February 15, 1927, pp. 3876, 3880, and 3882.

[12] Wichita *Beacon*, February 26, 1927.

[13] The following leaders were present in Washington at least part of the time during the second session of the Sixty-ninth Congress: Sam Thompson, Ed O'Neal, Charles Hearst, and Chester Gray for the American Farm Bureau; Ralph Snyder of the Kansas Farm Bureau; C. O. Moser, B. W. Kilgore, and W. W. Pitts, legislative committee of the American Cotton Growers Exchange; Xenophon Caverno, president of the Missouri Cotton Growers Association; W. H. Settle of the Indiana Farm Bureau; J. N. Kehoe, vice-president of the Burley Tobacco Growers Co-operative Association; Geoffrey Morgan, general manager of the Dark Tobacco Growers Co-operative Association; George Duis, president of the North Dakota Wheat Growers Association, and Thomas Cashman of the Minnesota Council of Agriculture. Of course, Peek, Hirth, Murphy Peteet, and Davis were continually on hand. Hirth wrote that "Peek, Davis and Peteet are in truth the 'Three Musketeers' who emerge laurel wreathed from the combat and never will the farmers of the United States be able to repay them even in part for the brilliant and outstanding service which they have rendered." *Missouri Farmer*, Vol. XIX (March 1, 1927), 3.

fight as an old time Texas steer." At 9:30 P.M. the final roll call began and, as everyone expected, the bill passed by the substantial majority of 214 to 178.

Peek triumphantly announced that the result was an "intellectual justification" of the principles for which he had fought. His wife, who had watched both the House and Senate debates from the galleries, wrote in her diary, "It was the inarticulate voice of suffering farm populations making themselves heard at last." Writing from Chicago, R. A. Cowles told Peek: "Whatever the President may do, . . . the principles you have advocated from the inception of the effort . . . has [sic] now been accepted by Congress. . . . You have won a great fight." And Lowden wired Peek, saying, "my heartiest congratulations it would be very hard overstate credit which is your due for great victory."[14] Henry Wallace was on hand so he could report an eye witness account to his anxious readers. The story of how the bill had been passed, he wrote, without much money or "party machinery is one of the most astonishing things in American history."[15] Peek had every right to feel proud.

Support from southern congressmen and senators had made the difference between defeat and victory. Twenty-two Democratic senators and ninety-seven representatives voted yea. The McNary-Haugenites made their greatest relative gains in Arkansas, Louisiana, Oklahoma, and Texas. This reflected the low price of cotton, as well as pressure from the rice interests.

There were other factors, however, which helped pass the bill. In the first place, there had been vote-trading between supporters of the McNary-Haugen bill and those who wanted the McFadden branch banking bill. And probably some legislators voted for the measure in disgust at the administration's failure to offer any plan that promised real relief for agriculture. Undoubtedly, too, the bill got votes from men who wanted to embarrass President Coolidge and his administration.

Perhaps more important was the general belief that the President would veto the bill. Thus opponents of farm relief could vote for the McNary-Haugen bill to satisfy their constituents, yet

14 Cowles to Peek, February 19, 1927; and Lowden to Peek, February 18, 1927. Davis Papers.

15 *Wallace's Farmer*, Vol. LII (February 25, 1927), 299.

do so confident that Coolidge would not let the measure become law. During the Congressional debate, it was frequently stated that Coolidge would disapprove any bill containing the equalization fee. Democrat O'Connor said that "on both sides of the House men are going to vote for this bill who . . . snicker at its absurdities and who know that it is unworkable on the theory that the President will veto it."[16]

But would he? This was the question in everyone's mind? Peek wrote on February 22 that "the general impression seems to be that he is going to veto the bill, although I am not going to be surprised either way." One thing was certain. Coolidge did not lack for advice.

During the Congressional debate, and immediately after the bill passed, farmers bombarded him and Jardine with demands either to approve or veto it. An Indiana farmer advised Coolidge to "get the viewpoint of the broad prairie farmer. Don't be a narrow minded hill billy from Vermont dominated by selfish money and manufacturing and union labor interests all your life." A Topeka bank official told Jardine, "it is undeniably true that 90% of our Kansas farmers are solidly back of this measure. It is my best judgment that you should encourage the President to sign the bill."[17]

Even some of those who were lukewarm toward agricultural relief legislation explained to Coolidge that the McNary-Haugen bill should be tried. The Grange had refused to endorse the measure after 1924. However, Master L. J. Taber told the President, "it will be the part of wisdom to give the McNary-Haugen bill a trial." The Grange still preferred the export debenture plan, he said; but if the McNary-Haugen measure became law, it would stimulate rural morale and, more important, it would remove farm relief as a political issue.[18]

Some of the bill's staunchest enemies reluctantly agreed that Coolidge should let the legislation become law. The editor of the *Grain Dealers Journal* declared that the President would be charged with favoring a "small minority," [millers, packers and

16 *Cong. Rec.*, 69 Cong., 2 sess., February 15, 1927, p. 3876; and February 17, p. 4081.

17 A. L. Sheridan to Coolidge, February 24, 1927; and C. B. Merriam to Jardine, February 19. Files of the Secretary of Agriculture.

18 Taber to Coolidge, February 19, 1927. *Ibid.*

other opponents] if he vetoed the measure. "He is left on a limb. The obvious course for him is to yield to the will of the people as expressed by Congress."[19]

On the other hand, a great many people strongly urged Coolidge to kill the bill. The President's underlying strength among the rank and file was indicated by one farmer who said that the bill looked "dangerous" to him, but he added, "what you do will convince me whether it is good or bad for I believe in your judgment."

Two days after the bill passed, Everett Sanders asked Secretary Jardine "whether there is any objection to its approval." The same day Jardine sent Coolidge a twenty-one-page memorandum with a covering letter which concluded, "I do not feel that the bill should be approved." The interesting thing about this exchange of communications is that they took place the same day. Still more interesting is the fact that the memorandum had been typed on a machine similar to that used in the office of Herbert Hoover. The typescript was especially large. It seems certain that Jardine took Hoover's comments and passed them on to the President as his own. Probably Jardine, Hoover, and Mellon had talked over the problem, and this memorandum represented their joint views.

Coolidge sent his long, stinging veto message to Congress on February 25. Could the author of this fourteen-thousand-word document be "Silent Cal"? The first half of the message followed the Jardine-Hoover memorandum almost word for word. Coolidge's main objections, he said, were that the bill was designed to help only a few crops; it involved government price-fixing; the equalization fee represented "the most vicious form of taxation"; that by increasing prices production would be stimulated and consumption would decline, which was "to fly in the face of an economic law as well established as any law of nature"; he expressed opposition to giving a board power to raise farm prices, a scheme which ran counter "to our traditions, the philosophy of our government, the spirit of our institutions, and all principles of equity"; finally, the President said, it would breed a cancerous bureaucracy, and besides, it was unconstitutional. The entire discourse was a promulgation of the laissez-faire position for agriculture.

Reaction to the message depended upon one's attitude toward the bill. Peek and his followers stormed at Coolidge and blasted

[19] *Grain Dealers Journal*, Vol. LVIII (February 10, 1927), 152.

him unmercifully. Coolidge had set up a straw man, and then knocked him down, Peek declared. By March 1 officials of the Executive Committee of 22 had written an answer to the President, attacking his main contentions. This was incorporated in a speech by Congressman Dickinson and distributed widely. One section of the reply said, "The veto message is part of the program that is industrializing America at the expense of agriculture." If this was an exaggeration, at least Coolidge was not forgetting industry. Two days before he vetoed the McNary-Haugen bill, he raised the tariff on pig iron 50 per cent under the flexible provision of the Fordney-McCumber tariff, and within a few days the price rose 50 cents a ton! He signed the McFadden banking bill the very day he disapproved the farm measure. These actions maddened the farm crowd, and were considered further proof of the administration's willingness to sell out agriculture.

But, as was to be expected, the President had a lot of support. Carl Williams, editor of the Oklahoma *Farmer-Stockman,* praised the veto message and said that the McNary-Haugen bill "may be regarded as dead."[20] After congratulating the President, an Iowa farmer accused the Corn Belt Committee of being "the worst bunch of hypocrites that ever met together."[21] Another critic said the entire campaign reminded him "of 1896 and 16 to 1."[22] That was the worst thing he could say!

The administration meant to wring every ounce of political influence out of the veto message. By May 11, the Department of Agriculture had distributed 87,200 copies, and friendly publicity organs throughout the country gave generous space to the President's economic wisdom. Perhaps this would help head off any possible political revolt. However, Coolidge was confident of his position. Despite some signs of dissatisfaction in the Midwest, the mid-term elections held only a few months before had resulted in a general endorsement of his administration.

One problem that continued to plague the McNary-Haugen group was the matter of acreage limitation and production control. This idea gained renewed impetus with the drop in cotton prices. Cries were heard throughout the South during the winter

[20] Williams to Jardine, March 1, 1927. Files of the Secretary of Agriculture.
[21] H. A. Riggs to Coolidge, May 23, 1927. *Ibid.*
[22] C. S. Booth to Jardine, March 9, 1927. *Ibid.*

of 1926–27 that cotton acreage must be reduced at least 25 per cent. A vigorous campaign was waged by farm leaders, bankers, businessmen, and publicists, but cotton acreage fell only slightly in 1927. Here was another example of the futility of voluntary crop restriction.

Nonetheless, there was a growing demand for "balanced production." Most thinking on the subject was fuzzy and indefinite, but the idea gradually gained ground. Somehow price-destroying surpluses must be *prevented,* not dealt with *after* they occurred, it was argued. Jardine, Hoover, Mellon, and other Republican leaders had advocated this idea for several years. Commenting on the McNary-Haugen bill in January, 1927, Jardine had told Senator McNary that if any farm relief scheme was to be permanently successful, it "must include definite provision for stabilizing acreage and production in line with effective demand."[23] He failed to explain how this might be done.

The idea of adopting some type of farm relief which would definitely keep acreage in check was strengthened early in 1927, when W. J. Spillman published his little book, *Balancing the Farm Output.* Although he was an economist in the Department of Agriculture, he explained that his views did not represent the official position of the department. Spillman had much to say about production control. "It must be thoroughly understood," he wrote, "that any plan that will markedly stimulate increase in acreage will fail." He suggested a plan of giving farmers acreage allotments. On production from his allotment a farmer would receive tariff protection and higher prices, but on any excess output he would only receive the world price. This, Spillman believed, would retard acreage expansion and halt production increases.

The agitation for some kind of acreage regulation, however, continued to meet with stern opposition in the strongholds of McNary-Haugenism. Peek would not tolerate it. The only reference to production control in the 1927 bill was one which instructed the board to advise producers "in the adjustment of production and distribution." This provision had been included in most of the surplus-control bills, but was not really important in the minds of Peek and his backers.

[23] Jardine to McNary, January 11, 1927. Files on McNary-Haugen bill, Legislative Branch, National Archives.

Now that the battle had been brought into the open between Coolidge and the advocates of government aid to agriculture, what course should the farm lobby follow? Peek declared that failure to get farm relief rested squarely on the President. He urged the farmers to hold him responsible. He was as determined as ever to carry on the fight, but he was willing to consider compromise proposals so long as the equalization fee was retained.

There were some, however, particularly those wanting to embarrass the Republican party as it was then constituted, who were in no mood to compromise. Hirth wrote to Senator McNary, "Hell will be indefinitely frozen over before I consent to any farm relief measure which does not deal fairly and honestly with the present agricultural situation." If necessary, he said, he was willing to work four more years to compel "common decency at the hands of the Pig Iron crowd who express themselves chiefly through Mr. Hoover."[24] When one of Jardine's friends urged him late in 1926 to confer with the McNary-Haugen leaders and reach some mutual agreement, the Secretary replied, "To get together with these leaders you have got to be for the McNary-Haugen bill."[25] This was true on the fundamental question of financing surplus operations.

Whatever the precise moves of the McNary-Haugen supporters might be, one thing was fairly certain. The McNary-Haugen bill could be passed at the next session of Congress. The farm lobby had never been stronger than in the spring of 1927. Late in 1926, Agricultural Service, a high sounding name for a lobby, had been created. Chester Davis ran the Chicago office, and Walton Peteet headed the one in Washington.

A smooth-working organization, Agricultural Service was aided in late 1926 and early 1927 by more numerous and generous contributions to pay salaries and provide for other expenses. Lowden gave $2,500 to the farm lobby up to March 1, 1927, and was paying it to the Executive Committee of 22 at the rate of $500 a month. Later he gave more. Baruch contributed an additional $2,500, which brought his total up to at least $7,500. Alex Legge gave $2,500; Burton F. Peek, George's brother, $1,500; and S. S. Davis of the Rock Island Plow Company, $1,000. These and various

24 Hirth to McNary, April 23, 1927. Davis Papers.
25 Jardine to J. W. Searson, October 12, 1926. Files of the Secretary of Agriculture.

other contributions were received during the period from July, 1926, to March 1, 1927.

And during the summer of 1927, the co-operatives began donating substantial sums to Agricultural Service. By October over $7,000 had been contributed. The Missouri Farmers Association and Burley Tobacco Growers Association each gave $1,000, and the Mississippi Staple Cotton Growers Association sent $2,286. And Peek continued to make large gifts. Whenever the coffers were empty, he paid the bills out of his own pocket. Of the $15,668 spent by Agricultural Service between March and October, 1927, Peek contributed $4,696, plus paying all of his own expenses. For him the cost of farm relief came high.[26] The largest individual contributors to the fight for farm parity in the 1920's were Baruch, Mark Woods, Lowden, and Peek, all of whom gave $5,000 or more each. Peek spent several times that amount, although he never kept any account of his outlays.

From records available in the Peek and Davis files, it is not possible to determine accurately the total amount of money spent by the farm lobby between 1924 and 1928. From the scattered evidence, however, it does not seem likely that direct expenditures exceeded $50,000. This does not include money spent by individual farm organizations, such as the Farm Bureau, Farmers Union, Illinois Agricultural Association, the Missouri Farmers Association, and others which spent hundreds of dollars. But farm leaders were discovering what other pressure groups already knew —it cost money to lobby. The figures given here seem rather inconsequential to Americans living in the second half of the twentieth century—a generation which saw the American Medical Association spend $267,747, and the American Farm Bureau $63,988 for lobby expenses during the first nine months of 1952. But in the 1920's, when farmers were only beginning to grasp the importance of lobbying on a national scale, expenditures of $10,000 to $15,000 a year seemed quite substantial.

The various farm groups interested in the McNary-Haugen bill did not always work in entire harmony. Some members of the Corn Belt Committee were jealous of the publicity and credit which went to Peek and the Executive Committee of 22. Hirth explained to Davis that some leaders "had it in their craw that the

26 Financial Records. Davis Papers.

farm organizations have not been put into the picture as much as they deserve to be."

Davis, however, replied that "no man in America can fairly charge that Mr. Peek sought or seeks any credit for what he has done. What he wants is results." The reason Peek had been in the limelight, Davis reminded Hirth, was because the regular farm groups had not kept effective organizations in Washington. "The man or committee that does the job," he said, "must be in Washington and stay there." Then Davis concluded: "The fact of the matter is—and you well know it—that newspapers do not take anyone's word for what has happened in Washington. They knew that the campaign was being directed not from the American Farm Bureau Federation and not by some non-resident and absent committee, but from 1133 Investment Building, Washington."[27] And truly that had been the case.

It can hardly be overemphasized that one of Peek's outstanding traits was his ability, as Davis said, "to keep that agglomeration of dissimilar forces pulling like a team." Some of the farm leaders were prima donnas, concerned over their place in the picture and nursing little feuds and jealousies. "I never ceased to marvel at George's patience," Davis wrote, "and his ability to handle them without appearing to do so." In the fall of 1927 the farm lobby, under Peek's skillful guidance, was not only ready to repass the McNary-Haugen bill, but, if necessary, to try to pass it over a presidential veto.

[27] Hirth to Davis, May 20, 1927; and Davis to Hirth, May 21, 1927. *Ibid.*

Chapter XII

Final Defeat

IF THE farm relief campaign had accomplished nothing else by 1927, it had at least forced many national leaders to reorient their thinking on agricultural problems. They had been driven, however reluctantly, to accept the principle that the federal government had some responsibility for the welfare of American farmers. No longer was it a matter of whether the government should do anything. The question was, What kind of federal aid?

And more than ever before, businessmen were giving farm problems serious attention. In April, 1926, the National Industrial Conference Board published an admirable survey of the agricultural situation entitled *The Agricultural Problem in the United States*. It emphasized the significance of agriculture in the total economy, a point which Peek and other farm leaders had persistently stressed. The following month, the National Industrial Conference Board organized a businessmen's commission on agriculture to make a further study of farm problems. Reporting in November, 1927, the commission recommended gradual tariff reduction on manufactured goods and approved the principle of making the tariff effective on agricultural commodities. The report suggested establishing a federal farm board to help stabilize farm prices, but warned against the government directly "buying . . . farm products for this purpose until it is conclusively demonstrated that the result can not be accomplished in any other way." While the commission repudiated the McNary-Haugen bill, it did concede that the federal government had some responsibility for helping to solve farm problems.

Late in April, 1927, Peek, Davis, Sam Thompson, Earl Smith,

Hirth, and other farm leaders met in Chicago to consider the prospects of repassing surplus-control legislation. They agreed unanimously to stand behind the McNary-Haugen bill, and to fight harder than ever to preserve the vital equalization fee.[1]

One of the crucial questions in the spring of 1927 centered around the attitude of Senator McNary. Strong rumors persisted that he was about to support a bill which would please the President. Was McNary weakening? Fearing that he might be, Hirth sent him an urgent plea on April 23, saying that half a loaf would be worse than nothing. But McNary replied that he had been misquoted in the press, and that he would not desert the McNary-Haugen cause.[2] At the same time, however, Chester Davis said that McNary intended to do everything possible to work out a plan which the administration would accept. This seemed like political common sense.

During the early summer, Frederic P. Lee, legislative counsel of the Senate, worked out a new McNary-Haugen bill. Lee had been the strong right arm of Peek and Davis in framing farm legislation. Because of the widespread belief that production would be stimulated under legislative price-raising, Senator McNary insisted that something be added to the bill which would penalize increased output. He also wanted to include more commodities in order to meet Coolidge's objection that the bill favored a few crops.

While the McNary-Haugen leaders were drawing up a new bill and laying plans to pass it, Senator Norbeck attacked the problem from another angle. During the spring, he and Congressman William Williamson induced Coolidge to spend his summer vacation in the Black Hills of South Dakota. It was thought that if Coolidge visited the Midwest, he might become more sympathetic to legislative schemes for lifting farm prices. Norbeck also wanted to get presidential support for the Mount Rushmore National Memorial, which was being carved by the flamboyant and unpredictable Gutzon Borglum.

However, this stategy backfired. The first day Coolidge appeared at his temporary offices in Rapid City, he met State Senator J. L. Robbins, who warmly grasped his hand and said, "Mr. Presi-

[1] Chester Davis to McNary, May 2, 1927. McNary Papers.
[2] McNary to Hirth, April 29, 1927. *Ibid.*

dent, I wish to congratulate you for your courage and wisdom in vetoing the McNary-Haugen bill." Norbeck was deeply chagrined. But this was only the beginning. An increasing number of summer White House callers praised Coolidge for his veto. If anything, the President's trip to South Dakota convinced him that his action had been much more popular than some of the vocal farm spokesmen would have led him to believe.[3]

While Coolidge was in South Dakota, he announced that he did not choose to run for another term. His decision gave an added political cast to the farm relief question. Thinking of Hoover, Peek declared that Coolidge's withdrawal should warn "other anti-farm relief members of the administration" not to seek the Republican nomination in 1928. Peek claimed that his contact with farmers indicated strong support for Governor Lowden. Thus, as the agricultural forces mustered their strength to repass the McNary-Haugen bill during the fall of 1927, the political implications of farm relief were constantly in the forefront.

Meanwhile, Jardine was actively promoting his own farm relief ideas. His plan, similar to the Curtis-Crisp bill, provided for establishing a federal farm board which would encourage co-operative marketing along commodity lines. It also called for creating stabilization corporations which in emergencies would buy and hold farm surpluses to keep prices from falling to unprofitable levels. He advocated "an ample revolving fund" to be supplied by the government to finance carrying surpluses from year to year. Jardine also stressed the importance of adjusting production to demand. This was essential, he argued, to achieve "that economic stability of agriculture which we all hope to attain."

While these ideas had been favored by the administration for several years, Jardine began pushing them with unusual vigor in the summer of 1927, as a means of counteracting the McNary-Haugen scheme. An interview with the Secretary appeared in the Washington *Star* in August, 1927, and in September he outlined his position in an article for the *Farm Journal*. The Department of Agriculture sent out hundreds of reprints of these articles to friendly farm leaders, editors, economists, and politicians.

Among those who had been asked to comment on Jardine's

[3] Gilbert C. Fite, *Peter Norbeck: Prairie Statesman* (Columbia, Missouri, 1948), 128.

plan was Carl Williams. Although he favored the scheme, Williams wisely explained to Jardine that government loans to co-operatives might never be repaid. The government, he said, "by loaning money to surplus-control organizations, is actually in the business of handling farm crops and of bearing the loss, if any." Williams added, however, that he had no objection to the government going "into partnership with the co-operatives financially as well as morally."[4] The Oklahoma City editor had analyzed the situation accurately, but it sounded strange coming from the camp of those who opposed the McNary-Haugen bill on this very score.

Despite Jardine's strong backing for his co-operative marketing measure, it won only scant support at the grass roots. Eric Englund, department economist, reported to his chief in July that people in the Midwest had only a "hazy idea" of the Secretary's proposals. The Fess-Tincher and Curtis-Crisp bills, he said, had not impressed farmers. Englund admitted that the McNary-Haugen leaders had kept their idea alive "with real skill," and urged the Secretary to carry out "an offensive pushing of your program."[5]

Acting on Englund's advice, Jardine promptly contacted many of the co-operative leaders to gain support for his farm relief plan before Congress met. But the response was disappointing due to the effective work of the McNary-Haugen group. Ernest Downie, general manager of the Kansas Co-operative Wheat Marketing Association, wrote that every farm organization in Kansas except his own, was working for the McNary-Haugen bill. "At the present time," he explained, "I have no hope of uniting the farm organizations of this state in favor of a large pool or in favor of anything except the McNary-Haugen bill."[6]

Jardine was also unsuccessful in winning southern support. Actually, many co-operative officials in the South favored the idea of liberal government loans to co-operatives. They would have been satisfied with the Jardine type of legislation. But midwesterners kept them in line. C. O. Moser, general manager of the American Cotton Growers Exchange, admitted that his organization felt "friendly toward Secretary Jardine's proposal." He considered it "futile and foolish" to continue advocating legislation

---

4 Williams to Jardine, March 30, 1927. Files of the Secretary of Agriculture.
5 Englund to Jardine, July 25, 1927. *Ibid.*
6 Downie to Jardine, September 12, 1927. *Ibid.*

which would probably be vetoed by the President. But then he explained the predicament of southern farm leaders:

> The Mid-Western group are unalterably opposed to any kind of a loan plan. It appears that they are accepting nothing except the equalization fee with the right to raise the American price of food stuffs to the world price, plus the tariff, to what they designate an American price. Of course, in cotton we have no such views. We only want to take off of the market temporarily unneeded surpluses, and are not thinking of the American price as being higher than the world price. . . . However, we are in this difficult position, . . . and that is, we can get no legislation that will be of any great benefit to us if, at the same time, wheat is not benefitted equally, and the Mid-Western farmers claim that nothing will help wheat except an effective tariff added to the world price. You will, therefore, observe that we are in a most embarrassing position. They do not want a loan bill and say it will not serve their purpose—we can not get anything less without their approval and the support of their legislative representatives. Even if we could get something, and it would not help wheat—it would not long help cotton. In the meantime, we have the highest personal regard for Secretary Jardine. We do not share the views that some of the farm leaders express concerning the Administration. It looks as though we are in a serious deadlock, but if we must choose defeat by one way or another, our Committee has decided, as difficult as such a decision is, that they must go along with the other farmers.[7]

It is clear that Jardine knew even before Congress assembled that he could not woo southern cotton and tobacco co-operatives away from the McNary-Haugen fold.

Agricultural representatives of the South and West met in St. Louis on November 1 and 2, and declared that the McNary-Haugen bill "embodied the only practical method yet proposed to extend equality to agriculture." This meeting, however, was not without political implications. After citing broken platform pledges, the farm delegates said that agriculture needed "a fair,

[7] Moser to Eric Englund, November 7, 1927. *Ibid.*

sympathetic and courageous" administration. Southern influence was more evident in St. Louis than at the 1926 gathering. The main promoter, at the suggestion of Peek and Davis, had been George Donaghey, former governor and president of the Arkansas Farm Relief Club.

Peek and his supporters had been able to hold their lines secure, despite the tactics of their opponents. During November and December, the principal farm organizations, except the Grange, passed resolutions reaffirming their devotion to Peek's legislation. When Congress met in December, farm relief spokesmen were on hand to present their usual plea. Congressional hearings, where differences between the authorized farm leaders and representatives of the administration were brought into sharp focus, were held intermittently throughout January and February, 1928.

The McNary-Haugen proponents made it clear that they would be satisfied with nothing less than a bill which included the equalization fee. Speaking for the Farm Bureau, Chester Gray said it would be better to have no farm legislation if the fee were omitted. On the other hand, many congressmen and senators were strongly considering a compromise measure which would leave out the controversial fee. But farm leaders would not budge on this question. They kept exerting pressure on the House Agriculture Committee until on March 20 it voted 13 to 8 to retain the equalization fee. That finally settled the issue for all practical purposes.

On other issues the farm spokesmen were more willing to compromise. In the first place, much more emphasis was placed on production control in the 1928 bill. In the revised measure one of the principal duties of the federal farm board would be to "advise producers through their organizations or otherwise in the development of suitable programs of planting or breeding, so that burdensome crop surpluses may be avoided or minimized." Furthermore, if the board found that farmers were ignoring advice on planting and production of a given commodity, it could "refuse to make loans for the purchase of such commodity." The demand for production adjustment, which had been advocated by the administration and others, was finally accepted by the agrarians in letter if not in spirit.

Moreover, the 1928 bill applied to all crops, although equaliza-

tion fees were not to be collected on perishable fruits and vegetables. Help to these commodities could come only from loans to
their co-operatives. By eliminating the idea of including only basic
crops, the McNary-Haugenites hoped to meet the President's
charge of favoritism for special commodities. To be provided was
a larger revolving fund of $400,000,000, not over half of which
could be loaned to co-operatives at any one time. These loans were
to help the co-operatives carry seasonal surpluses and to expand
their marketing services.

The board was also empowered to make marketing agreements
with co-operatives or other agencies in order to dispose of surpluses. Any losses arising from the "purchase, withholding, and
disposal" of a commodity were to be paid out of the revolving or
stabilization fund. If this fund was insufficient, then equalization
fees were to be levied. Actually, the 1928 bill included the Jardine
plan of federal aid to co-operatives, but as a second resort equalization fees could be levied to raise sufficient money to pay export or
storage losses. Peek and his backers were certain that government
stabilization funds would not be sufficient to finance the program
and fully expected, if the bill became law, that an equalization
fee would be necessary.

The McNary-Haugen supporters had made important concessions to Coolidge and Jardine. The bill applied to all crops, and
co-operative marketing, the administration's answer to farm problems, was to be given strong backing. Only on the equalization fee
did the farm lobbyists remain unmoved, and even it was to be used
as an alternate device in case the revolving fund was insufficient.
Looking at the four-year history of the McNary-Haugen bills, one
sees some important shifts of position. These were prompted by
administration pressure, political expediency, and a desire to satisfy the co-operative marketing associations.

As originally drawn, the McNary-Haugen bill was an emergency measure. Later versions were designed to put agriculture
on a permanently prosperous basis. Emphasis was gradually
changed from price-raising to price-stabilization. Nothing was
said in the 1927 and 1928 bills about ratio-prices or making the
tariff effective. Peek and his group were still thinking in terms of
equality for agriculture or parity, but political expediency had
forced them to omit this concept from the bill. Furthermore,

greater stress was placed on orderly marketing and the later measures were tied in closely with the co-operative organizations. Peek's first plan had called for giving help to only a few basic commodities which were burdened by a chronic surplus, but in the later bills all commodities were included and different methods were provided to deal with the special problems involved.[8]

Although Peek and the farm leaders had made significant modifications in their scheme, they still had the substance of the original proposal. The board had sufficient power to engage in price-lifting operations, and the idea of dumping surpluses abroad at below domestic price levels—the two-price system—was still retained.

In the spring of 1928 the farm lobby was less evident around Washington than during previous sessions. Chester Davis declared, "It looks as if we are not backed up by very much interest in the country when all the Senators can see around are George Peek, Frank Murphy, Dr. Kilgore and myself."[9] It really did not matter, however, since congressmen and senators were already committed, one way or another, to the measure. Those who were still unconverted would not have changed their minds if all the farm representatives in the country had descended on Washington.

The farm lobby was strengthened, too, by the approaching presidential campaign. The specter of an aroused electorate was an unpleasant and disturbing thought to many federal legislators, and they hardly dared to return home without at least a gesture toward farm relief. Likewise, the virtual certainty that Coolidge would veto the measure again prompted some congressmen and senators to vote favorably, although they disliked it.

On April 12 the Senate passed the last McNary-Haugen bill 53 to 23, and on May 3, the House approved it 204 to 122. Some minor differences in the House and Senate bills were resolved in conference committee. The conference report was accepted by the House on May 14, 204 to 117, and by an unrecorded vote in the Senate two days later. A most interesting aspect of the 1928 vote was the large number of senators and representatives who did not vote. Although supporters in the Senate picked up six votes over 1927, 17 senators did not record a preference. Actually, most of these opposed the bill. In the House 108 did not vote, while only

---

[8] 70 Cong., 1 sess, *Senate Doc., No. 141.*
[9] Davis to Earl Smith, April 5, 1928. Davis Papers.

39 were in that category in 1927. The number of yea votes was slightly less in 1928 than in 1927.

It was common gossip that the President would again veto the bill. On May 5, before Congress took final action, a large delegation of farm leaders visited Coolidge. Among those who urged him to approve the measure were Peek, Senator McNary, Sam Thompson, Davis, Kilgore, Murphy, Earl Smith, William Settle, Hearst, and Hirth. They told Coolidge that their new bill represented an honest effort to meet every objection expressed by him "without departing completely from the fundamental principles for which the farm groups . . . have been contending for years." Turning to the problem of the equalization fee, they said that experience had proven that co-operatives could not handle price-depressing surpluses without it.[10]

But Coolidge was true to his principles. On May 23, he sent a considerably sharper veto message to Congress. The bill in some respects, he said, was less objectionable than its predecessor, but it still contained features, particularly the equalization fee, which were "prejudicial . . . to sound public policy and to agriculture." Moreover, he declared that the measure was still unconstitutional, and was "as repugnant as ever to the spirit of our institutions, both political and commercial."

The President's main criticisms were that the bill attempted to fix prices, that the equalization fee was an unjust and dangerous tax, that extensive bureaucracy would result, that it would encourage profiteering by middlemen; and that it would stimulate overproduction and aid foreign agricultural competitors. Coolidge advised Congress to follow his farm program which was essentially one of loans to co-operatives, plus reduced production. His plan of assisting farmers to help themselves, he said, was within the framework of American traditions.[11]

At this point it is appropriate to analyze briefly President Coolidge's veto messages. Any study of the Coolidge discussions forces one to conclude with agricultural economist John D. Black that some of his arguments were valid, while many of them were naïve and irrelevant. It must first be emphasized, however, that

10 Statement in the McNary Papers.
11 70 Cong., 1 sess, *Senate Doc. No. 141.* An attempt to override the veto in the Senate lost by a vote of 50 to 31.

the President's messages reflected a philosophy, a definite point of view, regarding the function of government in economic affairs, especially in relation to price and income received by particular groups. Farmers might be encouraged to help themselves, Coolidge thought, but he denied that the federal government should fool with agricultural prices.

On the other hand, Peek and many of his farm followers believed that the government did have some responsibility for maintaining a prosperous agriculture. If this required government aid to lift farm prices, they favored it. As shown earlier, Peek had been greatly influenced by his wartime experiences that had revealed the effect which government could have on economic trends and price levels. He saw no economic fallacy, or departure from American tradition, in a program whereby the government aided agriculture, since it helped other economic groups in various ways. And throughout the 1920's Peek and other farm leaders constantly insisted that the country could not be permanently prosperous if agriculture was depressed.

The philosophic conflict between the McNary-Haugenites and their opponents was a gulf that no legislative compromise could bridge. Much of the importance of the fight for farm relief lies in the basic differences over the role of the national government in American economic life. Surplus-control advocates recommended a degree of planning for American agriculture which was designed to give farmers more control over agricultural prices. However slight this planning may have been, it was nonetheless repugnant to such rugged individualists as Coolidge and Hoover. Thus, besides the agrarian-versus-industry theme which ran through the farm fight, an equally important conflict was the fundamental difference of opinion over the function of government. It is significant to add, however, that many of Coolidge's most bitter critics, including Peek, were about as conservative as the President on major political issues, except on the matter of aid to agriculture.

To Republicans, such as Coolidge and Hoover, who were still worshipping at the shrine of William McKinley, the McNary-Haugen bill represented a dangerous change in the traditional relationship between economics and government. Hoover felt so strongly on this point that he was almost blinded to reason. In discussing government operation of business, socialism, fascism, and

Sam H. Thompson
president of the American Farm Bureau Federation
1926–31

collectivism, Hoover later wrote in his *Memoirs,* "My colleague, the Secretary of Agriculture [Henry C. Wallace] was in truth a fascist, but did not know it, when he proposed his price- and distribution-fixing legislation in the McNary-Haugen bill."[12] To have made such a charge in the heat of the campaign against farm relief would have been one thing, but to state it as reasoned opinion in the light of history demonstrates a bitterness and ignorance unworthy of Hoover.

Considering Coolidge's specific objections, it is plain that his charge of unconstitutionality was largely irrelevant and that he merely added this point to strengthen arguments which he considered entirely sufficient on other grounds. His charge of price-fixing, and that the board could "raise the domestic price to the consumer, not only the full amount permitted by the tariff but as far above that as the board might deem proper and expedient," was gross exaggeration and a half-truth. The board could not have raised prices above world levels more than the extent of the tariff which was determined by Congress and the President under the flexible provision. To a degree it could be considered price-fixing, but, as Professor Black has pointed out, only in "the same way that the tariff is price-fixing." And the degree to which prices could have been lifted was definitely limited.

Coolidge was bitterly opposed to the equalization fee, which he called a "sales tax upon the entire community" designed to benefit producers. It was not a tax for revenue purposes in the ordinary sense, he declared, but a levy for the help of a few. One could argue against the protective tariff with equal logic, and this was a weak approach coming from the stronghold of protection.

What the President considered administrative complexities of the measure aroused his sharpest language. This charge does not carry much weight as it might be made against almost any government device. Simplicity of administration is desirable; yet, as Rexford Tugwell later observed, "lack of it ought not to prevent the adoption of a desirable policy." It might be better, Tugwell said, to do something difficult than to do nothing at all.[13] In light

12 Herbert Hoover, *Memoirs, The Cabinet and the Presidency* (New York, 1952), II, 174.
13 R. G. Tugwell, "Reflections on Farm Relief," *Political Science Quarterly,* Vol. XLIII (December, 1928), 481–97.

of developments in administration during the following quarter-century, it seems certain that an intelligently selected board could have properly administered the law.

Actually, Coolidge did not stress his most fundamental objections to the measure in either of his veto messages. He was basically opposed to raising the cost of living and the price of raw materials because of the adverse effect this would have on the competitive position of American industry. Secretary Mellon had stated this plainly in June, 1926. Undoubtedly, he had expressed Coolidge's views. Coolidge was bound by what Tugwell called "a stubborn determination to do nothing." There were sound economic arguments against the measure which he might have expanded, but his real opposition stemmed from "a doctrinaire unwillingness to depart from laissez faire" for American agriculture.

What about the bill's major weaknesses? While much of the presidential argument rested on flimsy evidence, he did touch on two glaring faults. Increased prices, he said, would stimulate production and intensify the surplus problem. Moreover, he emphasized that export dumping would encourage antidumping and other restrictive trade measures by foreign countries, thereby reducing our export markets. These two basic objections were enough to condemn the plan in the minds of most people.

In this connection it is of interest to consider the attitude of economists. There was no dearth of comment from this quarter. Tugwell, Irving Fisher, B. H. Hibbard, George F. Warren, Joseph S. Davis, Alonzo E. Taylor, Edwin G. Nourse, John D. Black, Eric Englund, E. R. A. Seligman, Allyn A. Young, and Bernhard Ostrolenk were among the better known professional economists who gave serious consideration to the McNary-Haugen proposals. Generally speaking, most professionals opposed the plan. Allyn Young of Harvard explained to President Coolidge early in 1927 that he believed "practically every competent economist in the United States" thought it was unsound. "Not since Mr. Bryan's free silver campaign of 1896 have the American people been asked to agree to an unsounder economic proposal."[14] In this connection, Henry A. Wallace once summed up the opinion of agricultural economists held by most farm leaders. Wallace said that he was tired of

[14] Young to Coolidge, February 4, 1927. Files of the Secretary of Agriculture.

economists who could find a hundred reasons to oppose a bold move to help agriculture but who never had a constructive idea of their own!

As mentioned earlier, in 1923, Eric Englund, who was then at Kansas State College, fired one of the opening guns against the ratio-price plan.[15] He cited the higher cost of living, artificial stimulation of production, and public opposition as major weaknesses of any government program to increase farm prices.

The next year Rexford Tugwell began publishing a series of articles on farm problems. He pointed out the disadvantages suffered by agriculture in the over-all economy, and was more favorable to social planning than most of his professional colleagues. He tried to show that production was not so sensitive to the price mechanism in agriculture as in most industries, and that farmers were inclined to produce despite low prices. He admitted that farmers needed special help, but he criticized the McNary-Haugen bill because it aimed at extending an unfair system of favoritism to a special group like those already enjoying tariff protection. He also attacked the economic nationalism of the McNary-Haugen supporters. By 1928, Tugwell had modified his views. He believed that the plan might have succeeded if some way could have been found to keep higher prices from increasing production. "I should liked to have seen it tried as a beginning," he said. Then he concluded, "As a piece of social legislation it surpasses anything an American Congress ever formed."[16]

Analyzing surplus-control legislation in 1925, B. H. Hibbard of the University of Wisconsin, like most of his colleagues, argued against the McNary-Haugen bill's economic feasibility. He said that the measure was "woefully inadequate to fit the complexities of the market," particularly regarding the many kinds and grades of farm products. If prices were raised on a few crops, he believed that other growers would also demand help. Passage of the measure would put the nose of the camel under the tent, he said, and the government would ultimately become the country's greatest

[15] Eric Englund, "Fallacies of a Plan to Fix Prices of Farm Products by Government Control of the Exportable Surplus," *Journal of Farm Economics,* Vol. V (April, 1923), 86–101.

[16] R. G. Tugwell, "The Problem of Agriculture," *Political Science Quarterly,* Vol. XXXIX (December, 1924), 549–91, and "Reflections on Farm Relief," *ibid,* Vol. XLIII (December, 1928), 481–97.

dealer in farm commodities. Privately, Hibbard was more critical. He told Chester Davis that the McNary-Haugen bill was an "ill-conceived preposterous bill." "Of all the ways not to . . . help the farmers I would give this bill either first rank, or, at least, honorable mention."[17]

The two economists who gave the most intensive study to the McNary-Haugen bills were John D. Black of Harvard and Joseph S. Davis of Stanford. Black wrote several articles on farm problems with special reference to surplus-control legislation, and he included a chapter on the subject in his unsurpassed book, *Agricultural Reform In The United States,* published in 1929.

Black never openly endorsed the McNary-Haugen plan, but he was much more sympathetic to its aims and possible success than most others in his field. If raising farm income is a legitimate end, and "if the measure will accomplish this," he wrote, "then on such a basis it is economically sound. . . . If economic soundness implies the value of ends, then reasons enough in terms of broad national policy can easily be found for asking the cities to subsidize the country a little for a few years. If it has been good policy to subsidize industrial developments for so long, why is it not good policy to subsidize agriculture for a change, in view of its recent history and present status."[18] But Black raised a word of caution. "The attendant consequence most to be feared would be expansion of production in the newly subsidized lines, followed by abandonment of the plan, leaving the grower in a worse plight than now."[19]

Joseph S. Davis and Alonzo E. Taylor made a most detailed analysis of how the plan might be applied to wheat. Skeptical of long-range proposals for economic planning in agriculture, these economists referred to the McNary-Haugen bill as "a far-reaching departure in American agricultural policy," and a "huge experiment." They concluded that the scheme could be made to work but "that its net outcome, within a few years, would be a

17 B. H. Hibbard, "Legislative Interference With Prices," Academy of Political Science *Proceedings,* Vol. XI (January, 1925), 184–97; and Hibbard to Davis, March 1, 1926, Davis Papers.

18 John D. Black, "McNary-Haugen Movement," *American Economic Review,* Vol. XVIII (September, 1928), 425–27.

19 John D. Black, *Agricultural Reform in the United States* (New York, 1929), 254.

serious disadvantage to wheat growers and would create fresh maladjustments in American agriculture. The greater the early success of the measure, the greater would be the prospect for its ultimate failure." They also argued that higher prices would stimulate acreage expansion and aggravate the problem of surpluses. The effect on acreage, they said, "was the crucial point of the entire proposition."[20]

Therefore, when President Coolidge stressed the matter of growing surpluses resulting from higher prices, he was repeating the position of most professional economists. Also he was describing economic realities as revealed in American agricultural history. It had been clearly demonstrated that price increases of sufficient weight would cause a major expansion of wheat acreage, as well as increases in other crops and certain types of livestock.

There was every probability that if the McNary-Haugen bill had been successful in raising prices to any appreciable degree, surpluses would have developed, obviating most, if not all, of the prospective benefit. The McNary-Haugenites never really answered this argument. In fact, even Peek was forced to admit the validity of it, although in public he claimed that the equalization fee would deter expanded production. Writing to Chester Davis, he said, "I think it is true that a substantial increase in price will bring additional production and that unless the situation is intelligently handled there is danger of breaking down the plan."[21]

It has not been generally known but this question worried the McNary-Haugen leaders much more than they would openly admit. Hirth wrote to Henry A. Wallace in 1926 that if equality for agriculture were achieved, "we will undoubtedly be brought face to face with the problem of overproduction in a manner far more serious than many of the friends of agriculture realize at this time. . . . And if after we succeed our ship encounters rough seas because of overproduction, (as I feel it will) then we must demonstrate that we have enough intelligence to 'sweat our way out.' "[22]

The equalization fee would not have held farm production in check. This is true because the farmers would not have felt the

20 J. S. Davis and A. E. Taylor, "The McNary-Haugen Plan As Applied to Wheat: Operating Problems and Economic Consequences," *Wheat Studies of the Food Research Institute*, Vol. III (February, 1927), 177–234.

21 Peek to Davis, July 31, 1925. Peek Papers.

22 Hirth to Wallace, July 29, 1927. Davis Papers.

cost of the fee directly. And as far as the board advising farmers to produce within certain limits, experience of the Farm Board under Hoover showed that it would not have met with any success. It seems certain that if the plan had been adopted it would have ultimately broken down under increasing surpluses, unless some means had been found to limit acreage and breeding.

An aspect of the problem which never received adequate attention by either the opponents or supporters of the McNary-Haugen bill was the matter of vanishing farm export markets. Foreign demands particularly for American wheat, beef and pork were disappearing. This was due to greater production in European countries, to nationalistic policies of self-sufficiency, to competition from Canada, Australia, and Argentina, and to trade barriers, which were erected partly as a reaction to the American high protective policies.

To build a farm program on the idea of nearly unlimited agricultural export markets was to build on a delusion—unless the United States would have been willing to lower her tariffs so there could have been a freer flow of goods. If exports were to continue high, somehow international trade barriers of high protective rates, quotas, and embargoes had to be reduced or eliminated; or the United States would have to finance its own exports, as it did to a considerable degree in the 1920's, through about seven billion dollars in private loans abroad. The changing position of the United States from a debtor to a creditor nation during and after World War I, placed American international trade in a new light, and most people, including farmers, did not comprehend the significance of this shift.

Nonetheless, assuming that the objective was to raise the prices of certain farm commodities, it is reasonable to conclude that the McNary-Haugen bill, if made law, would have worked for a short time. There is no doubt but that a federal farm board with the taxing power envisioned in the equalization fee could have forced up the prices of farm commodities. Under the prevailing tariff, however, prices could not have been raised as much as many McNary-Haugenites supposed. After making careful calculations on wheat, J. S. Davis and Alonzo Taylor concluded that in 1923–24 and 1925–26 the increase per bushel under the 42-cent tariff could not have been more than 10 or 12 cents at Buffalo, New York. As long as opportunities were available to dump surpluses in foreign markets, the equalization-fee plan would probably have benefited farmers in the United States. If the bill had been passed in 1920 or 1921, there is a strong possibility that it would have worked for the next three or four years, or perhaps a little longer. Farm income might have been increased millions of dollars. But opinion is almost unanimous that in time growing surpluses and falling export markets would have ruined the plan.

There was a chance, of course, that had the bill become law, it would have been revised after trial and error to meet the problem of increasing output. Some plan of acreage restriction or production control might have been added. It must be recognized, however, that political pressure would have worked against any production control amendment, since farmers and their spokesmen bitterly opposed such a policy. As shown earlier, they considered this a part of the program of industrializing America at the expense of agriculture. Further proof of this is seen in the fact that farmers had to sink to the awful depths of the depression of 1932–33 before they would consent to acreage control, and then they did so only reluctantly and half-heartedly.

Yet in considering the McNary-Haugen bill, its many ramifications, and the position of its critics and supporters, judgment must not be made on the basis of available knowledge at mid-century. The scheme must be judged in light of understanding in the 1920's, and of the predominant political and economic philosophy. Peek and the other McNary-Haugenites were struggling, somewhat haltingly, toward a definite goal. Their objective was to formulate an intelligently constructed farm policy which would give farmers greater control over the price of their commodities, and to place agriculture in its proper relationship to the rest of the economy. The very nature of farming, however, made it extraordinarily difficult to frame a program which would permit agriculture to regulate prices as successfully as business and labor. Much more government action was necessary to achieve their ends than envisioned by supporters of surplus-control legislation between 1924 and 1928.

But Peek never lost faith in the McNary-Haugen principles. Russell Lord has recorded a revealing conversation between Peek and Davis during the last Congressional fight over the bill. Davis remarked somewhat wearily: " 'George, this is the last heat I trot. We can't dump surpluses over the sort of tariff walls they're rearing over the water now.' George Peek plodded on, putting his feet down slowly, firmly, as if there were a plow before him. 'The hell we can't!' he said shortly. He never changed."[23]

[23] Lord, *The Wallaces of Iowa*, 273.

Chapter XIII

*Appeal to the People**

PRESIDENT Coolidge's vitriolic veto of the second McNary-Haugen bill assured farm relief a prominent place in the presidential campaign of 1928. Peek had already decided that if Coolidge disapproved the bill, farmers must turn to the ballot box for relief. He had often discussed the role of agriculture in national politics with his old friend and adviser, Baruch. By 1928 they had agreed that unless farmers became politically articulate, they would never obtain their economic rights. So now Peek and Baruch, backed by numerous supporters, were determined to plead their case before the final judges of public policy—the American people. Although Peek had attempted to keep the farm question out of *partisan* politics, he had repeatedly urged farmers to support senators and representatives who voted for the McNary-Haugen bill.

With the presidential vetoes, however, it was obvious that the election of friendly legislators, regardless of party, was not enough. If the McNary-Haugen type of farm relief was to be enacted, a man with an entirely different outlook must be placed in the White House. Midwestern farm leaders hoped they could force the Republicans to nominate a confirmed disciple of McNary-Haugenism. Their favorite candidate was Frank O. Lowden, who, immediately after the 1928 veto, reiterated his devotion to surplus-control legislation. But if the farm relief crowd could not nominate Lowden, it was prepared to trade its influence to the Democrats for support of the McNary-Haugen principle.

* Most of the material in this chapter was previously published under the title, "The Agricultural Issue in the Presidential Campaign of 1928," in the *Mississippi Valley Historical Review*, Vol. XXXVII (March, 1951).

For at least two years Peek and a few others had been pushing Lowden's nomination, sometimes openly but more often quietly. Even as early as 1926, one reporter at a Des Moines farm gathering wrote: "This talk is heard in every group that gathers; . . . that the farmer's hope lies in Frank O. Lowden."[1] Throughout the next year farm leaders wrote and talked constantly about nominating Lowden. Shortly after the first veto, L. F. Greenup of Montana informed Chester Davis, "we have been forwarding telegrams to the Honorable Frank Lowden requesting him to get into the presidential race at the next election."

Peek explained to a friend in South Dakota that people there should get behind the Lowden movement. "I think Lowden knows more about the farm situation than any man in public life, . . . he would make it his first job if elected, to see that agriculture was given a square deal," he wrote. Then Peek, who found it hard to violate his traditional Republican conservatism except on the farm issue, added, "He is safe and sound and his record as Governor of Illinois was remarkable."[2]

Thus the farm leaders worked during 1927 to commit as much political strength as possible to Lowden. And they were not without success. On October 31, 1927, Senator Norbeck announced that he would support the former Illinois governor. This was a clear signal for other midwestern progressives to follow his lead. Some important political figures shortly did declare for Lowden. Among these were Senator Nye, Governor McMullen of Nebraska, and Governor Hammill of Iowa.

But the courageous and independent Norris, one of agriculture's greatest champions, refused to heed the pleas that he support Lowden. He explained to Hirth that Lowden, besides being embarrassed by heavy campaign expenditures in 1920, did "not represent . . . what I want to see in a President of the United States. He does not belong to that faction in the Republican party that, it seems to me, ought to be favored with the nomination." Later Norris declared that, in his judgment, Lowden belonged to the selfish interests in the party. "He is as satisfactory to them as Mr. Mellon or Mr. Hughes, if we exclude the one proposition of the

1 Chicago *Tribune,* July 20, 1926.
2 Peek to C. W. Croes, August 6, 1927. Davis Papers.

McNary-Haugen bill."[3] Lowden did not arouse excitement among many genuine progressives.

After Coolidge announced that he would not seek another term, support for Hoover's nomination mounted rapidly. Therefore, while the McNary-Haugen backers were trying to build Lowden strength, they had to make every effort to thwart the Hoover candidacy. No candidate was more unsuitable from the viewpoint of the militant corn and wheat belt farmers. In April, 1928, as a means of forestalling the growing Hoover popularity, Peek prepared a lengthy statement on the farm problem which was inserted in the *Congressional Record* by Senator Norbeck. Since 1917, the account read, Hoover had been the "arch-enemy of a square deal for agriculture." This and similar charges were repeated thousands of times before the election was over.

No amount of preconvention campaigning, however, could stem the mounting tide in Hoover's favor. When the Republican national convention met in Kansas City on June 12, his nomination was virtually assured. And to the disgust and disappointment of most farm leaders his ideas on agricultural relief were accepted. After a spirited battle in the resolutions committee, the equalization-fee principle was omitted from the farm plank by a vote of 35 to 15. The majority plank, however, was full of promises and sympathy for agriculture. The party pledged to create "a Federal Farm Board clothed with the necessary powers to promote the establishment of a farm marketing system of farmer-owned-and-controlled stabilization corporations or associations to prevent and control surpluses through orderly distribution." The plank further stated: "We favor, without putting the Government in business, the establishment of a Federal system of organization for co-operative and orderly marketing of farm products." This proposal did not even begin to satisfy the McNary-Haugenites, and they prepared to carry their fight to the convention floor.

Some of those representing the left wing of agricultural revolt hoped that a popular demonstration might influence the convention. Several hundred individuals marched through the streets, hotel lobbies, and finally to the convention hall, shouting, "We don't want Hoover." But they were denied admittance. William

[3] Norris to Hirth, November 8 and 15, 1927. Norris Papers.

Allen White observed that these protestants did not represent the lunatic fringe of the farm movement. They were simply obsessed with the idea that only surplus-control legislation of the McNary-Haugen type could save the farmers.[4]

Meanwhile, Earl C. Smith of Illinois was presenting the farmers' side to a noisy and unsympathetic convention. After praising the McNary-Haugen idea, he concluded that if his party hoped to retain the Republican farm vote, it must "fairly and squarely face this issue." Frank W. Murphy, Dan W. Turner of Iowa, and Governor McMullen also spoke in favor of the equalization-fee proposal. Murphy shouted that farmers were tired of sitting in Lazarus-like fashion, begging for the crumbs that might fall from the tables of industry, finance, and commerce. These pleas for a McNary-Haugen-type farm plank were answered by Senator Borah and Congressman Fort of New Jersey. With the oratory over, the convention voted 806 to 278 in favor of the majority plank.[5] So far as the Republicans were concerned, McNary-Haugen principles were cast into outer darkness. Lowden's candidacy now collapsed and he withdrew, leaving Hoover a clear field except for scattered favorite sons.

The Republican convention had not adjourned before Peek and the farm relief leaders were packing their bags to leave for Houston. Settle of Indiana declared, "We are going to Houston and if the Democrats adopt the farm plank they'll get our votes." Chester Davis carried an agricultural plank in his brief case as he left for the Texas city on June 19. "I can not help feeling considerably discouraged over the outlook," he wrote, "I am somewhat skeptical over the willingness of the Democratic party to adopt the right kind of a platform at Houston."[6] But Davis was too pessimistic. Democratic leaders were already planning to capitalize on Republican unrest and dissensions. Perhaps if a suitable farm relief plank could be adopted a large number of normally midwestern Republican votes might be captured by the Democrats. Consequently, the farm leaders were welcomed with open arms in Houston. "We were shown every courtesy from the New York delegation down," Davis wrote.

4 *Daily Emporia Gazette,* June 14, 1928.
5 *Official Report of the Proceedings of the Nineteenth Republican National Convention* (New York, 1928), 145–60 and 175–76.
6 Davis to B. W. Kilgore, June 19, 1928. Davis Papers.

Peek played the key position. In reviewing his activities, Davis explained: "He was the keystone of the structure, although I am sure many of the farm leaders there did not know what was going on. Backed by Mr. Baruch and with the support of Pat Harrison, Senator George and others, George sat with the inside few and they finally accepted the plank as we prepared it with a few changes of their own."[7] He added that if the Democratic farm plank was not satisfactory, "it is because we do not know how to use the English language."

The Democrats did not specifically endorse the McNary-Haugen bill or the equalization fee. However, they recognized the principle of segregating farm surpluses so as to make the tariff effective. The cost was to be borne by the "marketed units of the crop whose producers are benefited." This seemed to be approval of the equalization fee. Peek thought it would be a political blunder to mention the McNary-Haugen bill and the equalization fee by name. He apparently reasoned that Smith would poll more votes if he could be presented as favoring McNary-Haugenism, yet not alienating eastern voters by specifically mentioning it. But he sincerely believed that if the Democratic plank could be enacted into law, it would mean the adoption of his brand of farm relief. Peek and other farm leaders left Houston determined to support Smith, but withholding public endorsement until after his acceptance speech.

A meeting of sixty-two farm representatives in Des Moines on July 16 indicated that at least fifty agricultural leaders were going to vote for New York's Governor Smith.[8] However, could they influence Republican senators and representatives in the Midwest and the average rural voter? It soon appeared that most of the McNary-Haugen supporters in Congress would line up behind Hoover. McNary, Haugen, Brookhart, Dickinson, Nye, and others who had favored surplus-control bills were soon actively supporting the Secretary of Commerce. Governor McMullen described the trend as a general "exodus for the band wagon." Thus, it quickly became apparent that Peek would have a very difficult time holding the farm ranks secure.

In their acceptance speeches both Hoover and Smith devoted

7 Davis to Hirth, July 3, 1928. *Ibid.*
8 Des Moines *Register,* July 16, 1928.

more time and attention to the agricultural issue than any other single problem. After declaring that "the most urgent problem in our nation today is agriculture," Hoover traced his familiar views. Besides an adequate tariff, his plan was to establish a federal farm board with power to aid co-operatives and to build up "farmer-owned and farmer-controlled stabilization corporations which will protect the farmer from the depressing demoralization of seasonal gluts and periodical surpluses." According to Hoover, this program would permit the farmer "to control his own destinies"; best of all, it would not put the government in business.

Speaking several weeks later from the steps of the capitol in Albany, Governor Smith lashed out at the failure of the Republicans to provide adequate farm relief. Like Hoover, he promised government aid to co-operative marketing, plus a plan of dealing with surpluses. He was extremely vague on the latter point, but declared that each "marketed unit" must bear part of the benefit expenses. This appeared to be support of the equalization fee, although Smith said there were "varying plans" for accomplishing the desired objectives.

Hoover and Smith both recognized the importance of the problem, both were sympathetic, and both believed that the federal government was the only suitable agency to bring about effective relief. Hoover was more specific regarding a remedy, but Smith's approach pleased most of the McNary-Haugen leaders because he leaned toward their solution. The Oklahoma *Farmer-Stockman* was not far amiss when it declared: "The McNary-Haugenites will not support Hoover. They will support Smith because they hope that, knowing nothing as to cures, they can get him to take their medicine."[9]

Late in July, Peek was called to New York to confer with John J. Raskob, chairman of the Democratic National Committee, and other leaders. On August 1 he and Raskob were closeted for four hours working out tentative plans for bringing disgruntled Republican farmers into Democratic ranks. The next morning Peek breakfasted with Smith at the Hotel Biltmore. Leaving the conference "beaming and elated," he announced shortly afterwards that he would support the New Yorker.[10] At the same time Smith

9 Oklahoma *Farmer-Stockman*, Vol XLI (September 15, 1928), 660.
10 *New York Times*, August 3, 1928, p. 1.

New York Herald Tribune Syndicate

"They've Tried It on Most Everybody Now,"
by "Ding" Darling
The issue over another bottled product helped lose Al the election

New York Herald Tribune Syndicate

"The Decoy," by Darling
Other matters in the campaign concerned farmers
more than farm parity

declared that he favored the "principle" of the equalization fee.

This satisfied Peek. But much to the chagrin of many McNary-Haugenites, Smith declared two days later that the equalization fee as found in the bills of 1924, 1927, and 1928 was "not acceptable." Further embarrassment resulted when he added that he had no detailed farm relief plan of his own. He proposed to rely on a committee of experts to develop a policy after his election. These statements did not perturb Peek, and he was hard at work with the Democratic National Committee developing plans to carry the corn belt for Smith.

Many promoters of the McNary-Haugen plan, however, were shaken by Smith's wobbly position. Chester Davis told Henry A. Wallace that, while he was personally satisfied, he "did not like the way Smith's statement on the equalization fee came out of New York." About all of the satisfaction Davis could convey to the doubters was that "George seems satisfied that Governor Smith will stand on the principles of our legislation."[11]

On August 2, the same day Peek came out for Smith, Raskob announced that "an aggressive fight to corral the disgruntled Corn Belt farmers" would be launched immediately. The Democrats realized that it was essential to carry some of the midwestern farm states. This could be done only if many of the normally Republican farmers voted for Smith. Under these circumstances, "Peek seemed like a heaven-sent emissary to foment the revolt," wrote columnist Frank R. Kent. The Democrats enlisted his services.

The preliminaries for launching a full-fledged agricultural campaign were started by the Democrats around August 15 under the direction of Chester Davis. Peek was also active, and on August 22 he sent a memorandum to Raskob outlining the financial needs for organizing and canvassing eleven vital farm states from Ohio to Montana. He asked for $499,800.[12]

By the first week in September state-wide independent organizations had been formed in Indiana, Illinois, Iowa, Missouri, and Minnesota to gather the farm vote for Smith. This support for the Governor had developed more or less spontaneously with no special backing from the Democratic National Committee. In order

11 Davis to Wallace and Davis to B. W. Kilgore, August 6, 1928. Davis Papers.
12 Peek and Joseph M. Proskauer, "Memorandum for Mr. [John J.] Raskob." Davis Papers.

to co-ordinate the work of these independent agricultural leagues and farm clubs, the Democrats, on September 10, formed the Smith Independent Organizations Committee with headquarters in Chicago. Peek was named chairman and Davis, vice-chairman. The committee was to direct the farm campaign in the Midwest states, channel funds from the national committee to local workers, supervise advertising and publicity, and, in general, foment revolt against the Republicans in the farm belt. Peek explained that the committee must destroy the claims that Hoover was a friend of the farmer, while building up a constructive picture around Governor Smith. Farmers must be convinced that agricultural relief was paramount in the campaign and that a vote for Smith was a vote for McNary-Haugenism or something closely akin to it. The Smith Independent Organizations Committee was to confine its activities exclusively to farm relief.

The Democratic National Committee was not in a penny-pinching mood and readily agreed to give Peek the nearly $500,-000 which he had requested. Beginning late in September he was to receive $100,000 a week until the election.[13] This amount proved to be about one-fourteenth of all the campaign funds reported by the Democrats. It was a bold but not a reckless move by the Democratic high command, and it was good strategy even if the midwestern farmers did not jump at the bait. Not often in the country's history had such a concentrated campaign been planned to influence a specific class of voters on a single issue in a definite area. A tremendous burden rested on Peek. However, he was equal to the task. Under his aggressive guidance, independent agricultural leagues were soon formed in Ohio, Indiana, Illinois, Missouri, Iowa, Nebraska, Wisconsin, Minnesota, the Dakotas, and Montana for the sole purpose of electing Smith and Robinson. These leagues co-operated closely with the state Democratic organizations, but were completely independent of local control.

In each state the agricultural or independent league functioned under a president or chairman. Wherever possible a prominent Republican farmer was asked to head up the agricultural campaign for Smith. When the proper organization was effected, an initial contribution, usually $2,500, was sent to the league's

[13] See "Report on Audit of Accounts," appended to the "Report of the Smith Independent Organizations Committee." Davis Papers.

state headquarters by the Smith Independent Organizations Committee. More funds followed as they were needed, but each state was to keep approximately within a $25,000 limit. The money was used to carry on state-wide, county, and township organizational work. State and local workers were paid, the former as much as $100 a week, the latter $3 to $5 a day, plus expenses. Naturally there were many volunteer workers who were active because they believed that "farm relief was the real issue."

Minor problems quickly cropped up to plague Peek and his organization. Some states were slow in organizing, and effective work was delayed well into October. In other cases, officers of the agricultural leagues were dilatory and unenthusiastic and had to be replaced. And there were temporary financial difficulties which greatly annoyed Peek, but in the long run did not handicap his work. The Democratic National Committee finally provided the $500,000 promised, but often Peek had to plead for funds. On October 1 he wrote to Hugh Johnson, who was then working with Baruch, urging him to impress Herbert H. Lehman with the importance of getting money to Chicago immediately. "We must have this money quickly. . . . I can not go ahead with the work unless I am assured that these funds will be forthcoming." Two days later he told Johnson, "this annoyance about funds must be removed. . . . I am giving my 'guts' to this thing and I do not think it is fair for me to be subjected to the unnecessary annoyance."[14] Peek got the money he needed and by careful planning he was able to return $100,000 to the Democratic National Committee after the election.

The basic problem which Peek faced was convincing farmers that agriculture was the most significant question in the campaign. Would the farmers place economic interest above considerations of liquor and religion, as well as traditional party fealty. Even before the national conventions some observers recognized the difficulty of isolating the farm issue. Sam L. Morley of the Oklahoma Cotton Growers' Association warned, "Our farmers are being misled, and are having their attention called to the Wet and Dry issue; and a lot of them are falling for this propaganda."[15] The editor of the Des Moines *Register* saw that no ref-

14 Peek to Johnson, October 1, 1928. Peek Papers.
15 *Oklahoma Cotton Grower* (Oklahoma City), June 10, 1928.

erendum could be achieved on the farm relief question. While he believed that the McNary-Haugen bill was the best relief measure proposed, he argued that it would be futile to try to fight the campaign on this issue. "Too many other things enter into the choice of the next president to make anything like a farm movement for one candidate or the other successful. Our presidents are not chosen on single specific issues."[16] How well Peek was to learn this! It proved to be impossible to overcome the powerful prejudices against Smith's religion and his stand on prohibition in the conservative-thinking, largely protestant, rural areas.

Peek and the Smith Independent Organizations Committee were flooded with letters showing that in most rural areas the liquor and religious questions overshadowed the farm problem. An anti-Hoover Missouri farmer asked, "If Smith is elected will the Pope of Rome rule the United States?" "I am shocked," wrote an indignant Kansas farm wife to Mrs. Verna L. Hatch, who headed the women's work of the committee, that "we have a woman among us who would lay aside such matters as Prohibition [and] Catholicism as mere nothing . . . and even think that farm questions are foremost." An Iowa farmer lamented to Chester Davis, "if there is any one class that will defeat Governor Smith it is the Methodists of this country."[17] The pro-Smith farm leaders who favored prohibition were constantly challenged as to how they, as drys, could support Smith, a wet. Julian Friant of Missouri replied that he was doing more farming than drinking, and was more interested in obtaining better prices than in keeping "some fellow in New York from getting a glass of beer."[18]

Peek had hoped that most of the farm organization heads would bolt to Smith, but here, too, he was disappointed. While a large number of this group did vote for the Governor, most farm leaders in the Midwest saw that their constituents would not follow them so they refused to campaign against Hoover. Charles E. Hearst, president of the Iowa Farm Bureau and a close friend of Peek's, explained, "Believe me, George, if I felt we could do other than is being done here, we would be doing it . . . but let me repeat, the dry, protestant, republican State of Iowa can't be stam-

16 Des Moines *Register,* July 17, 1928.
17 Letters in the Davis files, October, 1928.
18 Julian Friant to Peek, August 21, 1928. Davis Papers.

peded into going back on their former principles without more definite assurance than they have now that the act will accomplish the purpose."[19] Such reports from the grass roots and leadership levels should have dampened any enthusiasm of Peek and his helpers in Chicago, as well as that of their superiors in New York.

Smith's equivocal stand on the McNary-Haugen bill and the equalization fee caused some of his supporters much embarrassment and weakened his position, both among farm leaders and ordinary dirt farmers. His attempt to promise more than Hoover without alienating conservative interests met with little success. Smith announced early in August that the equalization fee was unsatisfactory, but that he favored the principle. He repeated this in several campaign speeches, including his major agricultural address at Omaha on September 18. He declared time and again that he favored establishing "an effective control of the sale of exportable surplus with the cost imposed upon the commodity benefited." A reporter in Oklahoma City asked him if that was not the equalization fee, but Smith shot back, "not necessarily." When questioned if he could be quoted as not favoring the fee, Smith impatiently retorted, "I don't think I should say that."[20] Smith kept insisting there were "four or five plans" for achieving the principle which he favored. He never elaborated on any of these, however; in fact, he admitted that he was not familiar with them all!

Smith's straddle on the agricultural issue did not instill confidence nor win the ballots of wavering farm voters. Rather it resulted in confusion. Peek apparently favored this strategy as did Smith's eastern supporters. Peek traveled with Smith from Chicago to Omaha and declared that the Governor's speech there was just "what I wanted." Smith evidently had privately assured Peek that, if elected, he would back the equalization fee, but his public utterances were sources of confusion and misinterpretation. Therefore, it was up to Peek and other leaders to convince the farmers that Smith was sound on the main features of McNary-Haugenism. Peek's correspondence reveals that this was not a simple task. Such a close friend as Sam P. Bush of Ohio said that, "if I thought Smith would truly support the equalization fee I should feel inclined to vote for him."[21] Bush was clearly in doubt as to Smith's position, even after assurances from Peek.

19 Hearst to Peek, August 10, 1928. *Ibid.*
20 Chicago *Daily Journal*, September 21, 1928.
21 Bush to Peek, October 2, 1928. Peek Papers.

One of the worst results of Smith's "agricultural straddle" was that it left the way open for many prominent Republicans who had favored the McNary-Haugen bill to support Hoover in good faith and without the least embarrassment. Many were sincerely convinced that there was little difference between the Republican and Democratic positions. Smith failed miserably to make the farm issue clear cut.

The main reason he could not bring the agricultural question into sharp focus was because he never really understood it. Smith could recite the McNary-Haugen jargon and repeat the farm shibboleths, but that is about all. Besides Peek, Rexford Tugwell and Hugh Johnson tried to explain the agricultural question to Smith and his advisers. When Tugwell went over the McNary-Haugen plan with Mrs. Henry Moskowitz, one of Smith's advisers, her immediate reaction was, "why, that will raise the price of food won't it?"[22] Such was the grasp of farm problems by some of those close to the New York Governor.

Senator Norbeck declared that Smith's apparent disapproval of the equalization fee had materially hurt his chances in the Midwest, because most farmers believed there was no difference between him and Hoover on agriculture. Henry A. Wallace and Senator Nye were among other farm leaders who agreed. "I have not been able to see any material difference in the platforms or public utterances of the two parties and their candidates," Nye wrote. Norbeck and Nye were undoubtedly influenced by party considerations, but Smith's position was not one to arouse enthusiasm and confidence in tried and trusted McNary-Haugen supporters who would have the responsibility of placing future legislation on the statute books. Although Senator Norris backed Smith, he did not do so primarily because of the Governor's stand on agriculture.

Most office-holding Republicans who had favored Peek's legislation were unwilling to risk party disfavor by bolting the G.O.P. on the farm issue. They had little to win and much to lose by such action. And when Governors Hammill and McMullen, and Senators Nye, Norbeck, Brookhart, and Shipstead, and Representative Haugen, to mention only a few, refused to support Smith, it left the Democrats with a dearth of farm leadership. The Inde-

22 Interview with Rexford G. Tugwell, June, 1952.

pendent Agricultural Leagues and the Smith Independent Organizations Committee were no match for the influence of Brookhart, Haugen, Dickinson, and Hammill in Iowa, to single out only one state. Senator Nye was frank in stating his position. "I am in entire agreement with you and your associates that the Republican party deserves a thorough whipping," he wrote to Peek, "but if I must help administer that whipping at the expense of rewarding Smith and Tammany I must postpone that whipping."[23] Smith's most vigorous agricultural support came from the Democratic farm leaders, or those Republicans, such as Peek, who had nothing to lose politically by bolting their party. After praising Senator Norris for his independent stand, Milo Reno bitterly declared, "It certainly should bring a blush of shame and humiliation to those jumping-jack peanut politicians, who have talked so loud and blatantly for farm relief legislation and at the crack of the party whip slunk into their kennel."[24]

Hoover had an abundance of capable and devoted campaigners in the entire midwestern farm belt to counteract the work of Peek and his committee. Senator Borah, whom Davis characterized as having no more understanding of farm problems than Andrew Mellon, was the most effective orator on the Hoover side. Throughout the Midwest, in city after city, he drew whoops and shouts of approval as he assaulted and smashed the equalization-fee proposal. His effect was deadly. When Borah spoke, the entire audience was likely to believe that he had just returned from a fresh conference with the gods!

And the erratic Brookhart praised Hoover and his proposed farm program, declaring that he knew "more about handling surpluses than any other man in the world." He criticized Peek unmercifully, saying that he was the "last man entitled to write a farm bill or lead a farm movement." Peek was also subjected to biting criticism from other quarters. "Mr. Peek is about through," said the editor of *The Northwestern Miller*. "His fetish is no longer a political threat. It is even losing caste in its lowly estate of political nuisance."

On October 2, the Minneapolis *Tribune* carried a two-column editorial entitled "A Peek at Mr. Peek." The editor sought to

23 Nye to Peek, September 19, 1928. Davis Papers.
24 *Iowa Union Farmer*, November 7, 1928.

prove that Peek, "the howling dervish" among farm leaders, was not even a real friend of agriculture, and had actually favored lower wheat prices in 1919, when he was head of the Industrial Board. And the charge was uncomfortably true, although then Peek had been concerned with problems of inflation and high living costs. He had written to Baruch that prices for raw materials must be lowered, and he announced in April that "there is every reason to expect lower food prices in the relatively near future."[25] The Minneapolis editor sharply criticized Peek for his inconsistent position between 1919 and 1928, and praised Hoover as a genuine and loyal friend of the farmer. This account probably had little effect on Peek's supporters, but it was nonetheless embarrassing.

Under Peek's energetic leadership, the work of the Smith Independent Organizations Committee was going full speed by mid-October. An extensive advertising and publicity campaign was designed to reach the vast majority of farmers in the eleven-state area. The committee's publicity department spent $75,941 advertising in thirty-five different farm journals, and nearly $50,000 more for newspaper publicity and pamphlet distribution.

"Vote as Farmers not as Partisans" was the theme of most material sent to rural voters. Over 3,200,000 booklets and pamphlets were distributed, mostly during October. When the mails proved too slow, enthusiastic Nebraskans showered one of Peek's addresses from an airplane. The radio was another medium used to reach farm voters, and just before the election scores of personal workers were put in the field. For instance, the Ohio Independent Agricultural League had about one hundred paid employees during the two weeks preceding the election, plus many volunteers. Most of the state organizations had over fifty paid workers.

However, the money, enthusiasm, organization, and hard work of Peek and the Smith Independent Organizations Committee seemed wasted in light of Hoover's striking victory. The Hoover landslide demonstrated that midwestern farmers were in no mood to vote for a New York Tammany Democrat who was a wet and a Catholic. There was little kinship between the sidewalks of New York and the corn fields of Iowa. Peek and his co-workers had been unable to persuade farmers that Smith was sound on farm relief. But more important, they had not convinced farmers that the

25 Peek to Baruch, February 19, 1918. Peek Papers.

agricultural issue was paramount. Rural voters were vitally interested in farm relief, but to many it was secondary to prohibition and religion. The vast majority of farmers favored some kind of a federal program to revitalize their sick industry, but they preferred that Hoover should implement any farm relief legislation.

This is by no means the whole story. Despite Smith's overwhelming defeat in the eleven states canvassed by Peek and his group, it is significant that the election showed signs of a Democratic revival. The most encouraging development for the Democrats was the fact that Republican majorities in most of these states were sharply reduced. In the eleven states under consideration, the Democrats gained 1,987,218 votes over their total in 1920; the Republicans added only 1,572,818. For example, in Iowa, Hoover polled slightly fewer votes than Harding, but Smith won 151,504 more than Cox. In Minnesota the Republicans picked up 41,556 votes between 1920 and 1928, while the Democrats gained 253,457. In North Dakota the Republicans actually lost 28,578 votes between the presidential elections of 1920 and 1928, while the Democrats were gaining 69,241. The election of 1928 clearly shows that from Illinois north and west into Wisconsin, Iowa, Minnesota, the Dakotas, and Montana the trend was definitely Democratic. In some local areas it was quite pronounced, although in others less so or not at all. There were definite signs that farmers had been awakened by Peek's efforts.

It should not be overlooked, of course, that in some of the rural counties which went for Smith there was a relatively large Catholic population. This was the case in Monroe County, Illinois, Traverse and Stearns Counties in Minnesota, and Dunn, Emmons and others in North Dakota. On the other hand, Union County, Illinois, and Mercer and Eddy Counties in North Dakota had comparatively few Catholics. Considering religious preference, no clear pattern emerges. It is difficult, if not impossible, to separate the influences which determined the result in a particular area, because probably in most cases several factors, including local politics, helped to shape the voter's final decision.

Much of the farm support given to La Follette in 1924, coming mostly from dissident or progressive Republicans, went to Smith four years later. Kossuth County in northern Iowa is a good case in point. It had never cast more than 1,861 Democratic votes after

1896. In 1924, Davis won only 1,369, but in 1928, Smith polled 4,-
736. The Republicans polled 2,930 in 1896, increased this to 6,018
in 1920, but dropped to 3,806 in 1924 when La Follette picked up
3,562. In 1928 the Republicans polled 4,878 or only about 142 votes
more than the Democrats. These figures indicate that most of the
La Follette strength went to Smith rather than back into Republican ranks.[26] The best example of this trend on a statewide basis
is found in Wisconsin where the Democrats polled only 68,115
votes in 1924 and 450,259 in 1928. This is not to say that the Democrats were adding only rural votes to their total, but much of their
increased support was coming from farmers. By 1928 farmers from
the Great Lakes to Montana were voting more strongly Democratic
than at any time in twelve or sixteen years.

How much of this can be traced directly to the special farm
campaign conducted by Peek and the Democrats cannot be judged
accurately. Probably the general farm depression of the 1920's,
and the constant spotlighting of agricultural relief by the McNary-
Haugenites, capped by the concentrated work of the Smith Independent Organizations Committee, had convinced many farmers
that they could expect little from the Republican Party. True, a
majority of these rural voters were unwilling to trust Smith, largely because of his religion and the liquor question, but in 1928
many farmers were more concerned about voting *against* Smith
than *for* Hoover.

The significant fact is that the drift was Democratic in a substantial number of farm states as early as 1928. A close analysis of
the voting in this area should have caused the Republicans grave
concern. Certainly, the depression of 1929 strengthened the Democratic trend among midwestern farmers, but it was not the sole
cause of it. Peek had been largely responsible for sewing anti-
Republican seed among farmers, Democrats and Republican alike.
When watered by falling prices and increased foreclosures, it bore
prolifically for the Democrats in succeeding elections, both in
good and bad times.

[26] Edgar Eugene Robinson, *The Presidential Vote, 1896–1932* (Palo Alto,
California, 1934), Table IX, 133–379.

Chapter XIV

The Farm Board Interlude

With the election of Herbert Hoover, an atmosphere of gloom pervaded the old strongholds of McNary-Haugenism. Yet, George Peek and his followers accepted the popular decision with a certain philosophic resignation. They could partially console themselves by the fact that both parties had been forced to give unusual attention to the farm problem. Furthermore, they believed that they would get another chance after Hoover's plans had failed.

But as a farm-policy maker, propagandist, and lobbyist, Peek had accomplished much more than he or his contemporaries then recognized. He had shown farmers and farm organizations that, with effort and sufficient money to form a proper organization, they were as capable of winning the attention of Congress as other special groups. Effective agricultural lobbying really dates from the 1920's with the activities of Peek and the McNary-Haugen group.

More than this, however, Peek had planted and nurtured the idea of parity, a concept which formed the basis of all succeeding farm legislation. The declared purpose of even the Hoover-sponsored Agricultural Marketing Act of 1929 was to place "agriculture on a basis of economic equality with other industries." While the means of achieving this end may have been faulty, it was nonetheless the stated objective. This indicated that the principle had been accepted by most responsible leaders in both political parties.

In order to achieve equality or parity, Peek had impressed farmers with the need for compulsory co-operation. This was the essence of the McNary-Haugen bill, with its equalization fee. The campaign for farm relief between 1924 and 1928 had gone a long way to weaken the reliance of farmers on traditional individualism. Thus by indoctrinating farmers with the idea of compulsory co-operation and group action, Peek helped to usher in an era of collective action among farmers. It is not too much to say that this was a major turning point in twentieth-century agricultural policy. The idea of forced co-operation set a precedent for the Agricultural Adjustment Act four years later.

Peek's insistence that the government had a fundamental responsibility to help agriculture gain a larger share of the national income was gradually accepted. This concept was implied in the price support programs during and after 1933. The attempt by the Federal Farm Board to peg wheat and cotton prices in 1930 was a timid acceptance of the principle that agriculture deserved special government help to maintain prices. Peek's campaign for farm relief did much to prepare farmers for more drastic legislation than that to which they had been accustomed.

The activities of Peek and other McNary-Haugen leaders also prompted farmers to give more careful consideration to the relationship of the tariff to agriculture than at any time since the 1890's. The propaganda about making the tariff effective had caused farmers to seriously question the benefits which they were supposed to receive under the protective system.

By stressing the importance of surplus production, and its effect upon farm prices, Peek unwittingly helped to stimulate consideration of acreage and production controls as a part of any national farm policy. As people pondered his plan of dumping surpluses abroad, some of them gradually concluded that it was more sensible to curtail production to near domestic demands. In other words, there was a growing shift of emphasis from the marketing aspects of the farm problem to those dealing with acreage restriction and production control. Despite Peek's bitter opposition to acreage regulation, the last McNary-Haugen bill had provided that the commodity advisory councils should advise producers on planting and breeding.

By 1928 the idea of compulsory co-operation, the parity concept, and the principle of acreage restriction had all entered the thinking of agricultural policy makers. These were fundamental in the Agricultural Adjustment Act of 1933. And it might be added that it was only a short step from Peek's equalization fee to the processing tax incorporated in the A.A.A. It can hardly be over-emphasized, therefore, that the New Deal farm program was not the work of wild-eyed radicals, eastern college professors, or impractical idealists. It resulted from the ideas and work of hard-bitten practitioners, many of whom leaned toward political conservatism.

George Peek, of course, could not see four years ahead, and in the late fall of 1928 he could not possibly have realized the full importance of his farm relief work. For the moment he was mainly interested in getting away for a long rest. The presidential campaign had been strenuous and tiring. So, in January, 1929, after cleaning up his work at the Chicago office of the Smith Independent Organizations Committee, he and his wife left for San Antonio.

The Peeks had spent several vacations in Texas, and by 1929 George said that he was through with Illinois winters. He thoroughly enjoyed the great Southwest. The winter sunshine was wonderful, the brightest he had ever seen, he declared. And the golf was good. Nearly every day he was on the golf links enthusiastically enjoying his favorite diversion. In the evening the Peeks liked to dine and visit with old friends who happened to stop by, or perchance entertain some new and interesting acquaintance. Peek had several visits with Gutzon Borglum, who was then working on his models for the Mount Rushmore National Memorial in his San Antonio studio.

After such a relaxing schedule for nearly four months, Peek left Texas late in April rested and refreshed. By July, 1929, the Peeks were getting settled back in their Moline house. And it seemed just a little strange. "Do you realize that we have hardly been home since the summer of 1924," Peek told William Hirth.[1] This offhand remark explains a great deal about the effort and sacrifice which he had made in connection with the fight for agricultural equality. After getting back to a normal schedule, Peek invited several friends to visit him in Moline. The contents of his cellar, he told Hirth, were in surprisingly good shape despite his long absence.

While Peek was enjoying the bluebonnets and other signs of

1 Peek to Hirth, July 9, 1929. Peek Papers.

spring in Texas, Congress was wrestling again with the farm problem in Washington. President Hoover called a special session of Congress for April 15 to deal primarily with the tariff and agriculture. After the election, Peek had taken the position that Hoover and his supporters should be permitted to tackle the farm question along the lines laid down in the presidential campaign. He had no faith in the success of Hoover's program, but "it is not my purpose to embarrass him," he wrote. "I only wish him Godspeed."

Others who had been in the front ranks of the McNary-Haugen battles agreed. Baruch said that the farm leaders should wait with open minds "and a kindly spirit for what Mr. Hoover has to propose. . . . Indeed, we should go further and aid him wherever we can, but certainly we should not permit any bunk to be put over by anybody." However, Baruch, like Peek, thought Hoover's plans were mostly "bunk."

The Agricultural Marketing Act was passed in June. It incorporated the main principles for which Coolidge, Jardine, and Hoover had been contending throughout most of the 1920's. It was much like the Fess-Tincher bill of the Sixty-ninth Congress which had been spurned by the McNary-Haugenites. The legislative battle was enlivened when some progressive Republican and Democratic senators attempted to amend the bill by adding the export debenture plan. But Hoover firmly opposed this move and it was defeated.

The new law was designed to aid and stimulate co-operative marketing, to deal with seasonal surpluses, and to stabilize farm prices. The main idea was to form great co-operative organizations for each principal commodity through which the crop would be marketed. A sum of $500,000,000 was provided to loan to co-operatives, so they could make heavier advances to members than was generally the case and so they could market their holdings in a more orderly fashion. It was also thought that if co-operatives controlled a large share of the crop, they could influence prices. In this respect the Sapiro philosophy was clearly evident. The law also permitted the formation of government-financed stabilization corporations to help control unusual surpluses. A federal farm board was set up to administer the law.

The Agricultural Marketing Act was similar to the last Mc-

Nary-Haugen bill in that both were essentially marketing measures. Much of the language was identical. It was "like sprinkling the stall with straw to make the old cow feel at home," said one agrarian leader. The two measures differed mainly in the method of financing surplus-control operations and in the fundamental objective. Of course there was no equalization fee in the A.M.A., and any losses in disposing or handling surpluses would be paid from the $500,000,000 revolving fund. Moreover, the McNary-Haugenites had intended to *raise* prices, while the sponsors of the A.M.A. proposed to *stabilize* them. Most farmers misunderstood the intent of the Hoover program and became extremely critical when the law failed to give them much direct relief.

Despite all of Hoover's talk about reduced production there was no effective provision to curb excessive output. In fact, the section dealing with production control was even weaker than that found in the McNary-Haugen bill of 1928. There was no threat of withholding prospective benefits of the law from those who ignored advice on production, as had been provided in the last McNary-Haugen bill. The provisions in either would not have been effective in materially restraining production. But it is interesting to note that when Hoover had an opportunity to determine the principles of farm legislation, he made no attempt to incorporate adequate means of regulating production.

Peek had no part in framing the new farm bill. McNary asked him to testify before the Senate Agriculture Committee, but he declined. His views were so well known, he said, that his appearance could serve no useful purpose. Only one aspect of the legislative battle keenly interested him. When it became clear that the debenture plan would be defeated, he wrote to Senator Norris and Representative Clarence Cannon that it was essential to "get these fellows on record who do not want to extend the benefit of the tariff to agriculture."[2] He was already seeking political ammunition for the mid-term elections of 1930 and the presidential campaign of 1932.

If Peek and other McNary-Haugen leaders had no faith in Hoover's legislation, friends of the measure were not much more optimistic. Carl Williams, who became the cotton representative on the board, warned his Oklahoma *Farmer-Stockman* readers

2 Peek to Norris, May 8, 1929. Norris Papers.

not to expect too much. The individual farmer might never feel the influence of the Farm Board's activities, he wrote. Even Senator Borah, who had performed so magnificently for Hoover in 1928, admitted that "no very near relief" could be expected, and that actually the Republicans, by passing the law, had not fulfilled their campaign promises.[3] Most everyone recognized that the Agricultural Marketing Act was essentially a political and not an economic answer to farm problems.

The Farm Board set out to weld the local and state co-operatives into regional or national farmers' marketing associations. Then national sales agencies were created to handle each commodity. Probably the most important of these was the Farmers' National Grain Corporation. The Farm Board at first made loans to qualified co-operatives which enabled them to borrow from all sources up to about 90 per cent of the market price on wheat and cotton. But in October, 1929, additional advances were made, covering the full value of the crop in the case of wheat. Prices soon dropped below the loan level, however, and the Farm Board was headed for serious trouble. As prices continued to decline, the board lost more and more money as it advanced the co-operatives funds to cover their margins and loan commitments. By early 1930, grain and cotton stabilization corporations were formed. By entering the market directly and buying wheat, the Farm Board temporarily pegged the price. Hoover had said that he bitterly opposed price-fixing when the McNary-Haugen bill was under consideration, but this was price-fixing with a vengeance.

When the depression grew worse and surpluses mounted, it became obvious that the board could not keep on supporting farm prices—not, at least, unless it had much more money, or unless farmers curtailed production. By June, 1931, the National Grain Corporation held 257,000,000 bushels of wheat and the board announced that it would not attempt to support the 1931 crop. Altogether the Farm Board lost about $345,000,000 trying to stabilize farm prices. Farmers did benefit to some extent, but at times, speculators profited handsomely. Basically, the law was a dismal failure.[4]

[3] Borah to A. S. Goss, July 12; and to R. A. Shepherd, June 12, 1929. Borah Papers.

[4] Theodore Norman, "The Federal Farm Board," Doctoral Dissertation, Harvard University, 1939.

Chester C. Davis
a leader in the fight for farm parity

The Farm Board sought to escape its dilemma by vigorously urging farmers to reduce production more in line with domestic demand. But the idea of production control met the uncompromising resistance of most farmers and their spokesmen. In July, 1930, Alex Legge, chairman of the board, and Secretary Arthur Hyde toured Nebraska, Colorado, Kansas, Oklahoma and Texas, telling farmers that if they expected fair prices, wheat acreage must be cut. They met with undisguised hostility. Although he did not say much, Peek agreed with the most violent critics of the Farm Board on the question of acreage restriction. He referred to the "talk we hear of controlling production" as "extremely dangerous."

By early 1931 enemies of the Farm Board were striking from every direction. From the beginning, members of the grain trade, livestock exchanges, and commission firms had led the fight against the Agricultural Marketing Act. Then, as it became more apparent that the Farm Board could not hold prices at what seemed to be profitable levels, farmers, agricultural leaders, politicians, business men, and others added their voices to the growing chorus of criticism. The board was hard put to find friends. Referring to the board's attempt to support prices, the editor of the Chicago *Journal of Commerce* called it "McNary-Haugenism at its worst." "The McNary-Haugen plan too radical!" exclaimed the indignant scribe. "In comparison with what is now happening, it seems as moderate as Elihu Root."[5]

Throughout the Farm Board interlude, Peek stayed quietly in the background. He really felt sorry for his old friend Legge, who, he said, was trying to administer an impossible law. Not wanting to embarrass Legge, he wrote in July, 1930, "I have not made a single public statement because I felt that the Administration was entitled to an opportunity to make good on its program." On November 11, 1931, Peek broke his long silence when he addressed the War Industries Board Association in New York. He declared that the Agricultural Marketing Act should be amended by adding the equalization fee. Then he warned his former associates that the economic situation was endangering everything they held dear in America. "Communism and other 'isms', " he said, "cannot be combatted successfully with oratory, but only by our providing and maintaining a better system. Sacred regard

5 Chicago *Journal of Commerce*, February 28, 1931.

for the property rights of a large number of small property owners rather than reverence for a small number of large property
owners, is insurance of the highest type for the capitalistic or individualistic system."

Even when the A.M.A. became an obvious failure, Peek did
not attack it directly. Rather, he declared that the farmers' only
real hope "is through a change in administration."[6] Beginning
early in 1930 his chief concern became the defeat of Hoover and
the Republicans. Several of his former supporters urged him to
lead another fight for McNary-Haugenism. But Peek refused.
When Henry Wallace consulted him on this matter, he replied,
"Would it not be better to put forth an effort to elect a president
who will sign a bill when it has been passed by Congress?"[7]

As the board floundered under growing surpluses, Peek quietly poked fun at his former critics. "It makes me smile," he wrote,
"when I think of the criticisms directed against the McNary-
Haugen bill—government in business, price-fixing, uneconomic,
etc." Was not the Farm Board guilty of all these things? he asked.
If the actions of the board were economic, "Adam Smith would
turn over in his grave."[8]

Despite the fact that Peek was temporarily out of the center of
things, he was not idle. In 1929 he, Frank Lowden, Burton F. Peek,
Chester Davis, and a few others established the National Corn-
stalk Processes, Inc. They planned to make wall board out of cornstalks on the basis of processes developed at Iowa State College.
Peek hoped not only to establish a profitable business, but also to
help farmers in Iowa realize cash from the sale of cornstalks. Ini-
tially, he invested around $50,000 in the project, and a plant was
established at Dubuque.

But the difficulty of obtaining a sufficient quantity of raw
material within a reasonable radius, plus the depression, doomed
the venture to failure. Peek and his associates not only failed to
make any profits, but they temporarily lost most of their capital.
In 1936, however, the firm was reorganized as the Maizewood Corporation. Time and circumstances were somewhat more favorable
then, and in the late 1930's. Peek recovered some of his earlier

6 Peek to Charles J. Brand, July 15, 1930. Peek Papers.
7 Peek to Wallace, November 21, 1930. *Ibid.*
8 Peek to Clarence Ousley, January 2, 1930. *Ibid.*

losses. In 1953 the Maizewood business was purchased by the Allied Chemical Company.

Meanwhile, a small group of farm planners were busy promoting the voluntary domestic-allotment plan of agricultural relief. This somewhat complicated scheme has been described as follows:

> . . . it involved raising the price the farmers would receive on the domestically consumed portion of their export crops by limiting sales of such crops in the domestic market. The part of the crop which farmers could sell in the domestic market was called the domestic allotment, and they were given certificates covering that allotment. In order to move a commodity into domestic consumption, processors had to cover the quantities offered for sale with certificates purchased from farmers. The increased return on each farmer's domestic allotment was to result from the fact that he received not only the world price, but also the proceeds from the sale of his certificates. No certificates were issued on production in excess of the domestic allotment, and on this quantity the farmers received only the prevailing world prices.[9]

Since farmers would receive only the world price for production above their allotment, the plan's promoters reasoned that growers would limit their plantings of surplus crops to the allotted acreage. When farmers became keenly aware of the price difference between the portion of their crop used at home and that sold abroad, it seemed logical that they would reduce their production of low price surpluses. This was generally considered the scheme's most important advantage.

Some of the principles of the allotment scheme originated with W. J. Spillman, economist in the United States Department of Agriculture, who outlined a limited-debenture plan in his book *Balancing the Farm Output,* published in 1927. At about the same time Beardsley Ruml, head of the Rockefeller Foundation, independently considered the same principles, basing his ideas on the German "import certificate" plan. He was anxious to find a plan

[9] Chester Davis, "The Development of Agricultural Policy Since the End of the World War," *Yearbook of Agriculture,* 1940, p. 316.

which could replace the McNary-Haugen bill. At Ruml's suggestion, Professor John D. Black of Harvard put the general ideas
into concrete form and incorporated them in chapter ten of his
book *Agricultural Reform in the United States*. It was Black who
coined the term "domestic allotment."

Black's discussion of the voluntary domestic-allotment plan
received wide circulation among the leaders of farm thought. In
March, 1929, Black testified before the Senate Agriculture Committee and declared that, in his opinion, the allotment scheme
was the most feasible thing thus far advanced to handle wheat and
cotton. His discussion of the plan, which was to appear a few
months later in his book, was published in the hearings at the
close of his testimony. After the book was released, Walter R. Mc-
Carthy of the Capital Elevator Company of Duluth paid for print-
ing and distributing some five thousand reprints of the domestic
allotment chapter.

The man who really led the fight for the domestic-allotment
principles was M. L. Wilson. As a professor of agricultural economics at Montana State College, Wilson had made a most intensive study of agriculture in Montana and the Northern Great
Plains area. Originally a supporter of Peek's surplus-control
scheme, he had gradually concluded that production must somehow be kept in check. After studying the allotment proposal, he
decided it was superior to either the equalization-fee or export-
debenture plans. Congratulating Black on his presentation, Wilson said in January, 1930, that the time was "psychologically
right" to depart from the farm relief principles advocated in the
1920's.[10] Wilson not only contacted his professional friends, but
he talked to numerous Montana farmers and won their enthusiastic support. Given the right opportunity, he wrote, "I can hook
them 100 per cent."

After more than a year of intensive letter writing and propa-
gandizing, Wilson had won such influential recruits as Henry A.
Wallace, Henry I. Harriman, president of the Boston Chamber
of Commerce, Senator Norbeck, and others. Harriman, who had
large agricultural interests in Montana, became one of the strongest advocates of the plan. He was a firm believer in economic plan-

[10] Wilson to John D. Black and to H. R. Tolley, January 29, 1930. Wilson
Papers.

ning for both industry and agriculture, and favored government regulation over "the destructive competition from which we now suffer." Harriman was among those in 1932 who were appalled at the spectacle of intelligent, civilized people starving on mountains of wheat and going naked amidst millions of bales of cotton.[11] Unless production was limited, he argued, no plan of farm relief would be of any great value in raising farm prices.

Wallace believed that the plan had most significant long-range implications. It was practical and could be made to work, he told Wilson, providing the country was heading toward state socialism. Then he added that it looked like the United States was actually going that route.[12]

While Wilson did everything possible to keep the idea before the country, economist Mordecai Ezekiel worked on it in the offices of the Federal Farm Board. In April and May, 1932, he prepared several memorandums for Chairman J. C. Stone of the Farm Board, urging the board to give the allotment proposal serious consideration. However, members of the board, as well as Secretary Hyde, refused to consider the scheme worthy of a trial.

By early 1932, Wilson had considerably modified the Ruml-Black plan. At the suggestion of Harriman and Stanley Reed, solicitor of the Federal Farm Board, the idea of trying to compel processors to buy allotment certificates was abandoned, because Reed believed that this was unconstitutional. In contrast, Harriman's legal staff of the United States Chamber of Commerce suggested that an excise tax be levied on processors of basic agricultural commodities, arguing that such a tax would be a constitutional use of the taxing power. Farmers were to receive benefit payments from this fund if they agreed to sign contracts limiting acreage. The tax receipts were to be distributed to producers of designated products on a prorata basis on that part of the crop sold for domestic consumption. The benefits were to approximate the amount of the tariff. Although this was not a particularly valid measurement of the desired price increases, Wilson contended that people had been so educated to "this tariff effective business" that it must be connected with the allotment plan. From that point,

11 Harriman to Wilson, March 12, 1932. *Ibid.*
12 Wallace to Wilson, April 20, 1932. *Ibid.*

he said, they could move more definitely toward production control.[13]

While tariff effectiveness on export crops was the objective for which Peek had been fighting, Wilson had changed the whole emphasis. The allotment plan sought to achieve agricultural equality by balancing production and consumption. Wilson was concerned primarily with production, not marketing. Here was the shift in policy which Peek bitterly opposed, but which through his farm relief efforts, he had done much to encourage. As the domestic-allotment backers worked tirelessly for their scheme, Wilson declared that they were actually "making history right now." How right he was. Acreage restriction and benefit payments were to become main features of the Agricultural Adjustment Act.

Wilson carried on much of his campaign for the allotment plan through W. L. Stockton, vice-president of the Montana Farm Bureau. At all times, however, Wilson was the key man behind the scenes. But when correspondence went out over Stockton's signature, it gave the impression that the allotment proposal had farm organization support. This, however, was not the case. The old McNary-Haugen group was suspicious and skeptical.

Farm Bureau officials were especially wary of the new proposal. Hearst of Iowa wrote to Stockton that he was "too strongly sold on the equalization-fee principle to readily change to another plan." The idea "staggers my imagination," said Ralph Snyder. Earl Smith insisted that he could see nothing in the proposal and suggested crystallizing "sincere thought behind the equalization fee." On the other hand, Hirth declared that the allotment plan would "prove more practical than the equalization fee." But he was an exception among leading McNary-Haugenites.[14]

In this situation Wilson considered it highly important to win Peek's support. Few other men in the country carried as much weight among farmers and agricultural leaders. And Peek had more than ordinary influence among congressmen and senators. It seems likely, however, that supporters of the domestic-allotment plan were more interested in Peek's political support than

[13] Wilson to John D. Black, October 7, 1932. *Ibid.* Harriman became president of the United States Chamber of Commerce in May, 1932.

[14] See Hearst to Stockton, April 13, and Snyder to Stockton, March 12, 1932, in the Wilson Papers; Smith to Peek, April 21, and Hirth to Peek, April 18, 1932, in the Peek Papers.

in his ideas for solving the farm problem. They liked him and respected his opinions, but they also knew of his bitter opposition to production control. Of course, they may have sincerely thought they could convert him to their viewpoint. If so, they did not know George Peek.

In March, 1932, Harriman suggested that the Domestic-allotment advocates hold a meeting in Chicago to discuss the entire situation and to frame a bill. Harriman and Wilson wanted also to consider problems of land use in which they were vitally interested. The official call went out from Stockton and naturally Peek was invited.

The most important outcome of the April conference in Chicago was the selection of a promotion committee, consisting of Wilson, Louis S. Clarke, an Omaha investment broker, Henry A. Wallace, R. R. Rogers, a Prudential Life Insurance Company executive, and W. R. Ronald, editor of the Mitchell [South Dakota] *Evening Republican*. Peek told the conference that he was not enthusiastic over the allotment proposal, but he temporarily kept an open mind. He thought the allotment scheme would be difficult to administer and that his own legislation was simpler. Another advantage of the McNary-Haugen bill, he said, was that it would bring "the least disturbance to existing channels of trade." But even so, because of the critical conditions of agriculture Peek was at least willing to consider plans which he instinctively opposed. "I have many deep prejudices, as you know," he explained to Earl Smith, "but if there is any possibility of getting legislation at this session of Congress, I am willing to lay them all aside."

Could Peek really abandon his "deep prejudices" on farm legislation? After his ten years in the front ranks it would not be easy. And Peek was not a man readily amenable to change. Besides, the increased emphasis on acreage restriction by the domestic-allotment promoters deeply disturbed him. By the summer of 1932, Peek was at odds in his own thinking. He admitted that world conditions had changed. Replying to Hearst, who insisted on clinging to the equalization fee, Peek conceded that foreign markets were no longer available to the same extent as they were when he had first advocated the McNary-Haugen bill. In light of the world situation, more "drastic remedies" were necessary, he wrote.

Despite his recognition of changes both at home and abroad, Peek bitterly condemned production control for agriculture. "I would not consent to arbitrary reduction [of production] at the expense of normal exports," he wrote. "I feel very strong on this point." He said that he would oppose any law which cut production unless a "relationship is maintained of say fifty per cent industrial exports and fifty per cent agricultural exports." In other words, he would not agree to reducing the output of exportable agricultural commodities unless industry was also forced to decrease its foreign sales. Agriculture should not be subordinated to industry by any such policy which, as Peek put it, encouraged farmers to give up their "normal export markets." He argued that the vacuum created by American withdrawal from the export markets would be filled by the products of other countries. He did not want to see American fields lie fallow while Canadian, South American, and Australian farmers took over markets which "had always been ours."[15]

Peek's position showed a degree of uncertainty and confusion unusual for him. In the first place, none of the acreage restriction proposals, including the allotment plan, anticipated complete withdrawal from foreign markets. The idea was to produce enough for home consumption, plus that which could be profitably exported. Furthermore, Peek talked as if, by reducing output, American farm products would be purposely withdrawing from world markets. Actually, United States farmers had *already lost* many of their former outlets even though they had produced at the lowest prices. Thus it was not a question of maintaining a position which the United States currently held, as Peek implied. Rather it was a matter of adjusting American policies to the existing situation and working to restore export markets through revised tariff policies.

Moreover, his idea of balancing industrial and agricultural exports had no particular merit. The country as a whole would not be helped by reducing industrial sales abroad just because they happened to exceed agricultural exports. Anyway, agriculture and industry were not competing for exports to the degree which Peek indicated. The United States exported the commodities for which there was a demand, and the world had greater need of industrial

15 Peek to Wilson, May 31, 1932. Wilson Papers.

products than those produced on American farms. To cut down industrial exports would not have made additional markets for agricultural products. In fact, it would probably have lessened the total sale because of reduced demand by industry at home.

For ten years Peek had talked about giving agriculture the same kind of influence and control over price which first business, and then labor, had been able to achieve in the modern industrial state. Yet, he was unwilling to follow the policies of business and restrict output in order to gain higher prices for farmers. Peek's position in the 1920's should have logically led him to support reduced production to maintain price, but his deep-seated antagonism to a program of economic scarcity for agriculture would not permit him to take this logical last step.

Peek's stand on farm problems must be judged on the basis of his agrarian prejudice. While he talked about a balance between agriculture and industry, farmers were his first concern. And the very fact that he talked of a balance between industry and agriculture indicated that he was thinking in the past, not the present. The balance which he sought had long been upset by a surging industry behind a protective tariff wall, and no government policy was likely to restore it. This was as futile as Woodrow Wilson's talk about "restoring competition." There was much, however, to his anxiety over government policies which might contribute to the *further* decline and inferiority of agriculture in the economy. It was a question of what kind of a balance should be achieved and the degree of industrial preponderance.

Peek had a deep, almost fanatical love for the kind of America which had provided opportunities for him and other young men in the early twentieth century. He believed that farmers were the nation's backbone, and that "the capitalistic system cannot exist without the independent land owning farmer." Unless this class remained strong in American society, he said in 1932, "we will have wide repudiation of debt and social and political disorder of such an extent that the repercussion will be far reaching."[16] And he pointedly warned that the rich would not be immune under such circumstances. If one really accepted the validity of Peek's basic premise that a class of independent, landowning farmers was necessary to preserve American democracy and capitalism, it was

16 Peek to Baruch, June 17, 1932. Peek Papers.

difficult not to agree that any policy which harmed agriculture would hurt the entire country. In any event, it was this belief which motivated Peek's whole farm relief campaign and forced him to oppose any program of restricted production.

Early in June, Peek received an urgent telegram from Earl Smith, asking him to come to Chicago at once to help draw up an emergency farm relief measure. Wilson had been in Washington a few days before presenting the domestic-allotment plan to the House Agriculture Committee, as well as to a group of congressmen and senators called together by Senator Norbeck. But since the allotment proposal lacked public and farm organization support, it seemed futile to work for it at that session. Therefore, Farm Bureau officials sought to push through a temporary price-lifting measure, and they wanted Peek's help.

The Rainey-Norbeck domestic-allotment bill was written by Fred Lee, a Washington attorney who had contributed much to the McNary-Haugen fight. The bill provided payments to farmers of 42 cents a bushel on wheat, 5 cents a pound on cotton, and 2 cents a pound on hogs for that portion of production used at home. The adjustment payments were to be financed by taxing processors. Since the crops were already planted, there was no need to provide for acreage restriction, a principle which neither Peek, Smith, nor Rainey would have then approved. This bill was strictly in accord with Peek's idea of an effective farm measure, since it struck directly at price enhancement. It should not be confused with the Wilson domestic-allotment proposal.

On the afternoon of July 13, Norbeck pushed his bill through the Senate on a voice vote. Within an hour a messenger was on his way to the House with the bill, accompanied by Lee. Friends of the measure in the House, however, were unable to get a favorable rule which would permit a vote, and the next day the Senate, under pressure from Hoover's supporters, voted to recall the bill for reconsideration. This meant the death of farm relief at that session since Congress adjourned two days later.[17]

With both Republican and Democratic opposition the Rainey-Norbeck bill really never had a chance. The Hoover Republicans bitterly opposed it in principle, and Speaker Garner and some other Democrats in the House did not want to pass any legislation

[17] Earl Smith to Henry T. Rainey, September 23, 1932. Rainey Papers.

which might help the Republicans in the approaching campaign. Just before adjournment the Hope-Norbeck bills were introduced to publicize the principles of the Wilson domestic-allotment plan. They were written by Ezekiel and Wilson with some help from Black.

By the middle of 1932, Peek and most farm leaders were more interested in the forthcoming election than in any stopgap legislation. Time and again Peek warned his friends that there would be no effective farm relief so long as the Republicans were in power. As early as 1931, he had said privately that Roosevelt was his first choice for president. On April 30, 1932, Peek wrote the New York Governor urging him to issue a statement saying that he favored some mechanism "to make the tariff effective on surplus crops," and to affirm that the depression stemmed largely from bankruptcy in agriculture. Roosevelt did not commit himself, but he invited Peek to confer with him "if you come East at any time."[18] Although Peek did not meet Roosevelt before his nomination, he was greatly pleased when Roosevelt, during the campaign, stressed making the tariff effective on farm crops and the importance of agriculture in the over-all economy. Peek was also urging Baruch to see that the Democrats adopted "sound" policies for agriculture in their platform. But Baruch said, "The farmer will still vote the Republican ticket, no matter what we put in the platform." He still favored the equalization-fee plan and believed it was the best yet proposed.[19]

After Roosevelt's nomination Peek left nothing undone to win the Midwest for the Democrats. He insisted that what he had tried to do in 1928 could now be accomplished. Farmers, he said, were sick of Hoover and the Republicans. His main theme was that prosperity could not be restored until farm purchasing power had been increased. Peek's own community offered an excellent example of the situation. Many people in the Moline, Rock Island, and Davenport area manufactured farm equipment. When purchases declined, production was cut, unemployment increased, banks failed, and merchants were without business. Reconstruction Finance Corporation money placed in the community would

18 Peek to Roosevelt, April 30; and Roosevelt to Peek, May 19, 1932. Peek Papers.
19 Baruch to Peek, June 13 and 16, 1932. *Ibid.*

not filter down to the working class. No fundamental change could occur, he argued, until "the farmer is in a position to pay his debts and buy something more."

In mid-August, Henry Wallace lunched with Roosevelt and they discussed Peek and his influence in the Midwest. Some of Roosevelt's advisers, Wallace said, tended to discount Peek's effectiveness because of Smith's defeat in 1928. However, Wallace and Henry Morgenthau defended Peek and explained the effect of the liquor and religious questions in that campaign. Wallace left no doubt in Roosevelt's mind about Peek's leadership and influence among farmers and agricultural leaders.[20]

During August, while Peek was helping to organize the agricultural campaign in Illinois, he was also responding to Henry Morgenthau's request for suggestions on farm policy. Roosevelt was preparing to deliver a major agricultural address at Topeka, Kansas, on September 14, and his advisers were seeking counsel from many quarters. Peek warned that Roosevelt should emphasize the general principle of a higher or "American" price for that portion of production domestically consumed, but that he should avoid recommending any specific plan for putting the principle into effect. "I have had a lot of experience with these different farm leaders and I know how opinionated some of them are. It would not do to accept the views of any one or two of them at the risk of offending some of the rest," Peek declared.[21]

At the very time Peek wrote, farm spokesmen who opposed acreage restriction, especially leaders in the Farm Bureau, were urging Roosevelt not to commit himself to any program of production control. Wilson, who had hoped that Roosevelt would vigorously support the principles of the domestic allotment plan, was openly worried. On August 3 he wrote that Roosevelt was receiving a "bombardment" from the "equalization-fee people." "I am a little afraid that he has the feeling that the equalization fee folks have the influence and the votes, although we have the right plan," Wilson said.[22]

Although Peek opposed production control, he did not join

[20] Wallace to Peek; August 29, 1932. *Ibid.*

[21] Peek to Henry Morgenthau, August 12; and Peek to Arthur F. Mullen, August 25, 1932. *Ibid.*

[22] Wilson to R. R. Rogers, August 3, 1932. Wilson Papers.

his old followers who were attempting to sell Roosevelt on the McNary-Haugen plan. He believed that, once elected, Roosevelt would treat agriculture fairly. Peek thought that the Democratic platform and Roosevelt's acceptance speech in which he alluded to the allotment plan, dealt with the farm situation "quite well." With farmers in such desperate straits, Peek was willing to forego any argument over plans. To him nothing could be accomplished until the Republicans were ousted. Therefore, he concentrated all his efforts on the campaign. "It looks to me as though in the campaign for Roosevelt . . . we are in the last line trenches and if he is not elected that agriculture is doomed to peasantry," he wrote.[23] Early in October, Peek, Chester Davis, Earl Smith, Ed O'Neal, and Clifford Gregory met with Roosevelt and Henry Morgenthau in Chicago. The meeting "did some real good," Peek wrote. He seemed convinced that Roosevelt was "sound" on farm relief.

But those who favored acreage restriction and benefit payments had the Governor's ear. Rexford Tugwell, who was advising Roosevelt on most economic matters, arranged for Wilson to visit Hyde Park late in August. Tugwell had "done a good job of selling him the idea," Wilson wrote, although he thought the Columbia University professor should have been a little more definite. But after Wilson's visit, there was no doubt about Roosevelt's position. Arrangements were made for Wilson to draft a speech for Roosevelt to use at Topeka. Following his own inclinations, as well as the advice of Peek and others, Wilson stuck to general principles. Recognizing that it was politically smart to confine his remarks to generalities and philosophy, Roosevelt incorporated the Wilson material nearly verbatim in his Topeka speech. He used about "everything I supplied him with minor modifications as far as the allotment plan is concerned," Wilson jubilantly announced.[24] Despite the general nature of Roosevelt's address, there could be no doubt but that he was referring to the domestic-allotment plan. Both Wilson and Tugwell were overjoyed. Between them, Tugwell told Wilson, they had really ac-

23 Peek to Earl Smith, October 18, 1932. Peek Papers.
24 Wilson to W. R. Ronald, September 15; and Tugwell to Wilson, September 30, 1932. Wilson Papers. The rough draft of Wilson's suggestions is located in the Roosevelt Papers at Hyde Park.

complished something for the farmer. And Tugwell gave credit where credit was due—to M. L. Wilson.

Peek likewise became enthusiastic over Roosevelt's performance at Topeka. After warmly congratulating him, he advised the Governor that "the principle of making the tariff effective for agriculture should be stressed."[25] Candidates running for office in the farm states, he argued, should support the program outlined by Roosevelt in Kansas. He predicted on September 22 that Roosevelt would sweep the country and that anyone who stood in the way would be buried under "an avalanche of votes."

Peek kept doing everything within his power to assure this result. He became a member of the finance committee of the Illinois Division of the Democratic National Committee, and contributed liberally. He also joined the National Progressive League for Roosevelt and Garner headed by Harold L. Ickes. "I shall probably join any and every other worth while movement which has as its purpose Mr. Hoover's defeat," he bitterly declared.

During October, Peek made a number of addresses throughout the Midwest. By radio from Davenport, Des Moines, and other corn belt cities, he urged farmers to elect Roosevelt. From long experience he knew what to tell them, and he had never been more in earnest about anything. For him this was the culmination of a ten-year battle against overwhelming odds. But his long years of work were about to pay off. Referring to the growing political alertness of farmers and their drift into the Democratic ranks, Hugh Johnson wrote, "George is responsible for more political progress in this direction than anybody I know."[26] The Democrats did everything possible to capitalize on Peek's continued bolt from his traditional Republicanism. They played up his agricultural leadership during the 1920's and his position in the campaign of 1928. Unlike four years before, however, practically all of the old McNary-Haugen crowd now joined him in deserting the Republican party.

Roosevelt's tremendous triumph—he carried all the Midwest farm states—pleased Peek more than anything since he had begun his fight for agricultural equality a decade before. For him it was like the return of spring after a long Harding-Coolidge-Hoover

25 Peek to Fred Davis, September 22, 1932. Peek Papers.
26 H. S. Johnson, *Blue Eagle From Egg to Earth* (New York, 1935), 142–43.

winter. Congratulating Roosevelt on the "magnificent victory," he declared, "I regard it as a victory for Americanism."[27] Then remembering Baruch's statement about midwestern farmers always voting Republican, he could not refrain from telegraphing his "dear chief," "Congratulations but do you still think farmers always vote Republican?"

At last the time had come when agriculture would get a new deal. Peek wanted nothing more. He had no desire for place, power, or patronage. On the farm question he did not have a single selfish motive. Truly he had said that he was in politics for agriculture, not in agriculture for politics. His reward would come when the farmers had been helped. He was intensely selfish and demanding for agriculture, but completely unconcerned about himself. When the administration had paid its debt to the farmers, Peek would consider that he had been rewarded for all of his effort and expense.

Did Peek want to be secretary of agriculture? Many of his farm friends insisted that he was the best qualified man and that, from the viewpoint of service to agriculture and to the Democrats, he should be appointed. Even Henry Wallace recommended him. On November 17, Wallace wrote Roosevelt that Peek had been the "most energetic and determined of all the men who have been fighting for 'equality for agriculture' since 1921. . . . When some of the farm leaders were ready to falter, he had stiffened their shaken morale." Wallace added that Peek had a deep appreciation of the economic situation and "it seems to me . . . that George Peek can be of extraordinary value to you in the cabinet with the situation as it now is."[28] The same day Wallace telephoned Hirth, asking what he thought of Peek's appointment. "I lost no time in shouting 'fine,'" Hirth replied.[29] Many other farm officials wholeheartedly agreed.

It is not likely that Roosevelt would have appointed Peek, regardless of his support from farm groups. The members of his brain trust probably did not want a man of Peek's dominance, persistence, and fixed ideas. And it is significant to note that Roosevelt never saw Wallace's letter of recommendation. At least

27 Peek to Roosevelt, November 9, 1932. Peek Papers.
28 Wallace to Roosevelt, November 17, 1932. Copy in *ibid.*
29 Hirth to Peek, November 18, 1932. *Ibid.*

Arthur Mullen reported this to Peek.[30] There was strong suspicion that Louis Howe intercepted it.

Peek certainly did not seek the office, although he would not have refused it as is evidenced by his statement that he would not "duck or run."[31] But he added, "I am not anxious to assume such responsibility." He wrote to Hirth: "About the job—do you not think I would be a d--- fool to accept it and all the grief which goes with it? My position has been vindicated and that means everything."[32] Indeed, his position did seem vindicated—at least for the moment.

[30] Peek Diary, entry for March 22, 1933.
[31] Peek to Charles Hearst, December 5, 1932. Peek Papers.
[32] Peek to Hirth, December 5, 1932. *Ibid.*

Seven Months in the A.A.A.

IT WAS understandable for George Peek to feel that he should have a major part in developing any New Deal for American farmers. No one in the United States had given so much time and money in trying to work out a national agricultural policy. "I had bought it and paid for it and wanted to have something to say about the kind of legislation we were to have," he told Henry Wallace.

Regardless of what one may think of Peek's ideas, his part in publicizing and dramatizing the farm issue had been of inestimable value. And many loyal friends and supporters believed his ideas were sound. They expected Peek to furnish the same kind of aggressive leadership which he had demonstrated so well between 1924 and 1928. He would not disappoint them.

By early December, 1932, George and Georgia, his wife, were back in Washington. They took an apartment at the Carlton Hotel and settled down to help finish the farm fight. Agricultural leaders were then considering emergency legislation along the lines of the allotment plan. It called for benefit payments to growers of basic crops on that portion of their production used in the United States, providing farmers agreed to reduce their output as recommended by the secretary of agriculture. The payment was to be sufficient to bring the average commodity price up to a fair exchange value, or parity. Wheat, cotton, hogs, and tobacco were considered basic, and money to finance the plan was to come from processing taxes. The major farm organizations, meeting in Washington, December 12 and 13, had approved these principles which were incorporated in the Jones bill.

The winter of 1932–33 was a tense and hectic one for Peek. Day after day, throughout December, January, and February, he worked and conferred on the principles of farm legislation. The Peek apartment was always a beehive of activity. Friends and acquaintances came at all hours of the day and night. It was not uncommon for visitors to show up early enough for breakfast or to be there until midnight, or past. The telephone was always ringing, so it seemed. Georgia Peek, who, like her husband, lived and breathed farm relief, not only served as wife and hostess, but as adviser, part-time secretary, and errand boy. If George was too busy to write a particular letter, she would do it, or if papers and plans had to be rushed to a senator or congressman, Georgia hailed a cab and went to Capitol Hill. Working together, the Peeks would sometimes become so engrossed in their task of preparing statements and data that everything else, including meals, was forgotten. "We worked so long over 'Comments' on the Agricultural Bill that we forgot to have any dinner and late at night we ordered up some oyster stew," Georgia Peek wrote in her diary. In some ways the feverish activity was reminiscent of the most exciting McNary-Haugen days. But now the atmosphere was more charged with excitement, and the pressure to do something—just anything—was greater.

Peek had not been in Washington long before it became apparent that he was in sharp disagreement with many of his old friends. The emphasis of Henry Wallace, who was to become secretary of agriculture, of Wilson, Ezekiel, and others on production control caused him deep dismay. After one conference, he declared that "farm leaders were being led off by economists." The winter had been one long, "unpleasant experience," he wrote in March, 1933.

Peek felt that he must fight the acreage-restriction and production-control group with all his might. Never accustomed to fencing, he struck with sledge-hammer blows. His first big punch against the trend of events was delivered on February 14, when he appeared before the Senate Finance Committee. He had been asked to discuss the relation between agriculture and the causes of the depression, a subject of paramount importance to Peek. Backed by pages of facts and figures, he told the senators that a major cause of the depression could be traced directly to low farm purchasing power since 1921. The disparity between agriculture and industry must be corrected, he said, by raising farm prices.

Then he took up the subject of production control. Peek maintained the widely held view that there was really no such thing as overproduction. If people both at home and abroad had sufficient food and clothing, he believed there would be no price-depressing surpluses. Therefore, the objective of any government program should be to maintain parity prices for that amount consumed at home, and somehow find markets for the surplus. Thus Peek took the position that the problem was essentially one of handling the supply after it had been produced, not controlling production.

A homely illustration of the underconsumption theory had been presented to Secretary Hyde in 1931 by a Texas cotton farmer. He urged that the government convert some nine million bales of cotton into blankets and overalls and distribute them to the needy through the Red Cross. The Secretary sat down and did some figuring. He replied that, if nine million bales of cotton were so converted, they would make 1,125,000,000 two-pound blankets, and 2,250,000,000 pairs of overalls weighing one pound each. Roughly, he said, this would be 9 blankets and 18 pairs of overalls for every man woman and child in the United States. "A family of five," he concluded, "would get forty-five blankets and ninety pairs of overalls!"[1] Hyde was not impressed with this solution.

Peek and all of those who opposed production control undoubtedly represented a majority of American thinking. The idea of forced scarcity was repulsive to most citizens. The files of the Secretary of Agriculture for that period bulge with complaints against policies of restriction. A railroad worker wrote to Henry Wallace on June 14, 1933: "Perhaps the railroad officials are getting enough to buy sail cloth for their yachts but we shopmen are not able to buy clothes, we are wearing rags and using flour and feed bags for towels and pillow slips. . . . We go to market once in a while to look at the nice vegetables then go home and eat macaroni and oatmeal. Is this the new deal? Give us decent wages and there won't be any surplus of either cotton or vegetables."[2]

Opponents of production control not only criticized the prin-

---

1 Arthur Hyde to a Texas cotton farmer, August 20, 1931. Files of the Secretary of Agriculture.

2 Railroad worker to Wallace, June 14, 1933. *Ibid.*

ciple, but argued that practically it was impossible. For example, Peek presented figures to show that about 75 per cent of the variation in wheat output was due to factors other than acreage. On this point William Allen White wrote satirically: "What is to be done with the young sow of subnormal intelligence and bad home environment—or the headstrong individualist who would set her own impulses above somber judgment of the Party and insist on having eight or ten little piggies instead of the allotted six?"[3]

Thus, in his testimony, the "Man from Moline" harshly criticized the general policy of production control. Speaking of wheat, he said:

> For many years I have protested against the expressed view of those who advocate the restriction of agricultural production to the demands of the domestic market, and I have pointed out the unfavorable effect such a policy would have, not only upon the farmer, but upon our whole economic structure—commerce, transportation and finance. The social effects, too, would be far reaching and destructive. I have pointed out also that the vacuum created in the world's agricultural market by our withdrawal would be—in fact is being—filled by other exporting countries. . . . Such withdrawal would dry up our own resources to the direct advantage of foreign nations.

A little later, he added: "Any plans for the restriction of agricultural production to the demands of the domestic market involving substantial curtailment of acreage, except occasionally in case of great emergency, as in case of cotton at present . . . should not be adopted as a permanent national policy." He argued that the government should adopt a program which would remove the price disparity for agriculture and restore foreign markets rather than cut production. These two policies were inseparably linked in his mind.

Having outlined his own views, he then scored the Jones bill. First, he said that, in the form it passed the House, too many basic commodities were included—wheat, cotton, hogs, rice, tobacco, peanuts, and butterfat. Peek believed that only wheat, cotton, hogs, and tobacco should be considered basic, meaning products

[3] Copy of White's statement in *ibid.*

on which benefit payments would be made. He declared that prices for these exportable crops were disproportionately low, and that "the prices of these commodities are believed to be a controlling factor in establishing prices for other agricultural commodities."

Secondly, he declared that marketing agreements should be added to the bill. This is signally important in light of his later insistence on attacking the surplus problem from this angle. "The purpose of such marketing agreements," he said, "is to put the agencies of government behind private enterprise (corporate and co-operative) in disposing of surpluses and to aid in maintaining for producers the fair exchange value for their commodity." Peek believed that price-raising agreements between processors and other agencies handling farm products and the government could be successful. He said that "if the results secured from these marketing agreements are such as to raise prices of agricultural commodities to the fair exchange value, there may be no occasion for the issuance of adjustment certificates and the collection of taxes from the processor." If under such agreements, however, prices did not rise to parity, then the difference between the fair price and "the prevailing market price should be paid to the farmer by the Government, and the Treasury should be reimbursed by means of an adequate tax on the processor," he declared.[4]

Furthermore, Peek argued that if in a great emergency the government did have to reduce the amount going to market, it should "arrest the harvesting of a part of any commodity by paying to the farmer the local market price, less the cost of completing production." If supply must be reduced occasionally, he said, it should be done in those states and areas producing the surplus. He also thought any restrictive provision should be administered on the state level and not from Washington.

Of course, Peek demanded at all times that farmers should have parity prices on that part of their production used in domestic consumption. In the first domestic-allotment bills, the idea had been to make the tariff effective. But the concept of equality or parity for which Peek had been fighting for ten years was incorporated in the Hope-Norbeck and Jones bills. The tariff idea had been superseded by the ratio-price or parity plan, because, even

4 *Investigation of Economic Problems,* Hearings before the Senate Committee on Finance, 72 Cong., 2 sess., February 14, 1933, pp. 108–45.

if the full amount of the tariff could have been added to the price of basic commodities, it would not have been enough in the crisis.

The Peek farm relief principles could be summarized as follows: marketing agreements, plus benefit payments sufficient to bring farm prices to parity; an aggressive program to find export markets; and restriction of production only as a last resort.

During the rest of February, Peek worked on amendments to the Jones bill, but the Senate took no action. It did not matter, since Hoover would probably have vetoed any legislation like that passed by the House. Action on agricultural relief had to await the new administration. Most Americans, and none more than Peek, waited impatiently and watched the Hoover regime pass unmourned.

On March 4, while Franklin D. Roosevelt was raising the hopes of millions by his stirring inaugural address, Peek was back in Moline. There, for the first time, he began to get rumors of why he had not been offered the job of secretary of agriculture. Paul Preston, one of his friends who had recently talked with Wallace, explained that Peek would have been asked to serve except for his friendship with Baruch. Secretary Wallace had remarked that President Roosevelt did not completely trust Baruch and his "New York connections." The new Secretary had also expressed the fear, according to Preston, that Peek would resent his appointment and refuse to co-operate. "I explained," Peek said, "that his fears were groundless and I would help in any way I could without stultifying myself."[5] Besides, Peek would rather have had Baruch's friendship and confidence than any public office.

There is no doubt, however, but that later differences between Peek and Wallace stemmed, to some extent, from Peek's resentment against the Wallace appointment. Perhaps Peek would have liked to be secretary of agriculture more than he cared to admit. In any event, he wanted a man in the post who was imbued with Peekian principles. Wallace was looked upon as kind of an outsider, an interloper, by the leaders of McNary-Haugenism. He had not been on the firing lines during the discouraging days when Calvin Coolidge ruled the White House. Peek's friends sensed this feeling, and he revealed it in his book *Why Quit Our Own*. He referred to Wallace as "a dreamy, honest-minded and rather

[5] Peek Diary, entry for March 4, 1933.

likable sort of fellow," but one who had "never been an active member of our farm group and had not gone through the days of battle." However, there was no sign of this feeling in the critical spring of 1933. The main thing was to get some farm legislation— at once.

On March 9, at Wallace's request, Peek left for Washington to help frame the new agricultural program. Two days before he had written to "Dear Henry" that he did not care about the details of legislation, but "I want to see the principle of fair exchange value become the law of the land so that never again may agriculture be subjected to another experience of the same kind we have passed through for the last twelve years."[6] On Sunday, March 12, Wallace met with Peek and a large group of farm leaders in his office. After the discussion, the Secretary turned to Peek and asked him if he would administer the new law when it passed. "I said 'no,'" Peek wrote in his diary, "but would be glad to help him in whatever way I could by advice and etc."[7] But he soon changed his mind.

Worry over administration, however, was slightly premature. First the principles of legislation had to be agreed upon, and then Congress must act. On March 16, the administration presented a bill which had been prepared in the Department of Agriculture. Peek appeared before the Senate Agriculture Committee on March 24, and repeated much of what he had told the Senate finance group a month earlier. He emphasized that broad administrative powers must be given to the secretary of agriculture "to deal with the various ramifications in this very complex industry." He thought the legislation must be flexible. No single prescription, he said, would fit every crop.

Peek made it clear again that he considered marketing agreements, not production control, the most important part of any new legislation. But the hearing revealed that some of the Senators thought otherwise.

SENATOR SMITH: Every element of this bill is to restrict our production to domestic consumption, . . . and we therefore, under these artificial methods can raise the price perhaps to a profit-

6 Peek to Wallace, March 7, 1933. Peek Papers.
7 Peek Diary, entry for March 12, 1933.

able level for that portion that is sold domestically. That is the logic of it.

MR. PEEK: Senator, your understanding of it is just exactly the opposite of mine. My understanding of it is that we are going to put the power of Government behind the farmers and the processors of farm products, to the end that we may raise prices to a fair level within the United States and meet world competition without having the price break down within the United States.

While Peek belittled the possibility of successful planned production in agriculture, he agreed that some provision for control should be in the bill.

MR. PEEK: It might be well occasionally to go in the particular areas in a particular season, after the prospect of the crop was well in sight, and remove a proportion of the maturing crop and destroy it rather than have that proportion destroy the whole industry. That is what happens with unregulated, uncontrolled supply. . . .

THE CHAIRMAN: . . . you don't mean to advocate, in order to maintain prices, the destruction of crops that are already produced, do you?

MR. PEEK: I would destroy them before I would let the slight surplus destroy our whole national economy; yes, sir.

The next day Wallace outlined his views on the new farm bill. Unlike Peek, he considered acreage control and regulation of production the cornerstone of the measure. He told the committee:

Production must be balanced with consumption if the price levels are to be maintained at any level that is fair to the farmer. This is particularly true when we face the burdensome carryovers of cotton and wheat. . . . It is necessary that the administration have not only the authority to control acreage planted, but also to control production marketed, in order to meet the varied circumstances.

However, Wallace did not completely discount the validity of marketing agreements. He said that the bill should provide for them and agreed with Peek that they "may in many instances assure producers a fair return without the necessity for the processing tax and rental or benefit payments." "The marketing agreements," he said, "also afford a means of providing relief for many minor commodities with respect to which acreage or production control and rental or benefit payments are not contemplated."

Despite Wallace's emphasis on production control, he did not favor a permanent policy of reducing output only to domestic demands. "I do not contemplate such reduction of acreage as meaning that we permanently forsake our foreign markets," he declared, "but only that we should face the fact of the existing carry-overs and control the acreage planted with a view of keeping the new production in accord with our potential domestic and foreign markets." But the question of developing additional foreign markets, he said, was "still at the mercy of an undetermined national policy."[8] From this testimony, it is clear that Wallace and Peek agreed in general on what ought to go in the farm bill, but they differed greatly on emphasis and on the possibility of increasing exports.

The Agricultural Adjustment Act, which was signed by the President on May 12, was broad enough to win the hearty support of those whose primary interest was acreage control and also that of those who advocated marketing agreements. The law sought to achieve agricultural equality by working toward the restoration of parity prices. The purchasing power of farm commodities was to be raised to the 1909–14 period, with the exception of tobacco, in which case 1919–29 was designated. This was to be done by limiting production and eliminating surpluses, by making direct payments to farmers who participated in the production control programs, and by working out voluntary agreements with processors and distributors of farm commodities in order to get higher prices and eliminate marketing abuses. The program was to be financed by processing taxes. The basic commodities on which benefit payments could be made in return for agreements to curtail acreage

---

[8] *Agricultural Emergency Act to Increase Farm Purchasing Power,* Hearings before the Senate Agriculture Committee, 73 Cong., 1 sess., March, 1933. See the Peek testimony, pp. 73–104; and Wallace, pp. 128–49.

or production were wheat, cotton, corn, hogs, tobacco, rice, milk, and milk products.

The law did not lay down any rigid formula for solving farm problems or raising agricultural prices. The secretary of agriculture was given wide powers to meet the various problems as they might arise. Furthermore, the law was flexible in that prices were not set at any arbitrary figure, but were to be maintained at a level fixed in relation to other commodities. The principle for which Peek had fought, equality for agriculture or parity, had been at last written into the law of the land.

Besides including the concept of parity and a provision for marketing agreements, the new law included another Peek-sponsored section. This was part of section 12b which permitted the use of processing taxes to pay losses on exports. Was McNary-Haugenism dead after all? Indeed not, if Peek could implement this part of the act.

It was generally known that Peek would get the number one administrative spot, even before the A.A.A. was approved by Congress. He took over as administrator on May 15. Peek was a natural choice for the job. Since the act was, in some respects, a sharp departure from previous farm legislation, its success might depend on effective and sympathetic administration. Certainly Peek's ability and experience in both industry and government, plus his devotion to the farm cause, qualified him for the post. And since he had such a large farm following, it was politically desirable to make him a member of the administration team. Besides, Wallace admired and liked his aggressive, hard-fighting friend from Moline, and appreciated what he had done for American agriculture. "I have known few men so determined and so little deterred by setbacks as George Peek in his long battle for the farmer," Wallace wrote in 1934.[9]

An additional reason why Peek was chosen to administer the A.A.A. has generally been overlooked. Many senators and congressmen accepted the idea of acreage restriction only reluctantly. Some of them considered parts of the law positively dangerous. The general knowledge that Peek would head the agency went a long way to allay the doubts, fears, and opposition of men like Senators Pat Harrison and Hubert D. Stephens of Mississippi.[10]

[9] Henry A. Wallace, *New Frontiers* (New York, 1934), 146.

Moreover, processors and distributors violently opposed the act, especially the licensing provisions. If they thought the program was going to be administered by a conservative businessman, their opposition might be lessened. Peek recorded in his diary a revealing conversation with an individual who had recently talked to representatives of the packers and other handlers of food products. "I asked him point blank," Peek wrote, "if they would object to the bill if they felt they would receive sympathetic and business-like administration of it. He said 'no,' but that they shuddered at the thought of Tugwell or Ezekiel."[11]

Generally popular, Peek's appointment was hailed as a victory for the conservatives and practical men of affairs in the Roosevelt administration. Here was a man, people said, who would help counteract the influence of theoretical college professors. "How should I address you, Mr. Peek? Doctor or Professor?" asked a publicity man in the Department. In reply, Peek could only snort, "Hell no!"

William Hirth said that Peek's selection was a "happy development" because Wallace's staff was "utterly unfitted" to administer the law, and because "it gives assurance to the farmers of the country that the question of higher farm prices has been placed in the hands of a strong and practical man."[12]

The old farm crowd, sometimes called "Henry's Father's gang" by the young liberals in the department, believed that the Department of Agriculture was too heavily loaded with idealists and social reformers. Had not the Secretary himself said that the new farm bill was "a major social experiment?" And then there was Tugwell, who became under-secretary. Many farmers and their spokesmen considered him radical, if not outright red, and wished that he was back at Columbia University.

But the more conservative farm leaders could relax now that George Peek was running the A.A.A. He was not interested in social experiments. If asked what he planned to do, he was apt to blurt out, "I'm going to try like hell to raise farm prices." In fact, two days after his appointment, he bluntly declared in his first

10 See Peek's account of his talks with Stephens and Harrison in his diary for March 22, 1933.

11 *Ibid.*

12 *Missouri Farmer,* Vol. XXV (June 1, 1933), 8.

press release, "The sole aim and object of this act is to raise farm prices." To be exact, he repeated it *three* times. That, and that alone, was Peek's idea of the law's purpose, and of his job as administrator. In discussing the profit system and the government's taking over more business, he characteristically remarked, "Unless it hustles, the Government has more hay down now than it will get up before it rains."

With the clear and undivided objective of lifting agricultural prices, Peek surrounded himself with old friends and other men in whom he had confidence. Charles J. Brand, author of the first McNary-Haugen bill, was brought in as co-administrator. The main administrative divisions under Peek's control were Information and Publicity, Production, Processing and Marketing, and Finance. These were headed by Alfred D. Stedman, Chester C. Davis, W. I. Westervelt, and Oscar Johnston, respectively. These men were not dreamy idealists. Peek also announced that he was going to depend heavily upon men such as Baruch and Lowden for advice.

In the late spring and early summer of 1933 haste was imperative. The growing season was well advanced by the time Congress acted. In many cases crops had been planted and the prospect of further staggering surpluses was frightening. "Wherever we turn to deal with an agricultural commodity, we have in prospect a race with the sun," Peek declared grimly.

Despite the confusion and lack of guideposts, Peek and his associates got the new farm program underway with amazing swiftness. Programs of production control were quickly inaugurated for cotton and wheat, and, a little later, for corn and hogs. Cotton was plowed under, the drouth cut wheat output, and young pigs and bred sows were slaughtered for food and fertilizer. And government checks began flowing into thousands of farm homes. On Thursday September 15, 22,122 checks were produced, but the number fell off the next day when a broken generator "stalled the machine for five hours!"[13] Looking at the spectacle of hundreds of employees busily producing and mailing out checks, a Russian visitor remarked: "Good Lord! This is a Revolution!"[14]

[13] H. P. Seidemann, memorandum for Mr. Peek, September 18, 1933. Files of the Secretary of Agriculture.
[14] Wallace, *New Frontiers*, 188.

No, there was nothing like it in all of American history. Millions of individualistic farmers were welded into a great co-operative effort through the vehicle of government benefit payments. In explaining that more than 500,000 cotton growers had signed contracts to take over 9,000,000 acres out of current production, Peek told a nationwide radio audience on July 14, "What has transpired . . . marks an epoch in American agriculture." Then he added, "I say history has been made during these days." And so it had been. This early success of the A.A.A. was a tribute to the work and resourcefulness of Peek and those who were working with him.

Peek had a good bit of adaptability in his make-up, and was not the inflexible administrator sometimes pictured. He had enough of a sense of humor and consideration for the opinions of others to get along well unless a matter of major policy was involved. For instance, when former Senator Brookhart was forced on his agency by the President, Peek accepted it despite his belief that Brookhart was not a good selection. Some of the A.A.A. officials watched Peek squirm. When the question of office space came up, someone asked, "Where are you going to put him, George?" With a doleful smile that was a combination of humor, satire, protest, and resignation, Peek instantly replied, "Oh, a way off somewhere in an attic room with a lot of God damn cobwebs in it."

Peek had a half-serious and half-humorous way of conveying his wish that the A.A.A. should take his conservative direction. He did this without asking men outright to change the color of their thinking. Alfred Stedman, his director of publicity, recalls that Peek was sometimes disturbed by his sympathy with the liberal views. One day Peek, noticing that Stedman was wearing a reddish necktie, said with a direct look but with a smile to take away the edge, "Your necktie is too red. I will send you one of a better color." A few days later Stedman received in the mail a handsome *blue* necktie, a gift from Peek.

In spite of the progress made in fighting the farm depression, these were extremely unhappy days for George Peek. Fundamental differences between himself and Secretary Wallace and between their respective followers in the Department of Agriculture, created a tense and disagreeable situation. From the beginning the A.A.A. was torn by internal dissension. Everyone was pulling hard, but in different directions. It is surprising that so much was accomplished.

As mentioned earlier, Secretary Wallace believed that production control was the heart of the law and that this phase should be stressed; Peek placed confidence in marketing agreements and the revival of foreign trade, while an aggressive legal staff of young urban liberals, headed by Chief Counsel Jerome N. Frank, wanted to use the A.A.A. as an instrument of long-range social and economic reform. Under these circumstances, it was natural for conflicts to develop.

Peek later declared that he had been completely surprised at Wallace's emphasis upon production control. But in trying to justify and defend his own position, he must have had a convenient lapse of memory. Before Peek took the post of administrator, both Wallace and Roosevelt had made their views abundantly clear. On April 7, Peek, Lowden, and Baruch were at the White House to confer on the pending farm bill. Referring to the President, Peek wrote, "He and I disagreed on the question of restricted production as a national policy." And Wallace explained to Peek on the day the A.A.A. became law, "it seems to me entirely clear that we ought to undertake acreage reduction in both cotton and corn but the extent to which this ought to go should again depend upon the outcome of our various conferences."[15] The fact that Peek insisted upon "direct access to the President" before he became administrator indicates that he believed he would have fundamental differences with the Secretary. Undoubtedly, Peek expected that, in a showdown on policy, he could win the President's support. And sometimes he did.

Regardless of the conflict of opinion, Peek set out to administer the law along the lines which he favored. He supported the acreage-reduction programs for cotton and wheat more out of duty than conviction. And on the corn-hog program he said, "there seemed nothing to do but go along with it in view of the existing emergency."[16] However, he shuddered at signing death warrants for juvenile hogs. Peek therefore concentrated on finding export markets and negotiating marketing agreements in order to get

[15] Wallace to Peek, May 12, 1933. Peek Papers.
[16] George N. Peek, *Why Quit Our Own* (New York, 1936), 132.

better prices and to dispose of surpluses. He had his assistants busy drawing up marketing agreements for fluid milk, fruit, tobacco, and other products. The thing to do, he argued, was to get processors and distributors to enter into voluntary agreements to pay parity prices for farm commodities. The first marketing agreement covered the handling of milk in the Chicago area and went into effect on August 1. It determined prices to be paid producers, consumer prices, and fair trade practices. This was typical of the agreements, and others soon followed.[17]

Peek was vitally concerned about increasing the percentage of the consumer's dollar received by farmers. By March, 1933, farmers were only getting 30 per cent of the consumer's dollar spent on farm products while they had received 50 per cent in 1929. It made Peek's blood boil to see the food industries in 1932 earn more than half their 1929 profits while farmers suffered ruin and foreclosure. Yet when it came to implementing his program, Peek was surprisingly charitable with the processors and handlers of food products. In his first press release on May 15, he declared that as far as the food and textile industries were concerned, he wanted "as little interference with established institutions and methods as is consistent with the fixed purpose of the law."

To supplement marketing agreements, Peek strongly advocated diverting surpluses not marketable at parity prices into special domestic or export channels. He would not admit that foreign markets were permanently lost. Through an aggressive export policy supported by the government, he thought that markets could be found. Peek still believed in the basic features of the McNary-Haugen plan and wanted to implement the two-price system. "It had been our original intention, . . .," he later declared, "to provide in the AAA the needed machinery to run the two-price system—an American price for American consumption and competitive foreign prices for exports." On September 20, he wrote Secretary Hull that "a strong, persistent, and well-planned policy looking toward the revival of international trade" should be undertaken at once. Since he based his policies partly on the assumption that foreign markets could be opened for surplus farm commodities, Peek brought himself into further conflict with Secretary Wallace, who held no such views.

17 Edwin G. Nourse, *Marketing Agreements Under the AAA* (Washington, 1935), 206.

Even before the A.A.A. became law, Wallace wrote to Peek, "there are extraordinary difficulties in building up at once an effective foreign purchasing power for our surplus farm products at a price which is at all satisfactory to our farmers. Also it seems that in case we indulge in a subsidized export trade in farm products, we can very promptly get into international jams of one kind or another."[18] And on May 12, Wallace declared that "we ought to act for the moment as if we were a self-contained agricultural economy." It appeared to many that Wallace was recognizing economic realities. To Peek the Secretary's position represented an admission of defeat and acceptance of the further decline of agriculture.

Peek argued that if the productive facilities of the farm were reduced, industry, not agriculture, would be the greatest beneficiary. His strong feelings on this point were expressed in a radio speech on September 1:

> My own view is that we are suffering in this country from an overcapacity of industrial facilities for which both the farmer and the consumer are paying. . . . Agriculture is cutting down its plant but a large part of industry is still trying to maintain boom-time capacity and capital values. This is being done at the expense of farmers and consumers. The public should no longer tolerate it. Industry must reduce its overcapacity. It cannot look for its relief by taking it out of the farmer's hide.

Peek never explained how he thought industrial overcapacity might be reduced, but his statement sounded good to bankrupt farmers.

The conflicts in the department which had been shaping up over policy and personnel reached a near climax in September with the negotiation of a marketing agreement for flue-cured tobacco. Officials of the A.A.A. drew up an agreement and presented it to representatives of the leading tobacco companies on September 15. Company officials objected to it on several counts, but especially criticized the provision which would have limited price increases on manufactured tobacco unless approved by the secretary of agriculture, and that provision which would have given

[18] Wallace to Peek, April 28, 1933. Peek Papers.

Bernard M. Baruch
friend and supporter of Peek
in his drive for a stable agriculture

A.A.A. officials limited access to books and records. In offering a counterproposal, the companies argued that they must be permitted "to manage, conduct and operate their respective businesses with freedom of business policy as heretofore."

Members of the legal department in the A.A.A. who had drawn up the original agreement favored strict control over the tobacco firms. In writing all of the marketing agreements, they took the position that food processors must be strictly regulated. They especially wanted to restrain price increases which might be passed on to consumers and to inspect company books.

There has been a great deal of misunderstanding on this matter of book and record inspection in the marketing agreements. The companies were willing for their books to be opened to the extent necessary to determine that the provisions of the agreement were being honestly carried out. But the legal division and consumer's counsel wanted unlimited right to investigate all of the companies' books and records, including those of affiliated firms in other lines of business not directly concerned with the marketing agreements. The companies did not object to the "standard books and records provision" in the license, just so they were not required to agree to it in the legal contract. They refused to sign away their legal defense against what they considered unwarranted and illegal fishing expeditions. This was considered unjustifiable interference with private enterprise. Peek agreed.

The tobacco buyers took the matter to Peek, and he supported them in objecting to those provisions which seemed like meddling with legitimate business. As finally accepted, the flue-cured-tobacco agreement provided that the companies would buy 250,000,000 pounds of tobacco at the parity price of 17 cents a pound. This was considerably above the current price and the agreement meant some $12,000,000 to this group of tobacco farmers over their 1932 income.

Chief Counsel Frank and members of his staff strongly opposed the agreement on the basis that it did not extend sufficient control over the tobacco industry. It looked like Secretary Wallace would refuse to approve it, largely upon Frank's recommendation.

Peek was fighting mad. In a memorandum to the President, written October 5, he reviewed the controversy in full. He declared:

The manufacturers feel, because of licensing and other provisions inserted by our group in the first draft of the present agreement and because of charts, specific comments on excessive profits, advertising, and other matters, there is a disposition by some members of our Administration to assume control of the industry as soon as possible. Therefore, they have attempted to determine by definition in the agreement the extent of control intended, because they state the possibility of their undertaking this agreement depends on the extent of the control to be exercised. . . . Some of our representatives have suggested, because of the apparent impasse with respect to these issues, that in lieu of this agreement—

(1) We take direct control of the markets by licensing all buyers at once.

(2) We enter the markets immediately to stabilize prices at or near parity by purchasing flue-cured tobacco.

Arguing that the agreement should be approved as it stood, Peek concluded, "I do not conceive that the Government should take over or control by license or otherwise, any industry which appears to be willing to co-operate with us in attaining these objectives."[19] A few days later he took the question directly to the President, who backed his stand. Wallace then reluctantly signed the agreement.

The fight over the flue-cured-tobacco agreement brought out the long smoldering feud between Peek and part of his legal staff. From the beginning Peek distrusted Jerome Frank, who, incidentally, had been a member of a law firm active in liquidating the Moline Plow Company. To provide himself with counsel in whom he had confidence, he employed Fred Lee on a personal basis. He gave Lee his full salary as administrator, which meant that Peek was serving without pay. He also hired Glenn McHugh, who had worked on the McNary-Haugen bill in 1925. McHugh did his best to serve as a buffer between Peek and Frank.

Difficulties were sure to arise when Peek tried to work around part of his legal staff. And conditions became worse when Frank brought in a number of young urban lawyers, some of whom were

[19] Peek, *Why Quit Our Own,* 148–49.

more concerned with social reform than with raising farm prices. Frank told Peek, "What we need are brilliant young men with keen legal minds and imagination." Then he added: "There are a considerable number of brilliant young men who would be willing to join us, partly because of the desire for experience, and partly because of the desire to help us meet the social problems arising from the emergency."[20]

As the A.A.A.'s legal staff was increased to about fifty-five lawyers, Frank employed Alger Hiss, Lee Pressman, Victor Rotnem, Francis J. Shea, and others. That they were bright young men, there is no doubt. And there is equally no question but that some of them held strong collectivist economic ideas. Their real interest was not so much to help raise farm prices as it was to protect consumers and control business.

These super-liberals believed that the capitalistic system was crumbling, that the profit motive was outdated, and that the place of government in the economy must continually increase. For example, Lee Pressman reportedly told some Detroit Milk distributors that the United States government ought to operate the milk business. When he was asked why the government should not also operate grocery and department stores, he replied, "Why not?"[21]

Disillusioned by the depression and its consequences, these young men had permanent ideas about relieving the nation's social and economic ills. It was later revealed that Pressman and some others in the A.A.A. became members of a Communist group in Washington. They would build a new world. They were not sure just how, but someway they would help usher in the millennium. If a new economic order was desirable, there must be a way. They were idealistic, impractical, and above all inexperienced. They had never plowed corn or met a payroll. Indeed, Jerome Frank's city lawyers had much to learn. One of them, working on a macaroni code, was supposed to have asked: "Just tell me this; is this code fair to the macaroni growers?"[22]

20 Jerome Frank, memorandum to Mr. Peek, June 16, 1933. Files of the Secretary of Agriculture.

21 Peek, *Why Quit Our Own*, 150; See also Arthur Krock in the *New York Times*, December 10, 1933, Pt. IV, p. 1.

22 Lord, *The Wallaces of Iowa*, 358. Actually, this person was probably re-

It quickly became clear to Peek that these leftwing urban law-yers were trying to use the A.A.A., particularly its power to li-cense processors, for purposes not originally contemplated. Their talk of limiting profits, regulating business practices, and inspect-ing books and records all seemed un-American to Peek. And when they tried to incorporate some of these principles in the market-ing agreements and codes which were under A.A.A. jurisdiction, Peek balked. The talk and ideas of the young liberals sounded like nonsense to him and he said so. Speaking before the Farm Bureau convention in Chicago on December 12, he strongly up-held the profit system and discounted the trend of government in business. He said that the "grave concern over the expression of a few ultra-liberals about the government taking over private busi-ness . . . is unwarranted." Then he concluded with his familiar statement, "I am in favor of the profit system, but I am in favor of starting with the farmer."[23]

Did Peek really know of Communist influence in the A.A.A.? There is no evidence in the Peek files to indicate that, while he was in office, he knew of any actual card carriers in his agency. Some of Peek's closest friends do not recall ever having heard him make such a charge while he was administrator. Peek had a ten-dency to group all leftwingers in that category, and "Communist" was a term which he frequently used to stigmatize extreme liberals with whom he disagreed. His belief, however, that there were some potentially dangerous radicals in the New Deal administration was borne out later. Peek was one of the earliest to notice that there were reformers around Washington who would solve the nation's problems in some authoritarian fashion outside of the American tradition. He warned against it, but his warnings went largely unheeded.

Besides the marketing agreements in milk, fruit, tobacco, and other commodities, Peek worked hard to export surpluses abroad.

---

ferring to durum wheat which was used for making macaroni. In speaking of this kind of wheat it was not uncommon to use only the word macaroni instead of macaroni wheat. But it made a good story and was repeated by the anti-Tugwell-Frank faction to show that the young lawyers knew nothing about farming.

23 G. N. Peek, "Speech before the American Farm Bureau Federation," December 12, 1933. Peek Papers.

Through the wheat export agreement consummated in October, 1933, he was responsible for sending some 28,000,000 bushels of wheat grown in the Pacific Northwest to the Far East. A subsidy of around 23 cents a bushel was paid to the export corporation at a cost of over $6,000,000, which came from processing taxes on wheat. China was able to buy American wheat because of a loan of $10,000,000 from the Reconstruction Finance Corporation, 60 per cent of which was designated for wheat purchases.[24]

Along with the tobacco agreement, Peek considered the export of wheat to China one of his most notable successes as administrator. To him it represented the type of government co-operation necessary to dispose of farm products. A regional surplus had been cut down and some $3,000,000 had been added to the pockets of northwestern farmers. Processing taxes, he argued, could better be used to subsidize export in this manner than to pay farmers to reduce production. But despite the apparent success of the agreement, it represented financing our own exports. Without the R.F.C. loan to China the deal could not have been made.

The fact that Wallace, Tugwell, and others in the department were hostile to export dumping did not deter Peek from further activity along this line. In November he authorized the use of $500,000 from processing taxes, in addition to previous sums, to pay losses on butter exports. Secretary Wallace was then at Warm Springs with the President, so Under-Secretary Tugwell was asked to approve the arrangement. He refused. But to make sure that he had the Secretary's support, Tugwell discussed the matter with Wallace by telephone on the evening of November 27. Wallace said that he did not favor subsidizing exports, and would not authorize dumping. This seemed to Peek like another example of interference by the liberals and idealists in the department. He wrote a sharp memorandum to the Secretary, but his arguments were unavailing and the proposal was dropped.[25]

Even a man possessed of much more patience than Peek would have been tried by these difficulties and frustrations. But this was

---

[24] Nourse, *Marketing Agreements Under the AAA*, 72–73.

[25] R. M. Littlejohn, memorandum for Mr. Peek, November 28, 1933; G. N. Peek, memorandum for Secretary Wallace, December 1, 1933; and R. G. Tugwell, memorandum for Secretary Wallace, December 2, 1933. Peek Papers.

not all. He believed that many policies under the National Recovery Act were militating against agriculture's welfare. Peek favored the general principles of the N.R.A., and he had suggested a voluntary partnership between government and business as early as 1918. However, he believed that industrial prices must be kept in check until farm prices were raised. Otherwise, how could farm parity be achieved? On this question he came into sharp conflict with his old friend and head of the N.R.A., Hugh Johnson.

In July the President announced his Re-employment Agreement to bring employers under a "blanket code." The important provision was for minimum-wage and maximum-hour agreements. Peek saw at once that if the food industries incurred higher costs under this code, they would likely pass them on to the farmer in the form of reduced prices for his products, or higher prices for what he had to buy. That, Peek said, would increase the disparity between farm and industrial prices. He recommended that food industries over which the A.A.A. had code authority should be exempt from the blanket code. His job, he told Johnson, was to raise farm prices, and he could not approve policies which worked against this objective.

The meeting of the Special Industrial Recovery Board on July 19 was hotter than the Washington weather. Johnson, Frances Perkins, Wallace, and Secretary Roper took the position that wages must be raised first. Peek argued that the A.A.A. and N.R.A. must be co-ordinated and wages and farm prices lifted together. The programs should not go in opposite directions, he said. "You mean," Johnson retorted, "you ought to start out and we follow you." "I resent that," Peek heatedly replied, "I resent it for the purpose of the record." On this issue Tugwell fought shoulder to shoulder with Peek, and representatives of the major farm organizations also supported his view. But Johnson's policy of placing labor provisions in the food industry codes prevailed.[26]

By November conditions had become untenable for Peek in the A.A.A. He disagreed with Wallace and Tugwell on so many points that it seemed hopeless to try to continue. The crisis came when Peek attempted to remove Jerome Frank. He wrote to Wallace on November 15, saying that Frank had become "impossible."

[26] Peek to Johnson, July 13, 17, and 20, 1933; and Proceedings of the Special Industrial Recovery Board, July 18 and 19, 1933. Peek Papers.

His complaints centered around Frank's alleged holding up of marketing agreements, and retarding enforcement proceedings under some of the milk licenses. But his real objection was that Frank almost always concurred with Tugwell and Wallace on important issues, and was in a key position to hamper or block Peek's plans.

It was quickly rumored, however, that Wallace would not dismiss Frank. Tugwell, more than anyone else, wanted to get rid of Peek, not Frank, and it was said that he was maneuvering so that Peek would be forced to resign.[27] Wallace had been deeply annoyed by the bickering within the A.A.A. He hated strife and discord. But most of all he was tired of Peek attempting to circumvent him by taking issues directly to the President as he had done in the case of the flue-cured-tobacco agreement.

As early as May 15, the day Peek took office, Wallace had written to Roosevelt, "Mr. Peek's insistence on using you as an umpire between him and myself will involve you unnecessarily in administrative detail." He said that he wanted "a clear and final understanding . . . that I am Mr. Peek's chief."[28] Thus it was not just a matter of firing the Chief Counsel, but a question of Wallace's authority as secretary. Peek always had been restive under the administrative arrangement. He wanted the A.A.A. established as an independent agency outside the Department of Agriculture and directly responsible to the President. Now he had raised the issue of Wallace's authority and would have to go.

On December 7, Peek had lunch with the President, after which they conferred for two hours. Wallace and Tugwell had been at the White House that morning, and Wallace returned for an hour after Peek departed. As Peek was leaving the President's office, reporters asked him about quitting the A.A.A. Peek replied abruptly: "I am going back to my desk now. I also shall be at my desk tomorrow morning. Beyond that nobody can ever make any plans."[29]

However, Roosevelt had asked him to resign. In fact, Wallace already had conferred with Chester Davis about taking the post. The only remaining question was what to do with Peek. It was

27 See Arthur Krock in the *New York Times,* December 10, 1933, Pt. IV, p. 1.
28 Wallace to Roosevelt, May 15, 1933. Roosevelt Papers, Hyde Park.
29 *New York Times,* December 8, 1933, p. 1.

a chilling prospect for Wallace and Roosevelt to think of a man of Peek's forcefulness and vocabulary running around outside the administration attacking the farm program. As it was, the A.A.A. had more than its share of troubles at the grass roots. Somehow, he must be kept happy and active within the New Deal framework.

Tugwell suggested sending him as minister to Czechoslovakia! From there he might travel around Europe and find some new markets for American farm products. But this idea was not seriously considered. It was finally decided that, since Peek was so vitally concerned about exporting agricultural commodities, he might be made special adviser to the President on foreign trade. That was it. Such a job would certainly appeal to Peek. It was dignified and sounded important; thus no one would lose face. It was encompassing enough to take all of his tremendous energies.

So on December 15, exactly seven months after he took office, Peek formally tendered his resignation. This was a victory for the "social outlook" group in the A.A.A. Three days later, President Roosevelt wrote, "I want to thank you very warmly for the high character of service you have rendered and to express my genuine appreciation of your willingness to take over the new duties I requested you to assume."[30]

In his last talk with Chester Davis before leaving the A.A.A., Peek said, "Get rid of Jerome Frank and the rest of that crowd as a condition to your acceptance." Davis, however, believed that he could "handle them." But in January, 1935, Davis called for and shortly got the resignations of Frank and Pressman, in the legal division, and of Fred Howe and Gardner Jackson, top men in the consumer's counsel. Peek's position on the question of personnel had been vindicated.[31]

[30] Roosevelt to Peek, December 18, 1933. Peek Papers.
[31] Peek discusses his problems with this group in his book *Why Quit Our Own*. In 1953 a subcommittee of the Senate Judiciary Committee quoted Peek in its report, *Interlocking Subversion in Government Departments*.

Special Adviser on Foreign Trade

I F Henry Wallace breathed a sigh of relief when George Peek trudged out of the Old South Agriculture Building, the same could not be said for Secretary of State Cordell Hull and his associates. State Department executives knew enough about Peek's views on foreign trade to suspect that the "Man from Moline" would be a thorn in their flesh. "If Mr. Roosevelt had hit me between the eyes with a sledge hammer he could not have stunned me more than by this appointment," Hull recalled in his *Memoirs*.

One of the principal objectives of the Roosevelt Administration was to restore American foreign trade, which had dropped from $9,640,000,000 in 1929 to only $2,934,000,000 in 1932. But how could this be done? Before and during the campaign, Roosevelt declared that he favored reciprocal trade agreements as a means of lowering commercial barriers. In a speech at Seattle, he said: "I have advocated and continue to advocate a tariff policy based in a large part upon the simple principle of profitable exchange arrived at through negotiated tariffs with benefit to each nation. This principle of tariffs by negotiation means to deal with each country on the basis of fair barter."

However, it was Cordell Hull, the new secretary of state, who spearheaded the drive to reverse the high protectionist trade policies of the previous administrations. For many years Hull had been a harsh critic of American commercial policy, and had futilely recommended gradual tariff reduction. As a means of lowering trade barriers, he favored reciprocal tariff bargaining, including unconditional most-favored-nation treatment.

Throughout 1933, the new administration moved slowly toward developing a reciprocal trade program. However, by the end of the year, Congress had not yet acted. In some respects, trade restrictions had even been tightened under the N.R.A. and A.A.A. Import quotas had been established for lumber, petroleum, and alcoholic beverages. Peek had dealt with this aspect of trade problems when he was put in charge of liquor quotas early in December. By the end of 1933 the time was approaching when a basic decision on trade policy had to be made. Were quotas, bilateral agreements, and other narrow, restrictive, nationalistic policies to be adopted, or would the administration follow the Hull philosophy of a broad program designed to lower commercial barriers throughout the world? This was a fundamental question. When Peek was made "special assistant" to the President, a title which he carried until late in March, 1934, the administration's commercial policy was in a fluid and unsettled state.[1]

As special assistant, Peek first headed a committee "to recommend permanent machinery to co-ordinate all Government relations to American foreign trade." On December 30, 1933, he recommended that a foreign trade administrator be appointed by the President to head a United States foreign trade corporation. He described the function of this corporation as seeing "that our domestic industries are assisted in developing foreign trade, guided in their related credit activities, and advised of the effect upon our agriculture and industry . . . of export and import trade." He also recommended that "fact-finding machinery" be set up to provide better statistical information on foreign trade, and that there be developed "a national system of bookkeeping of all the 'in' and 'out' items." Peek undoubtedly believed that if the President accepted his recommendation, he would become foreign trade administrator.

Roosevelt soon increased Peek's responsibilities by making him president of the Export-Import Banks. The first of these was created by executive order on February 2, 1934, to help promote trade with Russia; the second was established to stimulate commerce between Cuba and the United States. His bank duties, however, were most nominal. Because of differences with Russia over debt settlements, the trustees of the first Export-Import Bank

[1] Henry J. Tasca, *The Reciprocal Trade Policy of the United States* (Philadelphia, 1938), 27–28.

voted on March 16 not to do anything until the diplomatic questions were settled. The second bank was slightly more active and helped to finance some trade deals with Cuba.

In order to give Peek more specific duties in regard to commercial policy, the Office of Special Adviser on Foreign Trade was established by executive order on March 23, under authority granted in the N.R.A. Peek's main duties as special adviser, were, first, to gather and co-ordinate data on American foreign trade and to keep the President informed on developments. Secondly, he was authorized to "carry on negotiations with respect to specific trade transactions with any individual, corporation, association, group or business agency interested in obtaining assistance from the Federal Government through financing transactions, barter transactions, or other forms of Governmental participation authorized by law." Finally, he was to bring any trade deal which seemed "meritorious" before the appropriate government departments for their attention and action.

The Special Adviser's office was given $100,000 from the N.R.A. appropriation, and Peek quickly assembled a staff and began to work. His two chief assistants were Glenn McHugh, who left the A.A.A. when Peek did, and Wayne C. Taylor. He also had a legal adviser, public-relations officer and six other subdivisional heads. Although Peek had often ridiculed and belittled "impractical" college professors and Roosevelt's so-called brain trust, he invited several university men to join his staff. Dr. Alvin Hansen of Harvard, whom Peek later criticized in his book, was among the several professors who turned down his offer.

Viewing his task from the angle of a businessman just taking over a new firm, Peek considered that his first duty was "to assemble from . . . statistics an income account and balance sheet to show whether we had been doing business at a profit or a loss." No intelligent policies could be established, he reasoned, unless accounts, trends, and factors in foreign commerce could be studied as a whole. Thus, he sent his assistants to the Department of Commerce and elsewhere for statistical data.

Meanwhile, on April 5, he made his first major address on foreign trade to a nation-wide radio audience. However broad and complicated the problems may have been, it was obvious that

Peek's chief interest was doing something for agriculture. He felt that "eventually the proper development of foreign trade" could remove crop surpluses and perhaps be "used to kill off the acreage limitation and regimentation movement."[2] This was the only reason he took the job as special adviser. Dwelling on agriculture and foreign trade, Peek said: "I believe a sound foreign commerce is essential to the recovery and continued well-being of this country. Above all, in agriculture we cannot do without it. . . . We must seek outlets and more outlets at home and abroad. . . . I believe that no man denies today that we are in a position where our huge surpluses of agricultural products demand a world market."

Having stressed the importance of foreign markets to American farm prosperity, Peek then turned to specific recommendations. Conceding that there might be others who knew more about the problems than he did, including Secretary Hull, "my distinguished friend of many years," he urged that consideration be given to setting up "a co-ordinated and implemented Government clearing house for foreign trade matters." Then he declared that the United States could help restore world business by adopting a trade policy of "bartering or swapping." He also warned that, if this country hoped to increase its trade, "selected goods and services" must be accepted from foreign countries. "Trading is not a one-sided transaction," he said.[3]

Through his report to the President on December 30 and this first major public address, Peek had made his ideas on foreign trade clear. He wanted a centralized government agency on the order of the British Board of Trade to guide and control American foreign commerce. He favored reciprocal bilateral agreements with outright barter playing an important part. This aspect of Peek's program seemed to be essentially in line with Roosevelt's views.

The President had set up an executive committee on commercial policy in November, 1933, to co-ordinate the "commercial policy of this government, with a view to centralize in the hands of one agency supervision of all Government action affecting our import and export trade." And on several occasions, he had talked in terms of horse-trading and Yankee swapping. Roosevelt, Hull,

2 Peek, *Why Quit Our Own* (New York, 1936), 26.
3 Radio Address, April 5, 1934. Peek Papers.

Peek, and other Washington officials all favored reciprocal trade agreements. But the crucial question was whether such agreements should include the conditional or unconditional most-favored-nation clause. Hull and Peek were in fundamental disagreement on this matter and both sought the President's support. By early 1934, Roosevelt had not made up his mind.

These principles call for a brief explanation. Unconditional most-favored-nation treatment simply means that if the United States makes a trade agreement with country A lowering the rates on certain imports, it extends the same privileges to all other countries; that is, if the other nations give United States exports most-favored-nation treatment. This type of agreement is designed to encourage equality of treatment and to lower commercial barriers on a world-wide basis. Secretary Hull frankly hoped by this means to break down the American tariff walls and to reduce trade restrictions abroad.

On the other hand, conditional most-favored-nation treatment means that the United States will grant tariff concessions to country A, but will not extend them to country B unless B agrees to give concessions equal to those granted by A. This policy would necessitate bargaining nation by nation and tends to guard against a general reduction of American tariff barriers.

In his study of foreign trade, Peek began with certain basic assumptions which to him were almost axioms. He strongly upheld the soundness of the protective system and never tired of repeating how it had contributed to the economic greatness and prosperity of America. "We have been brought up on protection," he told the Women's Political Study Club in Washington. "If we are to abandon any measure of that protection it should be only in exchange for tangible advantages to us." Through bilateral agreements, he believed that trade could be expanded, while at the same time benefits of a high tariff system could be maintained. He favored admitting noncompetitive selective imports like tea, coffee, rubber, and silk "and such other commodities the importation of which will improve our standards of living and will not seriously affect our industries." Through a policy of selected exports and imports, he said, the United States could send abroad "those products we can best produce, particularly those agricultural products which are the backbone of our foreign trade and of our domestic prosperity."[4] After all, this was his main objective.

Secondly, Peek felt that, since other countries had increased their control over trade, the United States must follow similar policies. During the depression many nations not only raised tariff rates, but had resorted to much more effective regulations in the form of quotas, licensing, and exchange controls. Peek disliked these restrictions; but, since they were a reality, he argued that this country must operate on the same basis. "The United States has not kept up with the procession," he said. Thus, he believed that we should deal with foreign nations on a *quid pro quo* basis. For the United States to take the lead in trying to turn the world toward more freedom of trade seemed to Peek not only foolish but stupid.

On the basis of these ideas, Peek had developed a definite trade program, and, by the middle of 1934 he was advocating its official acceptance with all his might. This was at the very time that the Trade Agreements Act was being passed by Congress. His five-point program included (1) recognition that foreign trade was a definite concern of the federal government, (2) the establishment of a foreign trade board, (3) the publication of up-to-date statistical data on America's commercial and financial relations with each and every country, (4) pursuit of a policy of bilateral agreements on the basis of selective imports and exports, and (5) a satisfactory solution to the problem of a country's discrimination against the United States through exchange controls as a *prerequisite* to any general trade agreement with that country.

Peek considered this program so practical and sensible that he tended to view anyone who disagreed with him as a fool or a knave. In closing one of his principal speeches on foreign trade, he said: "I feel that they [five points] represent the starting point for a truly American foreign trade policy, based upon studies of facts which cannot be ignored. Their adoption will enable us to go forward. This would be a "new deal" in American foreign trade."[5]

Whether it would have been particularly "American" was debatable, but it did, indeed, represent some new developments in commercial policy. And Secretary Hull would have none of it.

[4] See addresses delivered November 21, 1934, and January 19, 1935. *Ibid.*
[5] *Ibid.*, January 19, 1935.

He detested the idea of greater government control over foreign trade which Peek advocated, and "his theories, if carried out," Hull wrote, "meant the death of the trade agreements policy."[6] The Secretary of State believed that there was more to be gained by combatting a strict *quid pro quo* basis of trade than by yielding to it. Nonetheless, Peek kept hammering his ideas into the ear of the President with his usual dogged persistence. From a political angle, he presented his case most skillfully by emphasizing that unconditional most-favored-nation treatment was a horrible Republican doctrine adopted in 1923. Then he attempted to show how Republican policies had contributed to the depression of 1929.

Peek had no real part in drawing up the Trade Agreements Act, but he did, incidentally, make a valuable contribution. As originally drafted, the measure was long and complicated. Having had a great deal of experience with Congress, Peek advised to "make the bill only two or three pages long, and it will stand a better chance."[7] He was right, and Hull was grateful for the suggestion.

On June 12, 1934, the President signed the bill. The law permitted the president to negotiate reciprocal trade agreements and to raise or lower the tariff as much as 50 per cent. Most-favored-nation treatment was specifically provided. "I watched our President sign our bill in the White House," Hull recalled in his *Memoirs*. "Each stroke of the pen seemed to write a message of gladness on my heart. My fight of many long years for the reciprocal trade policy and the lowering of trade barriers was won."[8]

But the Secretary's fight was not yet won. So long as George Peek had any influence with Roosevelt, Hull's program was in danger. Speaking over N.B.C. on the Farm and Home Hour, June 9, just three days before the President signed the Trade Agreements Act, Peek said, "The common sense approach through the maze of restrictions and barriers which now impede our trade with the world is through the old Yankee method of bartering—goods for goods, equal value given and received, . . ." The Secretary of State shuddered at the thought of this policy, and plodded ahead with his own program.

6 *The Memoirs of Cordell Hull* (New York, 1948), I, 354.
7 *Ibid.*, 356.   8 *Ibid.*, 357.

The same day President Roosevelt signed the Trade Agreements Act, he authorized Peek to release his first statistical study. It was entitled, "Letter to the President on Foreign Trade." A second "Letter," dated August 30, was made public in September and dealt with international credits. These reports covered the years from 1896 to 1933 and were divided into four periods, 1896–1914; 1915–22; 1923–29; and 1930–33. Peek presented figures to show United States exports exceeded imports by some $36,646,-000,000 during the thirty-eight-year span. However, considering both commercial and financial transactions, the picture was not so bright. After figuring tourist expenditures abroad, immigrant remittances, shipping, and other services rendered by foreigners, the favorable position of the United States was reduced to $22,-645,000,000 by 1933. Much of this was represented by war debts and other foreign securities of questionable value. Upon close analysis our creditor status did not seem so good, according to Peek.

There was nothing new about these figures, as the Department of Commerce had been releasing current data since 1922. However, it was valuable to have such summaries readily available. Also Peek revealed that there was no completely accurate inventory of American investment abroad and foreign investments in the United States. He recommended that provision be made to get more reliable information.

Peek's studies also publicized the policy of helping to finance our own exports through private investments abroad, while maintaining high tariff barriers against imports as was done in the 1920's. However, he did not use his figures to show that possibly American trade restrictions should be lowered so foreigners could pay their debts in goods. Rather, he tried to demonstrate how the United States had lost wealth by exporting capital, which had depreciated in value. The "draining off of our liquid resources by foreign nations," he later explained to the President, "rendered us vulnerable to the economic shocks which . . . overwhelmed us" in 1931–1932.[9] Peek failed to mention, however, how these loans might have been put to better use, and that domestic financial policies had also resulted in the loss of billions in liquid assets.

In any event, since Peek considered the export of "liquid re-

[9] Peek to Roosevelt, July 16, 1935. Peek Papers.

sources" as economically unsound, he argued that "we must pay close attention to the migration of capital and its relation to our foreign trade." To him this seemed to be further proof that a foreign trade board was needed to control American commercial and financial transactions abroad. He also insisted that "we must develop complete balance sheets between this country and each of the countries with which we are now dealing or with which we propose to deal." There was much to be said for better and more accurate bookkeeping of international accounts, and Peek sought to remedy an unsatisfactory situation. However, his reports were not as startling as he liked to claim, especially not to those who had studied the situation.

On June 13, the question of Peek's first letter was brought up at the President's press conference. Roosevelt seemed pleased with the result of his Special Adviser's work, and said that this was the first time our international account had been presented in such a clear, straightforward way. A reporter asked the president if there was any moral that might be drawn from the Peek letter. "None, absolutely none," Roosevelt replied, "we want the people of this country to think about these facts and get interested in them." Then he was questioned as to whether Peek's analysis would affect his own trade policies. He answered, "I haven't any more idea than you have."[10]

Indeed, at that moment, the President had not even decided whether Peek or Hull would administer the Trade Agreements Act. He was vacillating between influences exerted by his Special Adviser and his Secretary of State, and their respective supporters. For a time it looked as though Peek had won the battle for control over the reciprocal trade program, but on June 29 it was officially announced that the State Department would administer the law.

This did not mean that Hull had won the war over trade policy, just one battle. If he expected Peek to stop his campaign in favor of bilateral and barter agreements, he was sadly mistaken. Peek had been authorized to negotiate barter transactions under the executive order setting up his office. And he intended to proceed, although his agreements had to have presidential approval.

[10] Gardner L. Harding, "Notes on President's Press Conference, June 13, 1934." *Ibid.*

Peek sought backing for his policies both inside and outside government circles. On October 17, he addressed a large foreign trade conference in Chicago. The next week he spoke to a meeting of the American Bankers Association in Washington, and ten days later he was in New York to state his views before the Twenty-First National Foreign Trade Convention. The theme of Peek's speeches did not vary, and he always concluded by recommending his five-point trade program.

By the end of 1934, Peek was becoming more harsh in his denunciation of the unconditional most-favored-nation principle, and those who supported it. Speaking before the Association of Land Grant Colleges and Universities in Washington on November 21, he said that the United States had not worked out a plan to dispose of surplus wheat, "because we have in this country a school of international altruists which still believes in free trade as a means of raising the standards of living in all the world, notwithstanding the fact that such a practice can result only in diluting our strength with the world's weakness." Gradually, Peek was beginning to conceive of Hull's plan as something foreign and sinister, while his own was peculiarly "American."

Meanwhile, he kept pressing his views on the President, and with a measure of success. In letters dated November 12 and 14, he detailed his reasons for opposing the unconditional most-favored-nation principle. He also suggested that quotas be established on additional goods. "In view of existing world conditions," he recommended again that the "unconditional most-favored-nation policy be revised and that we return to the traditional realistic policy of conditional most-favored-nation treatment." The Hull policy had the effect of "unilateral economic disarmament," he said.[11]

There is no doubt but that Roosevelt was impressed by Peek's arguments. On November 19, he sent Hull a note which said:

Like most problems with which you and I have been connected during many years, there are two sides to the argument. In pure theory you and I think alike, but every once in a while we have to modify a principle to meet a hard and disagreeable fact! . . . I am inclined to think that if you and George Peek,

11 Peek to Roosevelt, November 12 and 14, 1934. *Ibid.*

who represents the very hard-headed practical angle of trade, could spend a couple of hours some evening talking over this problem of the most-favored-nation clause, it would be very helpful in many ways.[12]

Hull did invite Peek to discuss the matter, but, of course, they got nowhere. It seems clear that Roosevelt wanted his subordinates to reach an agreement so that he could be spared the displeasure of having to make the final decision. However, a crisis was at hand which would force Roosevelt to act.

During November and December, Peek's office had negotiated a barter deal with Germany to dispose of some 800,000 bales of cotton through the Export-Import Bank. Germany was to pay the bank 25 per cent in American dollars and the other 75 per cent was to be paid to the bank in German currency. American importers could then buy these German marks from the bank to purchase certain German goods. On December 12, after a conference with Peek, it was announced that Roosevelt had sanctioned the deal.

Peek was a strong and stubborn man, but so was Cordell Hull. Hull bitterly opposed this trade scheme. Besides having no confidence in the German government, he believed this was a discriminatory arrangement contrary to his ideas of trade equality. It would simply encourage more discrimination against the United States, he told the President, and the over-all consequences would be detrimental to American trade. The Secretary also considered the political implications, stating that Americans opposed to Hitler would resent a business deal so favorable to Germany.

None of these arguments impressed Peek. He had the single objective of selling surplus cotton, and his plan seemed like a practical way to do it. And many southern congressmen and senators thought he was right. Peek was just not bothered about the related problems which concerned Hull. Nonetheless, the President finally surrendered to Hull's position and withdrew his approval of the cotton agreement.

From that time forward, Peek's influence declined. The Hull philosophy of trade agreements had finally triumphed. However, progress in negotiating treaties under the Trade Agreements Act

[12] *The Memoirs of Cordell Hull*, I, 372.

was immeasurably retarded as a result of the Peek-Hull controversy which raged during the last half of 1934 and on into early 1935. The only reciprocal trade treaty signed in 1934 was with Cuba.

Though Peek may have been down, he was not out. He continued to make speeches and write articles in which he vigorously damned the Hull program. Yet, he remained loyal to the President and seldom let an opportunity pass to blast the Harding-Coolidge-Hoover regime. In fact, during late 1934, he did his best to play down the conflict between himself and Hull. After the Washington *Post* published an editorial on September 21 entitled "Mr. Hull and Mr. Peek," he wrote that his differences with Hull had been greatly exaggerated in the press. Peek felt that Roosevelt had the right inclinations, but that he was being led into the economic swamp by Hull and the "internationalists." Appearing before the Senate Agriculture Committee on February 1, 1935, he observed that there was a large "exportable surplus of theory" in the United States, but a great "undeveloped market . . . for facts."

Peek still hoped that he might get Congress to set up a foreign trade board. He prepared a bill which was introduced by Senator J. Hamilton Lewis of Illinois in August, 1935. In support of his measure, Peek sent bundles of statistics and copies of his speeches to sympathetic congressmen and senators. However, the bill never got out of the Foreign Relations Committee. Since the President had accepted the Hull policy, there seemed to be less excuse for such a board. If the Peek plan of negotiating numerous agreements country by country and product by product had been adopted, then a permanent foreign trade board could probably have performed a real service.

Meanwhile Peek's staff was preparing additional statistical data. A third "Letter to the President on Foreign Trade and International Investment Position of the United States" was published on April 30. Further studies were made on "Foreign Restrictions and Agreements Affecting American Commerce," and on "American Agriculture and Foreign Trade." Besides these, a series of studies was undertaken on the economic and financial position of various foreign countries. Peek continued to draw the same conclusions from his investigations; bilateral agreements and barter transactions were superior to the Hull program, and

American foreign trade and investment needed closer government supervision and control.

As Peek continued his blistering criticism throughout the spring of 1935, the country became acutely aware of the differences on trade policy. The controversy was taking the form of a "first-class government scandal," editorialized the *New York Times* on May 13. On June 5, Gardner L. Harding, Peek's public relations officer, reported on the results of his rather comprehensive study of editorial opinion dealing with the Peek-Hull conflict. His report showed that both men had strong nonpartisan and nonsectional backers, as well as bitter critics, in the nation's press.[13]

Congressional debate reflected a similar situation. Both Democrats and Republicans criticized the Hull pacts when certain special interests began to claim that these agreements hurt their particular businesses or industries. For example, Democrat John H. Hoeppel of California told his colleagues in February, 1935, that agriculture in his state was not being adequately protected. Across the continent in Massachusetts, Representative Allen T. Treadway, Republican, attacked the proposed agreement with Belgium, which would admit certain industrial items under lower tariff rates.

Most economists agreed with Hull. At the time, and later, Peek received harsh treatment at the hands of students writing on the reciprocal trade agreements. Some of them said that the Special Adviser's ideas were not "economics," but "Peekonomics."[14] However, among the academicians, Peek had the support of isolationist Charles A. Beard, a widely known scholar and writer on the economic interpretation of American history, who was rapidly developing an anti-Roosevelt obsession. Beard considered Peek "the realist among the administration men engaged on the foreign trade side. . . . Mr. Peek's mind does not seem to be encumbered by a thousand exploded economic dogmas that no longer fit the world of reality," he said.[15]

His strongest support, however, came from those who did not want any general downward revision of the tariff. Congresswoman

13 Gardner L. Harding, "Memorandum," June 5, 1935. Peek Papers.
14 See William S. Culbertson, *Reciprocity a National Policy for Foreign Trade* (New York, 1937), Chap. 6.
15 Beard to Gardner L. Harding, December 20, 1935. Peek Papers.

Isabella Greenway of Arizona was distressed by the fact that most of the favorable comments on Peek's stand were coming from Republicans! She might have added—high tariff Republicans. It was not only a matter of how best to expand foreign trade—by conditional or unconditional most-favored-nation treatment—but a question of whether American tariff barriers were to be generally lowered.

Despite the fact that Peek had some important support, by mid-1935, he was more than ready to leave government service. Probably no one had given so much advice and had so little of it taken. The time seemed ripe to leave the Roosevelt administration when the N.R.A. was declared unconstitutional on May 27, 1935. This wiped out the authority under which the Office of Special Adviser had been created, although the President made other arrangements for temporarily continuing the work.

Thus on July 16, after reviewing his ideas on foreign trade, Peek formally submitted his resignation as special adviser and president of the Export-Import Banks. "My fundamental reason for taking this step," he told the President, "is that I feel increasingly out of sympathy with the foreign trade policies now being pursued. I believe that national recovery will be impossible so long as these policies are continued."

The next day the President wrote one of his "Dear George" letters, congratulating Peek on his work and urging him to remain in government service. Probably thinking of the forthcoming election and not wanting Peek to leave in a bad frame of mind, Roosevelt insisted that there was still work to be done. He also held out the hope that at the next session Congress might pass a bill setting up a foreign trade board. Peek's services would be needed to study the problem further, he concluded.[16] But Peek replied that, since a major policy matter was involved, he could not reconsider despite the "cordiality" of the President's request. A few days later the President turned on the famous Rooseveltian charm and wrote:

> I know how very keenly you feel on the subject discussed and wish that I might be more entirely in agreement with you. As a matter of fact we are probably not so far apart in our views,

[16] Roosevelt to Peek, July 17, 1935. *Ibid.*

as I feel the impracticability of accomplishing in a short period, the things that you want to accomplish. At all events,
George, I want the benefit of your services, at least until the
management and policies of the Export-Import Bank can be
more definitely fixed and the work you have been doing as
Special Adviser definitely adjusted.[17]

Then he explained that he was leaving town and would discuss
matters more fully upon his return. "Carry on and see me when
I get back. Meantime, get a vacation," he concluded jauntily.
Peek acceded to this request and another victory could be chalked
up to the persuasiveness and administrative technique of Franklin
D. Roosevelt.

The President, however, had not pacified Peek. His resentment
against the Hull policies continued to smolder and it was only a
matter of time until it would break into an open flame. The more
he thought about it, the more convinced he became that Hull was
dominated by some evil internationalist and un-American point
of view. There must be some kind of conspiracy afoot designed to
wreck any truly national or American policy, he reasoned.

On Armistice Day he went to New York to make a few remarks
before some of his old War Industries Board friends. At the con-
clusion of what was otherwise a rather mild speech, he emphatically declared: "An American point of view calls for one policy, the
international point of view quite another. We have straddled long
enough. For my own enlightenment I have drawn up a list of
eight contrasting points. The 'deadly parallel' is a graphic method
of comparison. When we Americans choose—let us choose America." Then he listed eight contrasting points, saying this was
"America's Choice."

17 Peek to Roosevelt, July 17; and Roosevelt to Peek, July 25, 1935. *Ibid.*

A Policy for Internationalists	*A Policy for America*
I	I
Relaxation of immigration laws and regulation of immigration by international agreements.	Rigorous tightening of immigration laws: (a) To reduce American unemployment. (b) To reduce alien influences in our domestic affairs.
II	II
General reduction of tariffs: (a) Laissez faire. (b) Unconditional Most-Favored-Nation.	Preservation of the American market, American price levels and American employment: (a) Selective imports and exports. (b) Tariff reductions only for specific advantages in individual foreign countries (i.e. reciprocity or *conditional* most-favored-nation).
III	III
Stabilization of currencies by general international action (i.e. return to unregulated or foreign controlled gold standard).	Stabilization of American dollar at American price level—thereafter stabilization by agreement with individual countries or blocs where possible. (i.e. a managed currency based on national bookkeeping.)

IV

Free export of capital and resumption of general foreign loans. Multiplication of branch factories and American direct investments abroad.

IV

Control of export of capital:

(a) To conserve national assets and resources.

(b) To assist American trade, foreign and domestic.

(c) To minimize foreign influence or control over American securities market and American enterprise.

V

Naval limitation by international agreement to meet the requirements of Great Britain, Japan, France, Italy, and Germany.

V

Navy designed to meet American requirements including defense of the Panama Canal and the Pacific Coast.

VI

Dependence on foreign shipping and communications.

VI

Development of American shipping and communications systems.

VII

Submission of disputes to decision of foreign dominated tribunals such as the World Court.

VII

Settlement of disputes by arbitration confirmed by the Senate.

VIII

Automatic intervention in European or Asiatic political disputes, as under the Kellogg Treaty and Stimson Doctrine. Collaboration with League in naming "aggressors" anywhere in the world and enforcing sanctions.

VIII

In case of wars in Europe or Asia, strict neutrality and avoidance of "moral" judgments on belligerents. Cash - and - carry policy for direct or indirect trade with belligerents. For the Americas the Monroe Doctrine plus the Good Neighbor Policy.

Just before Roosevelt left on a trip to Warm Springs, Peek gave him a copy of the "deadly parallel." It all seemed ridiculous to the President. Writing on November 22, Roosevelt indicated that he had lost patience with Peek.

Dear George:

I do not know who wrote that little two page memo you gave men entitled "AMERICA'S CHOICE—Which shall it be?" but I must confess that I think it is rather silly. It sounds like a Hearst paper. . . .

The silly part of it is that in almost every case the "Policy for Internationalists" is not advocated either by the Government (legislative or administrative branches) or by the overwhelming body of public opinion.

For example:

1. Nobody is asking for relaxation of immigration laws or regulation of immigration by international agreements.

2. Nobody is asking laissez faire or unconditional Most-Favored-Nation general reduction of tariffs.

3. Stabilization of currencies by general international action is today impossible and, therefore, can be thrown out.

4. Free export of capital and resumption of general foreign loans and multiplication of American factories and investments abroad is advocated by no one of intelligence I know.

5. Naval limitation by international agreement *is* advocated, but it is a trick—an unfair thing—to say, that American policy would do this in order to meet the requirements of Great Britain, Japan, France, Italy and Germany.

6. No one in their right frame of mind wants dependence on foreign shipping and communications.

7. Submission of disputes to foreign dominated tribunals, such as the World Court, thus stated is unfair unless the writer of it is willing to come out against all multilateral international settlements of disputes.

8. "Automatic intervention in European or Asiatic political disputes, as under the Kellogg Treaty," is a deliberate lie. The Kellogg Treaty does not provide for automatic intervention.

In other words, this kind of statement amounts to nothing more than the setting up deliberately of straw men, who do not exist in reality, and then making a great show of knocking them over with a firing of salutes and a forefire of trumpets.

As ever yours,
Franklin D. Roosevelt

Four days later Peek resigned. In doing so, he denied that his speech had been intended as an attack on Roosevelt's administration. He was only referring to trends, he said, but added that "the issue is there."

The same day, November 26, the anti-Roosevelt Washington *Herald* splashed Peek's eight points and accompanying comment over half of its editorial page. The headline read: "Sane Nationalism or Fatuous Internationalism. Which Shall It Be?" The editor said that Peek may not have contributed much to a better understanding of some big national problems, seemingly justifying Roosevelt's judgment, but "we have never seen the sharp divergence of these viewpoints—the AMERICAN and the INTERNATIONALIST—more effectively presented. . . . Like a clear chart, it marks the hidden reefs of foreign entanglement and the shoal waters of weak and confusing policy; and, on the other hand, the true course leading to safe harbor and secure anchorage." The economic nationalists, isolationists, and various other critics of the Roosevelt administration had found a powerful recruit.

When asked at a news conference what he planned to do, Peek said he was going to stay in Washington all winter, or longer if necessary, and "fight it out." He announced that he was establishing an office in the Investment Building and would finance his own campaign to awaken the country to the danger of the New Deal farm and trade policies. He said he was ready to accept speaking invitations from agricultural and other groups, but that partisan politics would have no part in his campaign. When asked if he favored the re-election of Roosevelt, he said "no comment."[18]

[18] Press conference notes, December 7, 1935. *Ibid.*

Chapter XVII

New Deal Critic

Peek's resignation added just one more name to the growing list of New Deal "has-beens." Lewis W. Douglas, Hugh Johnson, Donald R. Richberg, and Raymond Moley were among the most prominent Roosevelt advisers who already had been relegated to the side lines. Peek was the last of the "Baruch Men" to leave the inner circles of New Dealism. Another conservative adviser had been lost.

No longer under wraps of loyalty to President Roosevelt, Peek at once began to attack the administration. The Canadian Reciprocity Treaty, which had just been negotiated, was the subject of his first blast. The pact seemed to favor American industry over agriculture because it lowered the rates on a number of Canadian farm commodities. The very thought of increased farm imports from Canada, while the United States restricted production, made Peek furious. He charged that the treaty was absolutely contrary to the President's pledge not to lower farm tariffs.

Peek was perfectly aware that, as a creditor nation, the United States must accept imports. However, he declared that agriculture was paying the cost of the reciprocal trade agreements while industry received most of the concessions. To him, this was only an additional example of government policy directed toward helping industry at the expense of the farmers.

Many agreed with Peek on this issue. A storm of protest met the Canadian agreement in the Midwest. Fred Brenckman, speaking for the Grange, said that the Trade Agreements Act should be amended to guarantee protection for American farm products, or the law should be repealed. At the annual meeting of the Illinois

Chicago Tribune Syndicate

Parrish's "Canada Gets the Better End of it"
Lowering of tariff barriers is never popular with everyone

Agricultural Association on January 30, 1936, a resolution was passed favoring "the possibilities of reciprocal trade treaties," but demanding that they should guarantee "a substantial balance of advantage in the exports of agricultural products over other industrial products." This was a clear expression of "Peekonomics."[1]

A more dramatic attack on administration trade policies came when the Sioux City Chamber of Commerce sponsored an eight-state conference on April 14. About seven hundred delegates gave enthusiastic approval to a formal resolution demanding the immediate repeal of the Trade Agreements Act. The meeting reached a climax when Peek was called to the platform, from which he excoriated the entire Hull program.[2]

After the Supreme Court declared the major features of the A.A.A. unconstitutional, Peek got Senator McNary to introduce a farm bill which he had written. His measure, which never got out of committee, called for federal aid to the states for soil conservation, higher import duties and quotas for farm commodities, an allocation of 30 per cent of gross tariff receipts to pay losses on exports, and payment of benefits on a domestic allotment basis. There was no provision for production control.

Peek told a group of farm leaders meeting in Washington on January 10 and 11, "It is my belief that the general principles underlying the fight for the McNary-Haugen legislation are deserving of careful consideration. The fundamental idea of helping the farmer under our American protective system to dispose of his surpluses in an orderly manner . . . is thoroughly sound." He made the answer to farm problems sound simple. Congress, however, ignored Peek and other critics, and passed the Soil Conservation and Domestic Allotment Act. Production control remained a vital part of New Deal farm policy, although it was camouflaged under conservation.

Most of the time during the spring of 1936, Peek was working on his book, *Why Quit Our Own,* the title of which was taken from George Washington's Farewell Address and indicative of his emphasis on nationalism. He collaborated with Samuel Crow-

1 Fred Brenckman, "Protecting the Home Market," a radio speech delivered February 15, 1936; and "Report of Resolutions Committee to the Twenty-first Annual Meeting of the Illinois Agricultural Association, January 30-31, 1936." Copies in Peek Papers.

2 Sioux City *Journal,* April 15, 1936.

ther. Crowther was a voluminous writer and one of the most vocal isolationists and economic nationalists in the United States. For several years he had been writing books and pamphlets discounting the importance of foreign trade to American welfare. His best known work on this theme was *America Self-Contained* published in 1933. While Peek and Crowther differed on a number of essential questions, their mutual support of protective tariffs and opposition to the New Deal trade program brought them together.

Peek supplied the material, including excerpts from his diary, documents, and other data, while Crowther did the writing. In a hard-hitting, swift-moving style, Crowther told the Peek story from the election of 1932 to when he left the Roosevelt administration in November, 1935. Chapter titles like "Broken Promises," "The Lost Opportunity," "The Plow-Up and Kill," "Founding an Un-American Policy," and "Internationalism Gone Wild," indicate that it was a highly personal and critical account of Peek's New Deal experiences. Arrangements were made to publish six articles serially in the *Saturday Evening Post* under the title of "In and Out," before the book was released.

Peek's account was somewhat more dramatic than he had really intended. In fact, it would have been far better if he had written it himself. He could not match Crowther's literary skill, but his presentation would have been less biased. Crowther wanted to stir up sentiment to increase sales. He warned Peek that the book could not be objective, because then no one would read it! Therefore, he insisted upon stressing personalities and such matters as radicalism in the New Deal. He often tried to carry his points by overemphasis and distortion. For example, Peek did not care to dwell on the subjects of plowing up cotton and killing little pigs. But Crowther wrote that these episodes ranked high in the public mind, and, regardless of their importance, they must be plowed up in the book! In some instances, Peek forced Crowther to tone down his exaggerated phrases and statements, but the published work was still filled with them. Nevertheless, *Why Quit Our Own* contained a substantial number of interesting documents from the Peek files which are of historical value.

The *Saturday Evening Post* articles appeared in May and June. Republicans and discontented Democrats were delighted at Peek's sharp indictment of the Roosevelt farm and trade policies. After reading the first installment one congressman telephoned Peek, "It was so damned good I read it twice." The entire book of 353 pages was published by D. Van Nostrand Company in July. The Chemical Foundation, Inc., of New York, which was vitally interested in high tariffs, bought 100,000 copies and simply flooded the country with them. Copies went to about every college and university library, to historians, business men, newspaper editors, and farm and political leaders.

Most everyone assumed that this was Peek's opening shot in the 1936 presidential campaign, and that he would return to the Republican fold. At least the Republicans were hopeful. The Chicago *Herald and Examiner* praised Peek and his book, as did the other Hearst papers. There was even an occasional suggestion that Peek should be nominated for vice-president by the Republicans, or perhaps be appointed secretary of agriculture if there was a change of administration. Fred Brenckman said that Peek's intimate knowledge of the New Deal would permit him to "throw confusion" into Democratic ranks.[3]

However, Peek had come to the place where acceptance of his principles on foreign trade and agriculture was a prerequisite for his support of any candidate or party. He refused to serve as a delegate to the National Republican Convention because, he said, "they may adopt some platform or nominate some damn fellow that I could not go along with at all."[4]

Still caring only for principles and nothing for party, Peek furnished a memorandum on agriculture and foreign trade to both the Democratic and Republican platform committees. The Democrats, of course, ignored his views. The Republicans, however, adopted his ideas with only minor modifications. The Republican platform promised to protect American farmers against competing imports, and to dispose of surpluses through tariff bargaining. "We strenuously oppose the so-called reciprocal treaties which trade off the American farmer," read the farm plank. Government payments were recommended as a means of giving surplus crops the benefit of the tariff.

With the adoption of this plank, it was no surprise when Peek

[3] Brenckman to A. M. Landon, June 5, 1936. Copy in Peek Papers.
[4] Recorded telephone conversation between Peek and Clarence Buck, April 19, 1936. *Ibid.*

announced that the Republican platform was entirely satisfactory. Would he campaign for the party's nominee, Alfred M. Landon, a reporter asked? "The entire subject now hinges upon the construction which . . . candidates place upon the planks of the platform," he replied.[5] In other words, if Landon would stand where Peek wanted him to, he could expect Peek's support.

Peek drafted suggestions for Landon's major speeches on agriculture and foreign trade which were delivered at Des Moines and Minneapolis respectively on September 22 and 24. Landon used the Peek material with relatively few changes. He promised, if elected, to exclude competing farm crops, to dispose of surpluses, and to make the tariff effective for agriculture.

These addresses were the signal for Peek to announce his support of the Kansan. In a radio address on September 28, he delivered a scathing attack on the Roosevelt farm record. He praised Landon and the Republican Party and said that the Republicans had promised an "honest fulfillment" of a sensible agricultural program. Was he being fooled by Republican promises which would be quickly broken? No, Peek said, "Governor Landon is the kind of a man who keeps his promises."

Many of his old friends out in the grass roots turned off their radios, scratched their heads, and wondered if this was the same George Peek who had set the prairies on fire for Al Smith and Franklin D. Roosevelt. Was "Old George," as they sometimes affectionately called him, becoming sour and cynical, with more interest in his own ideas and in the pride of authorship than in the over-all welfare of agriculture? It sounded strange to hear him praise the Republicans, after having raced up and down the country like Paul Revere for twelve years warning the people against Coolidge, Hoover, and Mellon. Was not Landon just a "Kansas Coolidge?" The only explanation for his action was his bitterness against administration policies, and his honest belief that he had a monopoly on the most workable and effective farm program which might be implemented by the Republicans.

Some may have thought that the Democrats were hitting below the belt when they asked Hugh Johnson to answer Peek. In his best swashbuckling manner, Johnson took to the air two days later and ridiculed his former friend, the prodigal who had "re-

[5] Moline *Dispatch,* June 12, 1936.

turned to his father's house." For twelve years, Johnson said, "Peek cursed the Old Guard," yet he now supported Landon, who had been nominated by "the very men who kicked him into a corner. . . . Farmers," he concluded, "will not go from the man who rescued them back to the men who ruined them—no, not even to gratify the wounded pride of a man who once served them valiantly."[6]

Johnson's speech undoubtedly was effective, but Peek said he would not dignify it with an answer. He continued to make other addresses for Landon, arguing that, despite three years of the A.A.A., farm income was still below the yearly average during the 1920's. Admitting that gross agricultural income had risen some $3,000,000,000 since 1932, he intimated that, under his plan, farmers would have received even more. Besides, the price that farmers had paid for this increase, he said, was government control and loss of freedom.[7]

New Deal supporters, however, held the trump cards, and Peek's oratory fell on deaf ears. When midwesterners picked up their copy of *Wallace's Farmer* on August 1, or later, they saw on the cover page a comparison of farm prices between 1932 and 1936. What did this show? Hogs had advanced from $2.50 to $9.10 per hundred pounds; eggs from 8 to 17 cents a dozen; and butterfat from 16 to 29 cents a pound. The oratory about loss of freedom could not match those figures; Bertrand H. Snell of New York could talk about citizens being "wearied and worn by three long years on the treadmill of New Dealism," but this vocal thunder all seemed ridiculous through the hindsight of Landon's 8 electoral votes compared to 523 for Roosevelt.

Peek said he was not "down-hearted" over the result, perhaps because he lacked complete confidence in Landon, although he confessed, "I was shocked at the extent of the New Deal victory." He was actually more glum and discouraged over the political outlook than he cared to admit. If Landon could just have carried a few farm states, it would have indicated a dissatisfaction with the Roosevelt farm program. Peek had desperately hoped for this result.[8] But in light of the election, what was there left to say? He

6 Hugh Johnson, radio address, September 30, 1936. Copy in Peek Papers.
7 G. N. Peek, "Farm Independence and American Freedom," radio address, October 22, 1936. *Ibid.*
8 Peek to Frank Lowden, November 9, 1936. *Ibid.*

later suggested that party lines should have been drawn more clearly. He even thought the country needed a new party.

Here was the expression of a man completely thwarted, one who could or would not adjust himself to changing times and circumstances. He was being driven further and further into a minority position because of the stubbornness with which he clung to his own convictions. Other Republicans, including a few farm leaders, were equally stunned by Roosevelt's sweeping victory. Lowden wrote, "I never dreamed of such an overwhelming defeat." Landon rationalized his experience as "a campaign of education" which "will bear fruit in the future."[9] But this offered scant comfort.

Most of the old McNary-Haugen crowd had stayed with Roosevelt. Men like Frank W. Murphy and William Hirth had no faith in Republican promises, even if Peek did vouch for Landon. Although they thought Peek was terribly wrong, they were charitable to their old associate. Hirth wrote to Wallace that although Peek had "strayed off after false gods," he had nonetheless "made more sacrifices for agriculture than any other living man."[10] The Des Moines *Register,* which had always supported Peek during the McNary-Haugen campaigns, agreed that he was sincere and a genuine friend of the farmer. The editor added, however, "We think Peek is wrong when he insinuates that Secretary Wallace is a dumb-bell, Secretary Hull an old fogey, and everyone else in Washington who disagreed with Peek either a fool or a knave."[11]

In an especially forgiving mood, Hirth suggested to Wallace that a new farm program be formulated and that Peek be asked "to once more sit in."[12] However, Peek had played his last hand, so far as agricultural policy was concerned. About six weeks after the election he closed his Washington office, which he had been operating since December 15, 1935, at a cost to himself of over $12,000, and boarded a train for Moline. He left with the firm conviction that Franklin D. Roosevelt and his lieutenants were leading the nation to economic destruction.

[9] Lowden to Peek, November 7; and Landon to Peek, November 12, 1936. *Ibid.*

[10] Hirth to Wallace, November 4, 1936. Copy in *ibid.*

[11] Des Moines *Register,* October 5, 1936.

[12] Hirth to Wallace, November 4, 1936. Copy in Peek Papers.

Peek stayed in Illinois only a short time before leaving for California. Early in 1937 he built a home at Rancho Santa Fe, and during the rest of his life he divided his time between there and Moline. But like most active men, Peek could never completely retire. The things which had monopolized his time and effort for so many years could not easily be put aside. Most of each morning was taken up by his voluminous correspondence, and in the afternoon he usually played golf.

Corresponding mostly with militant anti-New Dealers, Peek kept up with and helped to develop plans and strategy designed to upset the Roosevelt administration. Occasionally, between 1936 and 1940, he made a speech or wrote an article for a farm journal or popular magazine. He kept charging that lack of protection for farmers was the real gap in the tariff system. His views were constantly solicited by those who were fighting Roosevelt, and he became sort of a father-confessor on agriculture and foreign trade for the New Deal critics. Senator Arthur Vandenberg was among the leading Republicans in Congress who regularly sought Peek's advice.

Late in 1939, Peek came out of his semiretirement and began to make plans for the 1940 presidential campaign. He went to Washington in October to confer with John Hamilton, Senator Vandenberg, Joseph Martin, and other Republican leaders. He promised to do everything in his power to unhorse Roosevelt and the "internationalists."

He was not slow in getting on the political battlefield. On January 12, 1940, he addressed members of the American Livestock Association at Denver, where he charged that the administration was following a policy of "low tariffs, free trade and internationalism." The Roosevelt program of restricting production while permitting competing farm imports was not only inconsistent, he said, but crazy. About ten days later he attacked the Roosevelt farm and trade policies when he testified before the House Ways and Means Committee against extending the Trade Agreements Act.

Peek also joined with other isolationists in charging that Roosevelt was taking the country down the road to war. As one reads the correspondence of Peek and those of like mind, it becomes clear that part of the reason they began attacking Roosevelt on foreign policy was because he seemed most vulnerable there. It was hard to convince farmers, laborers, and small businessmen that the New Deal had ruined the country. The Liberty League had found in 1936 that not many voters were scared by the charge of socialism. However, if the President could be pictured as a warmonger or some kind of evil internationalist, a large number of voters might desert him. Thus by making the international question the major issue, Roosevelt might be beaten and his domestic policies reversed or scrapped. Of course, many of the isolationists were absolutely sincere in their belief that his foreign policies were unsound and un-American, but they also used this as an indirect method of fighting his domestic policies.

On July 20, shortly after the Republicans nominated Wendell Willkie, Peek was asked to confer with him at Colorado Springs. They spent the afternoon together going over agricultural and foreign-trade problems. Peek left Willkie bundles of statistics and memoranda containing his views. He emphasized that a farm program "substantially as provided in the McNary-Haugen Bill" should be advocated by Republican campaigners. He thought this would be especially appropriate since Senator McNary was Willkie's running mate.[13] Peek was as dogmatic as ever, and told McNary that unless his trade and farm policies were accepted the Republicans had no chance to win. He called his ideas a "procedure through which a Republican victory may be achieved."[14]

Peek's first reaction to Willkie was distinctly favorable. He referred to his "commanding personality, agreeable manner and . . . deep understanding of present day problems." But this was when he thought Willkie was going to support his program. As it became evident that Willkie was in essential agreement with Hull on reciprocal trade policies, and that he generally agreed with Roosevelt on the European situation, Peek's enthusiasm waned. One of Peek's friends said that Willkie had reduced the campaign to saying "that he knows how to cook a rotten egg better than Roosevelt does."

Letters in the Peek files written by leading Republicans indicate that Roosevelt probably became more apprehensive than was necessary over Willkie's strength. The Republican camp was filled

13 Peek to Arthur Vandenberg, July 25, 1940. Peek Papers.
14 Peek to McNary, October 2, 1940. *Ibid.*

with gloom from the beginning, despite optimistic press releases. Peek was complaining late in August that the Republicans had no chance to win, that they lacked enthusiasm and a spirit of victory. The Republicans seemed to be interested only in turning "the rascals out so we can audit the books," he wrote.[15] He made several nation-wide radio addresses just before the election, but more out of duty than confidence.

The fact that Willkie carried some midwestern states was a great encouragement to Peek. He believed Willkie could have done better, however, if he had made foreign trade and isolationism the principal issues. But only a few agreed with this view. Congressman Clifford Hope of Kansas, Republican leader on farm policy, pointed out that Willkie got the isolationist vote anyway because people though he was less likely to involve the country in war.[16]

Apart from the election, the fall of 1940 was a sad time for Peek. On October 27, he attended the funeral of his old friend Hirth at Columbia, Missouri. A month later Frank W. Murphy died in Minneapolis. The ranks of the old McNary-Haugen group were rapidly thinning out. By this time both Hirth and Murphy had joined Peek in criticizing and opposing the Wallace farm program. Hirth had written that he never held any man in such bitter contempt as he did Wallace. One catches the feeling of hopeless discouragement when he reads the last letters of these militant farm champions. Hirth, in ill health and about to die, believed that agriculture was on the verge of ruin; Murphy was disgusted and discouraged at the trend in government and was predicting woeful conditions ahead. They had not grasped what had happened in America during the brief span of twenty years. Repeating that the outcome of the election would depend on the farm vote, leaders of the old McNary-Haugen fraternity died without fully recognizing that a shift of political power had occurred. Franklin D. Roosevelt had built his strength around the urban masses.

Shortly after the election Peek was invited to join the America First movement. This was a natural alignment, since most of those in America First were anti-Roosevelt on domestic policy as well

15 Peek to Albert B. Wells, October 14, 1940. *Ibid.*
16 Hope to Peek, November 28, 1940. *Ibid.*

as in foreign affairs. Also Peek was influenced by some of his business friends. Throughout 1941, he made speeches, prepared material for pamphlets attacking the administration, helped to organize America First chapters, and contributed several hundred dollars to the movement. He became honorary chairman of the Moline chapter.

In his letters and speeches Peek argued that Hitler was no threat to the American economy and that our only need was to defend American shores. Once again, however, he found himself in sharp disagreement with some of his oldest and closest friends. Sam Bush of Ohio, who had served with Peek on the War Industries Board, wrote him that the United States must save herself by helping England. As early as December, 1940, Bush advocated getting in the war as a means of saving lives and money in the long run. Peek conceded that possibly the United States should help Great Britain, but our first duty, he said, was to get our own house in order. Likewise, Baruch thought Peek was badly mistaken in his attitudes. If Germany won, he wrote, "it will be an entirely different world in which we live."[17]

After the Japanese attack at Pearl Harbor and the America First Committee was disbanded, Peek wholeheartedly supported the war. He did not criticize the Administration's conduct of military operations. However, he was greatly concerned about the postwar world. Peek said that he would continue to fight for the "principles of Americanism" and "constitutional government," and to "prevent the infiltration of foreign ideas of government and economics."

Thus, in 1942 and 1943, Peek stepped up his assault on every movement which looked toward American co-operation in the postwar world. He warned that amidst wartime hysteria people might be led into commitments which would "dilute our strength with the world's weakness," as he described it. The main question, he said, was "Americanism versus Internationalism." He did not object so much to international political co-operation, but he feared economic entanglements which might "contribute our resources and our markets to a common pool in the management of

[17] Bush to Peek, December 2; Peek to Bush, December 11; and Baruch to Peek, May 21, 1940. *Ibid.*

which ours will be one voice and not the controlling one."[18] Believing that the Hull policies had been leading in that very direction, he fought harder and harder for high tariffs and quotas as a means of protecting American standards of living.

Peek finally concluded that there was no hope in the national leadership of either major party. Early in 1943, Landon wrote him that "we have got to be willing to meet other nations of the world in a reduction of our tariff." Peek replied sarcastically, but in good humor, "It sounds to me a little like Willkie and that is really the worst thing I can say about it."[19] Thus he put his faith and trust for the country's future in a few isolationist congressmen and senators such as Roy Woodruff of Michigan and C. Wayland Brooks of Illinois. He played a prominent part in Brooks' re-election in 1942.

Peek emphatically denied that he was an isolationist. He said that isolation was impossible. What he favored, he said, was "intelligent insulation." He meant that the United States must become largely self-sufficient, an economic island, refusing to "mesh our economy" into the economy of the world. If the Roosevelt-Hull-Wallace group maintained control, he visualized a postwar world where American wealth and standards of living would be dissipated through "idealism" and "internationalism." Peek thought only in terms of the United States—never on the basis of "One World." By the common meaning of the term, he had become an extreme isolationist.

It was a hard blow to Peek when Senator Vandenberg began turning his back on the isolationists in the Republican Party. Vandenberg wrote him in June, 1942, saying that he did not share Peek's concern over the United States selling itself short after the war. He explained to "Dear George" that Americans would mix their idealism "with large and ample doses" of enlightened self-interest. He did not think that the people would "permanently sacrifice their country to a foreign missionary complex."[20] But Peek had made up his mind and nothing could change it.

In December, 1943, Peek was working on a pamphlet with Dr. John Lee Coulter entitled "Alien Influences in America," and

18 Peek to C. Wayland Brooks, December 27, 1941. *Ibid.*
19 Landon to Peek, March 23; and Peek to Landon, March 30, 1943. *Ibid.*
20 Vandenberg to Peek, June 16, 1942. *Ibid.*

he was looking forward to purging the Republican Party of the so-called internationalists before the 1944 campaign. He was at Rancho Santa Fe, just turned 70. Toward evening on the seventeenth, he told Mrs. Peek that he did not feel well. They called a doctor who arrived about 8 P.M. After finding George's blood pressure over two hundred, the doctor administered appropriate medication and suggested that he sit in his chair by the radio and take a nap. Peek made small talk with the doctor about the political situation. Then he fell asleep. He never awakened. A cerebral hemorrhage brought the end.

THE death of George Peek ended a career alternately filled with success and disappointment; with accomplishment and frustration. He died still firmly consecrated to his theories on how farm problems could best be solved. However much one might disagree with his ideas and methods, he made outstanding and lasting contributions to American agriculture over a period of two decades.

He was a powerful force in compelling the national government to focus its attention on the plight of American farmers during the 1920's. Moreover, his insistence that the federal government had a definite responsibility for maintaining a prosperous agriculture has become generally accepted. Most people have forgotten that such talk sounded radical only three decades ago. He also did a great deal to activate the idea that farmers would never receive fair treatment until they became strong enough politically to force government acceptance of their demands. Peek demonstrated how this could be done when he and his supporters pushed the McNary-Haugen bills through Congress in 1927 and 1928.

His greatest contribution, however, was his demand for farm parity. Both major political parties finally accepted this principle and it has no doubt become a permanent part of American agricultural policy. In recent years no Republican or Democratic presidential candidate has dared to seek office without promising farmers parity or near-parity prices.

It would be gross exaggeration to imply that Peek accomplished these things alone, and he would have been the last to make such a claim. It is more accurate to say that he formed and guided a team of farm leaders, politicians, businessmen, and scholars who

299

were vitally concerned with agriculture's welfare. He relied heavily upon others, particularly Chester Davis, but Peek furnished the persistence, character, much of the money, and the driving force necessary to get results. He was the leader. Henry Wallace was right when he wrote in 1932 that Peek was the "most energetic and determined of all the men" who fought for agricultural equality in the 1920's.

Friends and critics alike lauded his devotion to agriculture. They might, and often did, disagree with him, but they conceded that farmers never had a more loyal or unselfish friend. Peek was interested in more than the immediate question of higher prices, which were just a means to an end. His underlying objective was to restore and maintain the independence and economic dignity of American farmers. In turn, he felt this would assure the nation's political stability.

The two-price system which Peek advocated was finally accepted in part, and even Secretary Wallace, to say nothing of his successors, was forced to use export subsidies. Despite acreage restriction, huge surpluses of wheat and cotton accumulated by 1938. During the crop year of 1938–39, over 100,000,000 bushels of wheat were exported with the aid of a 29-cent subsidy; and a bounty of $7.50 a bale was paid on cotton exports at about the same time. This was the "Peekonomics" which Wallace had so bitterly opposed in 1933 and 1934. Furthermore, the United States traded some 600,000 bales of cotton to Great Britain for 85,000 tons of rubber. Circumstances seemingly forced the Roosevelt Administration to accept even the principles of trade which Peek had proposed. Only the demands created by World War II saved the New Deal farm program from very critical times.

After the war the two-price system was used to divert surpluses abroad, and seems to have been accepted as one method of attacking the complicated agricultural situation. A good example is found in the International Wheat Agreement which provided for selling wheat at from 60 to 70 cents a bushel less than in the United States with the government paying the difference. In August, 1953, the National Grange endorsed a two-price system for wheat, and one of Secretary Ezra T. Benson's advisory committees recommended a similar program at about the same time.

What about other aspects of the two-price idea? Could a multiple-price system for farm products be developed in the United States to dispose of surpluses. So long as there are people who do not have an adequate, high-calorie diet, or while impoverished masses starve throughout the world, it seems sensible to distribute surplus food where it is needed rather than to destroy crops. Interestingly enough, Peek never gave this possibility much consideration, although it seems like a logical corollary to his theories of full production and export dumping. Some surpluses were given away to domestic consumers through relief channels in the 1930's. In the post-World War II period, Congress gave wheat to famine-ridden India and Pakistan. Thus, some attempts have been made to remove surpluses and at the same time to relieve human suffering. Peek's long agitation for the disposition of surpluses helped to stimulate consideration of some two-price mechanism for domestic consumers.

Peek emphasized some serious weaknesses in the New Deal program of maintaining prices above the world level and then restricting production. His charge that the United States was pricing itself out of the world market was, to a considerable degree, true. His further criticism that it was almost impossible to regain a market after losing it, was equally valid. As Peek liked to put it: "A lost customer is like a hooked trout that got away. You may hook him again but the chances are against it." Cotton is perhaps the best example of this. Between 1932–33 and 1938–39, foreign consumption of American cotton dropped 46 per cent.

Peek's greatest weakness as a farm leader was his over-simplification of the problems, and his belief that agricultural difficulties could be solved apart from those of industry, finance, and transportation. He fully understood the interrelationship of the different aspects of American economic life and he constantly talked about a balanced economy. Nevertheless, he did not sufficiently consider the necessity for changes and reform outside of agriculture. He believed one of the greatest virtues of the McNary-Haugen bill was that it would disturb the existing channels of trade very little, if at all. Peek had set out to give farmers some of the control over price which industry enjoyed, but he never seemed to realize that a simple government mechanism such as he proposed was not enough to accomplish this.

Peek, as well as many other farm leaders, failed to take adequately into account the effect of revolutionary changes in American agriculture. He saw clearly the effect on production of better machinery, improved plants, and animals, and, above all, the growing use of fertilizer; yet he did not give sufficient weight to these factors in trying to form farm policy. This fact is shown by his continued advocacy of about the same method for dealing with farm surpluses both in 1923 and in 1943. The surplus problem changed greatly over that twenty-year period. Peek never ceased studying the surplus problem, but he kept thinking too much in terms of seasonal surpluses, when actually the surpluses of several crops had become permanent, unless production control was inaugurated or consumption vastly increased. Peek continued to advocate full production without really considering what this meant in terms of increased output. His ideas of export dumping and marketing agreements were not enough to handle the ever-increasing surpluses.

Let it be said, however, that modern farm problems are tremendously complex. There is no easy answer and the entire question must be attacked from many different angles. Changing conditions in American agriculture demand constant experimentation with policies and programs. There is no one problem or any single answer. Even though Peek may not have found the final solution, his contributions to the whole thought and policy picture were significant.

Peek might have accomplished even more if he had adopted a broader view, and if he had been more compromising and less unyielding. Solutions to problems in a democracy come through a process of experimentation and give and take. He saw only black and white on the farm question—never gray.

Despite the fact that Peek came to disagree with many of his friends and former associates, he maintained their friendship and respect. Even his most bitter New Deal critics, not to mention the farm leaders, were all immensely fond of him. And he felt no ill will against them, despite their policy differences. Peek was not a small man. He could appreciate people who differed with him. Those who fought him on policy matters recognized that he was so honest, sincere, and unconcerned about himself that they could not help but like and admire him. No one expressed this better than Baruch. Upon Peek's death, he wired: "I loved George very

very dearly not alone for the magnificent qualities of his mind and spirit, but with an admiration born of the knowledge of outstanding service to his country not only in war but throughout all his days."

Farmers who enjoy parity or near-parity prices in the mid-twentieth century owe George Nelson Peek a heavy debt. The acceptance of the parity concept is a testimony to the impact which he made upon his times, and especially upon American farm policy.

Notes on Sources

THE source materials for this book were drawn largely from the correspondence and files, both public and private, of those who were involved in the farm fight between 1920 and 1933. The most important collections of papers used are those of George N. Peek and Chester C. Davis. These files are located in the Western Historical Manuscripts Collection at the University of Missouri. The Peek Papers are most useful for the period 1918 to 1924, and from 1929 to 1943. The Davis Papers, which are really the office files of the farm lobby, cover mainly the years 1924 to 1928. Besides original and carbon copies of letters, there are pamphlets, government documents, newspaper clippings, and other materials in both collections.

A second significant group of materials on the subject of agricultural relief is to be found in the files of the secretaries of agriculture, which are located in the National Archives. There I consulted the official correspondence files of Henry C. Wallace, William M. Jardine, Arthur Hyde, and Henry A. Wallace. Material on the various agricultural conferences, memoranda by economists in the Department of Agriculture, and other related data were also available. The best source of farm opinion is to be found in these files, where hundreds of letters written by farmers to the presidents and secretaries of agriculture are deposited.

Material of great value was taken from the correspondence files of the following important individuals: Senators Charles L. McNary, George W. Norris, Thomas J. Walsh, and William E. Borah; and Congressman Henry T. Rainey. All of these papers are located in the Manuscripts Division of the Library of Congress. The McNary Papers were especially important because of the key part McNary played in the battle for farm parity. Those of Walsh and Rainey contribute to a better insight into the attitudes and actions of leading Democrats.

Other private files studied include those of Frank W. Murphy at Wheaton, Minnesota; the papers of Senator Peter Norbeck at the University of South Dakota, Vermillion; William Hirth's files located in the Western Historical Manuscripts Collection, University of Missouri; John A. Simpson's remaining files, which are deposited in the Archives at the University of Oklahoma; the papers of Frank Lowden which are at the University of Chicago; and the M. L. Wilson files found at Montana State College, Bozeman. Bernard Baruch permitted me to examine some of the Peek correspondence in his files in New York City. One segment of the Franklin D. Roosevelt Papers was examined in the Roosevelt Library at Hyde Park.

Besides these correspondence files, I consulted the voluminous amount of standard literature on agriculture and farm relief found in books and periodicals. Newspapers, both large and small, were studied for editorial opinions, as was a cross section of farm journals. Government documents such as the *Congressional Record,* hearings of the Senate and House agriculture committees, official reports, and other data were all carefully examined. Finally, I interviewed scores of people who had a firsthand acquaintance with Peek and the fight for farm parity.